The First Jet Airliner:
The Story of the
DE HAVILLAND COMET

Aircraft
of
Distinction

SCOVAL
PUBLISHING LTD

© 2000 Scott Henderson
Written by Timothy Walker and Scott Henderson

British Library Cataloguing in Publication Data
A catalogue record for this book is available from the British Library

ISBN: 1 902236 05 X

Published by:
SCOVAL Publishing Ltd
PO BOX 36
Ponteland
Newcastle-upon-Tyne
NE20 9WE
England
Tel: (01661) 820 838
Fax: (01661) 822 911

Printed by Kyodo Printing Co (S'Pore) Pte Ltd
Singapore

Edited by S Henderson, R James and C Hymers
Produced and typeset in 11pt on 13pt Quorum by J.R. Taylor
Designed by Scott Henderson, for SCOVAL Publishing Ltd

CONTENTS

ACKNOWLEDGMENTS

The author and publisher wish to thank the following people for their help in many ways, for which we are most grateful — Captain A J Angus, Adrian M Balch, C A Hymers, N W Beatts, Ian Burns, John Cunningham, Captain John Dyer, Royal Canadian Air Force, A J Fairbrother, Sahra Foumba, Diana Gatchfield, Henry J C Geering, Mike Hooks, Roy James, John Martin, Eric McCarthy, Roger de Micardo, Francis Mseka, Nick Newton, M V Parker, Captain A J Perry, Henry Rolf, Johnny Walker, Captain Bryn Wayt, John Wilson and Julia Wood, John Wegg, Terry Waddington, Pam and Barry Guess at British Aerospace plc, Farnborough.— Also special thanks to Nick Webb for the Comet colour drawings and Doug Cotterell for the loan of his extensive memorabilia collection. For anyone who gave help and has not been acknowledged, please accept our sincere apologies.

PREFACE

My earliest aviation memories of travelling as a schoolboy on a Vickers VC10 helped to inspire the first book in the Aircraft of Distinction series 'Silent Swift Superb: The Story of the Vickers VC10'. However, in 1960, at the age of two, I was carried on board a BOAC Comet at Nairobi for a flight to London and it has been a pleasure to work on this, the second in the series. The Comet's place in aviation history is assured and yet there is still more to be said and admired about the aircraft. Conquest of the air has been one of the major achievements of the last century of the second millenium and the Comet's arrival in 1949 heralded an age of limitless travel for all. Its early success helped lift Britain out of its post-war blues and even after the tragic 'discovery' of metal fatigue, it rose Phoenix-like to fly for airlines all over the world. I hope you enjoy reading the story and viewing the illustrations as much as I enjoyed carrying out the research.

Timothy Walker
Caerleon 1999

FOREWORD

This book tells the story of the Comet, from the ill-fated Mk 1 through to the world's last flying example. The latter, a Mk 4C called Canopus, was operated from Boscombe Down as a flying laboratory and in her last three flying years, she took me east to Oman, west to Greenland and twice to the North Pole. One of her proudest moments was in June 1996, when Canopus led the Jet aircraft at Heathrow Airport's 50th Anniversary Flypast. Later on that year with retirement looming, she flew her last air display at the Fairford International Air Tattoo before I eventually took her to Bruntingthorpe in October 1997 where she remains on the ground to this day.

Everywhere Canopus went, she generated a surprising level of interest with enthusiasts both on the ground and in the air. With technologically advanced all-powered flying controls, she was delightful to fly and exhibited remarkably vice-free handling (apart from the occasional minor engine surge) which was all the more impressive given the vintage of her basic design. For the test pilot, further professional satisfaction could be found in abundance of design 'quirks' such as the electric starter system for the Avon engines, the elevator gear change mechanism and the antiquated compass display. The combination of an oddly shaped yoke and the small turquoise leather bucket seats required the pilot to assume an unusual and hunched position, which together with the limited field of view through the eight narrow windscreens further served to reinforce the Comet's eccentric charms, some of which still live on in the Nimrod Maritime Patrol Aircraft. In the ruthless search for efficiency, all of these traits have been designed out of modern airliners, perhaps taking with them some of the pioneering spirit of early aviation. However, no matter what advances lie in the future, it was the Comet which first helped to make the world the smaller place it is today,

Squadron Leader Mark Leonczek BSc RAF
Heavy Aircraft Test Squadron
Boscombe Down
July 1999

FROM THE BRABAZON TYPE IV TO THE DH 106 COMET 1

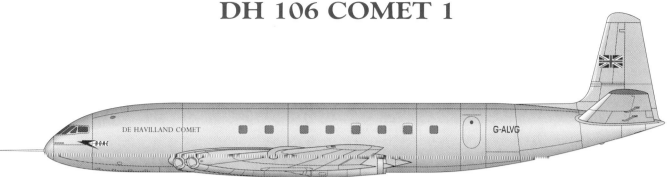

The concept of the de Havilland Comet evolved from the deliberations of two committees chaired by Lord Brabazon of Tara. The first Brabazon Committee was appointed in December 1942 by the Minister of Aircraft Production and the Secretary of State for Air. It was charged with the task of preparing outline specifications of the types of transport aircraft likely to be wanted after the war. The Committee was also asked to indicate which company should be invited to tender designs for each specification. At that time, by agreement with the US, transport aircraft development and production was at a standstill in Britain.

The report of the first Committee was submitted in February 1943. Among its recommendations was the use of the turbojet engine as a means of propulsion. Only one jet-propelled aircraft, the Gloster prototypes, E.28 and E.28/39, had flown in Britain at that time [1]. Eight new types of aircraft were proposed and the Committee recommended that they should receive immediate attention. The Brabazon Type IV proposal was for a jet-propelled mailplane for trans-atlantic use, carrying not less than one ton of mail, with pressurised accommodation for the crew and cruising at 400mph. The essence of the Brabazon Type IV proposal was to take advantage of wartime developments in engines and other

A dramatic night shot of the first prototype Comet G-ALVG, under construction in the flight hanger at Hatfield in early 1949.

An alternative view of G-ALVG displays clearly the single wheel bogie undercarriage used in the early flight trials.

aspects of aviation, in the hope of 'leapfrogging' the US aircraft industry and its monopoly of transport aircraft development.

The report noted that the detailed specifications of the proposed new aircraft should be drafted jointly by the potential users and the proposed constructors, in consultation with the Air Ministry and Ministry of Aircraft Production. Accordingly, the second Brabazon Committee was set up in May 1943 by the Secretary of State for Air. In the course of its deliberations, the Brabazon Type IV underwent considerable change. It was decided that while the turboprop engine might hold more promise in the long term, it would take longer to develop and the turbojet should therefore be used initially.

While the second Committee was in progress, de Havilland started to make design studies along the lines of the first Brabazon Type IV proposal for a trans-atlantic mail carrier. One of the first of these studies took the form of an all-metal enlarged Vampire, with three Ghost engines. Other novel layouts were a canard design powered by three Ghost engines in the rear fuselage, another using four Ghosts mounted in a swept wing, with a normal fin and rudder but no horizontal tailplane, and a similar design but with a conventional tail.

In May 1944 the second Brabazon Committee submitted its report. For the Type IV, it recommended a simple jet transport which would have an effective range of 700/800 miles carrying a 3,000lb payload including fourteen passengers. The aircraft was expected to have a gross weight of about 30,000lb, to be powered by two or more simple gas-turbine engines and to cruise at more than 450mph, at a cruising altitude of about 30,000ft. Since the turbojet engine was still in many respects an unknown quantity, the Committee concluded that it would not be helpful to prepare a detailed list of requirements for their Type IV. They decided to leave as much freedom as possible to the manufacturer and this was reflected in the specification, No. 20/44, issued late in 1944 by the MAP.

De Havilland had, by this time, informed the Committee of its design studies and indicated that a prototype could be built in fifteen months, starting early in 1945. One of the problems which confronted the designers at this stage was an almost complete absence of information on winds at high altitudes. Both BOAC and de Havilland were now thinking in terms of the North Atlantic again, but wind conditions at 45,000ft were a matter of opinion, yet they had considerable bearing on the size and shape of the project. In November 1944, BOAC made known to the Committee that they would require 25 of the Type IV aeroplane, and it was agreed that de Havilland should start work in February 1945 on an aeroplane as described in the specification 20/44 and to be known as the DH 106. In the early stages, the tail-less design was adopted and throughout

1945 BOAC supported this project and recommended that the Ministry of Supply should order prototypes. As the project grew in size, BOAC decreased its order to ten aircraft.

The first version of the Ghost jet engine was started up on one of the Hatfield test beds on Sunday, 2nd September 1945. Two of this version were built that year, but the wisdom of using a tail-less design was called into question and by the end of 1945 an alternative proposal had been drawn up. The redesigned aircraft had rather less sweepback and a sweptback tailplane was added. However, prior to abandoning the tail-less design, de Havilland produced the DH 108, sometimes referred to as the 'Swallow'. The aircraft was a modification of the Vampireand was used to test the behaviour of high speed tail-less aircraft in flight. Although one of the DH 108s later became the first British aeroplane to exceed the speed of sound, the results of the test programme in general confirmed de Havilland's decision to abandon the tail-less layout for the DH 106.

In October 1945, de Havilland proposed an aircraft of 82,000lb, to be powered by four Ghost turbojets of 5,000lb s.t. each and with a sweepback of 40° on the wing. The aircraft was for Empire or Atlantic service and formed the basis of negotiations between de Havilland, the Ministry of Supply and BOAC. Slight modifications were made, including an increase in weight to 93,000lb, and the type was embodied in the first de Havilland brochure for the DH 106, published in

May 1946. The MoS ordered two prototypes in September 1946 which they financed while de Havilland financed the rest of the Comet project.

BOAC stood by their decision to order ten aircraft but, before a contract was placed, de Havilland suggested a major redesign of the project to which BOAC agreed. This halved the degree of sweepback, lengthened the fuselage to increase the passenger capacity and substituted an orthodox tail unit in place of the earlier sweptback one. From the outset of the project, de Havilland had strived to strike the best possible compromise between conventional design and more radical concepts. While it was important to be ahead aerodynamically, it was also essential to be ahead chronologically. Any design features requiring a lengthy development period would delay the introduction of the type into service.

The choice of engine was also influenced by the need to be practical. De Havilland decided that the type of engine to adopt for a world airliner to serve throughout the 1950s was a centrifugal compressor turbine, with a single-sided impeller to simplify de-icing and fire prevention. They felt that the alternative type of engine, the axial flow turbine engine, was a risk. This was for two reasons. They did not have definite proof of its theoretically lower fuel consumption, and they considered that its rotors and stators made the axial compressor more vulnerable to small pieces of solid matter

VW120 was one of three DH108 aircraft adapted from the DH115 Vampire Jet Trainer to test the early swept wing tail-less configuration planned for the Comet in the first stages of its development.

This wind tunnel model clearly demonstrates the highly swept wing design tested in the early stages of development of the Comet, before a more conventional layout was adopted for the production aircraft.

that might be ingested, such as lumps of ice, rivets, birds or material from the runway surface. Much progress had been made by the de Havilland Engine Company with the Ghost engine and this was the engine they settled on.

On the basis of de Havilland's revised proposals of October 1946, BOAC asked the Ministry of Supply to give the makers an instruction to proceed for eight aircraft and this was issued formally on 21st January, 1947. De Havilland's Chief Designer, Ronald E Bishop, later recalled that he was told to "Forget about the cost, just get it right". The BOAC order was at a fixed price of £250,000 per aircraft, "Much too low, there's no doubt about it" Bishop later remarked. It was the market price plus £45,000 for four Ghost engines. Bishop did not recall any strict cost control discipline, and strains inevitably developed with the financial department. He was given the assistance of "someone to keep me informed of what things were costing" [2].

Bishop - known to senior colleagues as Ron or Bish - had joined de Havilland in 1921 and trained in the de Havilland Technical School. He held the design team's affection and respect and his own practical, hands-on shopfloor experience earned him the nickname 'Bellcrank and lever' Bishop. For his part, Bishop said "We had the best design team in the country by a very long way. They nearly all came up from our own

show", by which he meant the de Havilland Technical School. Right from the start of serious work on the DH 106, de Havilland adopted a policy of minimum publicity for the project and few technical details were published. For his part, Bishop kept a model of a tail-less, swept-wing airliner in his office to mislead visitors [3].

The two prototypes were owned and operated jointly by de Havilland and the Ministry of Supply. They had the constructor's numbers 06001 and 06002 and were registered G-5-1 and G-5-2 [4]. The Ghost engine commenced its flight testing in Avro Lancastrian IV, VM703, on 24th July 1947, being joined shortly after by Lancastrian VM749. The Ghost underwent flight trials in the outer nacelles of the Lancastrian with Rolls-Royce Merlin engines in the inner nacelles. 850 engine hours of flying were carried out. The test programme provided invaluable practical experience in such matters as fuel systems, air intake shapes and ram effect, re-lighting at altitude and many other problems for which in-flight experience was essential. The programme brought to light many faults in the installation of the engine and these were eliminated. The Lancastrian could fly on the twin turbines alone but, for safety reasons, the take-offs were with all four engines. Test flying was carried out by John Cunningham and Chris Beaumont, who joined the test programme with the second Lancastrian. The programme gave many on the technical and engineering staff their first experience of jet flight.

As time went on, the name Cunningham was to become synonymous with the Comet. He joined the de Havilland Aeronautical Technical School at Hatfield in 1935, and learnt to fly with No. 604 Auxiliary Air Force Squadron at Hendon on Avro 504Ns and later Hawker Demons. When he finished his course at the Technical School, he joined the Light Aircraft Development Department of de Havilland and later became a test pilot under Geoffrey de Havilland Junior. One of his first jobs was test work on the Moth Minor and Gypsy Minor engine and he continued as Assistant Test Pilot until the outbreak of war. He became known to the general public during the war as a result of his conspicuous success as a nightfighter pilot. Following the war he returned to de Havilland and in October 1946 he was appointed Chief Test Pilot. During a test flight on 23rd March 1948, in the Vampire specially fitted with a Ghost for high altitude research in the development of the engine, he set a world record when he flew to a height of 59,446ft.

Bishop took the view that de Havilland would be wasting their time if they set about designing an aircraft similar to the Constellation or the DC6. The inevitable delay, of around five years, of getting an aircraft into production, would have given the Americans a lead. Bishop had worked on the Mosquito and the Vampire and it was perhaps for this reason that he first conceived the idea of the Type IV as an enlarged Vampire with three Goblin engines.

Bishop would have preferred a slimmer axial engine and he had tried to persuade the de Havilland Engine Company to make one. They, and Sir Geoffrey de Havilland, preferred the robust simplicity of the centrifugal Ghost, a quality which Bishop also admired. He recalled the Ghost as "a simple, sensible, practical engine". One of the main drawbacks of the axial-engine at that time was that no research had been carried out into de-icing or tapping air from the engine for pressurisation. The decision to use buried engines on the DH 106 was taken by Bishop because the Ghost was a fat engine which induced drag. The Ghost was 4ft in diameter and breathed nearly 100lb of air per second. Since the jet aircraft is very sensitive to drag, every effort was made to keep this to a minimum. The Comet had a relatively thin wing, the thickness-chord ratio being 11%. All aerials were buried within the contour of the aircraft and the windscreen also formed part of the fuselage profile.

The engineering of the buried installation in the wing roots, tucked close to a thin pressure hull full of passengers, could be classified as high risk. The fuselage shell was made of thin twenty-two gauge sheet. The worst case mishaps would be the un-contained failure of an engine, with debris puncturing the fuselage causing decompression and possible fire.

The absence of propellers made it possible to adopt a short and simple undercarriage, the main units of which

A birds eye view of Comet aircraft, during production in the main assembly hall in March 1950, with 06045 displaying UAT titles on the forward fuselage. Notice the production of Heron and Vampire aircraft in the background.

In July 1952, G-ALYY takes shape in the erection hanger at Hatfield, only a matter of two months from the first flight which took place on 10th of September 1952. This aircraft was tragically lost off Stromboli on 8th April 1954.

retracted outwards to lie in wells in the wing. In May 1946, Bishop decided that the DH 106 must be equipped with hydraulically operated power boosted controls with no manual backup. This proved to be one of the major design problems of the aircraft. For safety reasons, three independent systems were installed with both engine driven and electrical pumps. In the early stages of the design, a complete control rig was built, representing the entire system from cockpit to control surfaces. For many months this rig buzzed away in the corner of a hangar, hour after hour and day after day, to eradicate faults and measure wear and its effects. Even so, when first installed in the aircraft, some minor faults appeared but the experience gained on the rig enabled these to be easily eliminated.

In its final form, the hydraulic system — which included the operation of the flying controls, the flap and air brake mechanisms, the undercarriage retraction, the nose wheel steering and the wheel brakes — was greatly simplified and compactly located in a pressurised compartment in the fuselage belly, which could be reached with ease, either from the ground or through the cabin floor. This space also contained the cabin pressurisation equipment and there was

ample room for two or three men to work without mutual interference. Very little trouble was encountered with the hydraulic system right from the start, and this was largely due to the amount of original thought which went into keeping the design simple and the refusal to accept preconceived ideas where these added complication without apparent compensation.

The level of cabin pressurisation for sustained flight at high altitudes exercised the de Havilland engineers from the early days of the project. They were faced with cabin differential pressures nearly double those in use on existing aircraft. The consequences of a cabin pressurisation failure were so serious that the fuselage had to be designed, according to Bishop, "rather like a submarine, so that it would never fail". Those parts of the fuselage that were to be subjected to pressurisation loads were designed to withstand 20.5 psi and sample sections were tested at pressures up to twice the operating figure. Windows were tested to a safety factor of 10 psi and all fuselages were tested to 11 psi as a matter of routine. In the early stages of testing, a full-size fuselage section failed while pressurised and this showed the risks inherent in such an explosive situation, and the subsequent difficulty in locating the failure origin. De Havilland adopted the water tank method for testing fuselages under pressure. They built the first water tanks in Britain for such a purpose. As a design requirement, all doors and hatches in the fuselage were designed to be inward opening so that the application of pressure in the cabin served only to seal them more thoroughly.

The effects of sustained flight in very low temperatures on certain materials also had to be carefully considered. Examples of such items were flexible hoses and bag tanks. For tests on such items, de Havilland built a decompression chamber which was large enough to accept a full diameter fuselage. In this chamber, it was possible to simulate altitudes up to 70,000ft and temperatures as low as -70°C. Extraordinary steps were taken with the testing of all components and pieces of equipment long before the first aircraft began to take shape in the shop. Unit by unit, equipment was tested in the decompression chamber at operating air pressures and temperatures. All components were subjected to exhaustive trials before they were installed in the aircraft. Windows are always a critical feature of a pressurised cabin and, to ensure that no contingency had been overlooked in the design stage, a specimen window was installed in a pressurised test frame. For two years the window was subjected to a proof pressure of over 10 psi during every working day. Each evening after the pressure was released, the window was cleaned according to the normal airline procedure. During the course of this long test, the window showed no deterioration. De Havilland

Comfortable and orderly, the cockpit of the Comet 1 was planned on the advice of John Cunningham, based on the Lockheed Constellation.

also built an accurate scale model for wind tunnel testing, and a full-size replica to help plan the layout for the crew and passengers and the details for the engine installations. The latter was built mainly of plywood.

The Aircraft Production team at de Havilland were as stretched to the limit as the Design team on the DH 106. One of their main concerns was the production of the tools

At eight o'clock on the morning of Saturday, April 2 1949, the Comet emerged from its hanger for the first time, so that engine runs could be made. Only the port engines were fitted on the occasion, as can be seen in this view.

A close up of the Comet nose fitted to the Horsa II glider (TL348), to test rain affect and visibility at low speeds.

required to ensure the high quality demanded by the project. Another was the development, within the planned period, of new processes and techniques which had not been fully established at the time. The door jamb and frame required the development of a drop hammer technique; fuselage rings were formed on a Hufford machine; the production of the wing and fuselage skins required the design and manufacture of suitable presses, a 35-ft-long press for the wing and two 25-ft-long presses for the fuselage and the production of the asymmetrical nose required the production of a drop hammer tool that had to be devised in three stages.

De Havilland took the decision to spend £1 million on tools. Plaster models were used for the development of drop hammers, stretcher presses and Hufford tools. To make these large plaster models, accurate information and loft plates were obtained from the Loft Department. The loft plates were then printed onto sheet metal which were then assembled into three-dimensional structures and filled with plaster. These accurate, solid models were used to make most of the tooling required on the aircraft. As well as being accurate, the method was relatively inexpensive. It was held to be as economic as riveting but offered a better strength-to-weight ratio. It was estimated that with the right combination of time, money and ingenious design work, de Havilland could produce the jigs and tools that would allow 80% of the production work on the DH 106 to be undertaken by semi-skilled labour.

The use of Redux metal-to-metal bonding for stressed joints, on the wing and the fuselage, produced a structure of low weight for the required strength and stiffness. It also produced a clean and pleasing appearance and reduced the need for maintenance. The Redux process consisted of using

suitable tools to apply heat and pressure to the parts that had to be bonded together. The mating surfaces of the top and bottom tools had to provide a 100% perfect fit and it was essential that every part of the surface, for which adhesion was required, received equal pressure. For this it was necessary to have accurately made tools. While the Redux process had proved highly successful in the Dove, it had not, however, been used on such a scale or on such highly stressed parts and de Havilland engineers conducted extensive tests to prove the strength of critical parts.

Another new process used on the DH 106 was that of glass cloth, which is known today as fibre-glass and which was used for components such as junctions and ducts. It was found to be strong and impervious to moisture. On some components, it replaced the old method of using canvas coated with resin, a method that dated back to the days of the flying boats.

Early in 1947, British South American Airways ordered six aircraft and this order was taken over by BOAC when the two Corporations merged, the total being finally adjusted to nine. BOAC's order was a valuable act of faith in the project as no other operator had ordered turbine powered aircraft, either turbojet or turboprop. BOAC's willingness to sponsor the DH 106 from the earliest design stage was of great consequence to the speedy production of the aircraft, and the early order by BOAC for a production batch, without waiting for the prototype, was an unusual and farsighted decision at that time. Although it was unlikely de Havilland would make a profit on the initial aircraft, the order was sufficient to start work on a production line such that other aircraft could be sold to other airlines, making it a justifiable commercial risk. At the time, BOAC operated the Lockheed 049 Constellation and Cunningham was sent to Lockheed's training facility at Dorval to train on the type. Much of the DH 106's layout — particularly the flight deck — was derived from the Constellation.

In March 1947, de Havilland established a team of design and development engineers purely for work on the Ghost engine. This team had an overriding authority over all other work carried out by the Engineering Division of the de Havilland Engine Company. In changing from the military to the civil edition of the engine, more than two thirds of the original detailed drawings had to be re-drawn. Owing to the buried nature of the engine, much longer exhausts were required than de Havilland then had knowledge of. In the event, the entire unit for the inboard engine was nineteen feet long. To insulate the engine temperature from the aircraft structure, cooling air was drawn through an annular space surrounding the jet-pipe, and

The de Havilland Comet mainliner, powered
by four Ghost turbines, opens a new era of
speed, smoothness and simplicity in airline
operation.   This picture serves to introduce
a survey of current de Havilland products

D E   H A V I L L A N D

The Comet prototype, at this time carrying the registration mark G-5-1, is prepared for its last engine runs prior to the first flight on 27th of July 1949.

the flow was induced by the extractor effect of the jet itself. The penalty of the long tail-pipe — as well as the air in-takes, made it necessary for the engine to give more than 5,200lb of thrust in order that the projected 5,000lb s.t. could be achieved.

The requirement of a higher rating necessitated a great deal of work on the turbine blades. At least four types of turbine blade were tested exhaustively and a slight concession to specific consumption had to be made in order that the mechanical reliability could be established. To achieve the extended life needed under such high-temperature conditions, the use of some of the very latest high-temperature materials, of which little was known outside the company's metallurgical laboratory, was needed. Following a series of blade failures, a very closely controlled system of heat treatment during manufacture was worked out which released the stresses built into the blades by the work-hardening process.

The scene at Hatfield on 27th of July 1949 at 6.48pm as the Comet prototype is seen on finals for its first landing.

THE DEVELOPMENT OF THE COMET 1

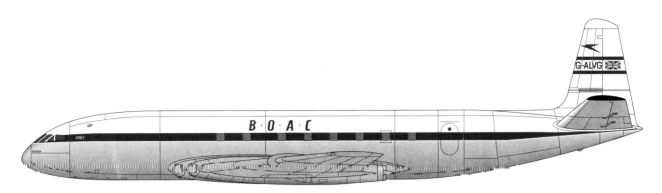

By December 1947, the DH 106 had been named 'Comet' but it was not the first time that de Havilland had used the name. In the early 1930s they manufactured five DH 88s, named the Comet, for entry in the MacRobertson race from England to Australia, in which Comet G-ACSS came first.

The components for the DH 106 Comets were manufactured in separate workshops and brought to the Assembly Shop — also known as the Erecting Shop — where the aircraft were assembled. The Erecting Shop was where Mosquitoes had been assembled during the War and it had a low roof. A crane was used when attaching the wings to the fuselage and once the undercarriage had been added, the tail of the aircraft was up in the roof girders, so to get the aircraft out, the tail had to be pulled down towards the floor with the nose up in the air. Once the aircraft had been wheeled out, it could not be fully re-housed and eventually a larger hangar was built which could accommodate the Comets.

Concurrently with construction of the two Comet prototypes, an extensive programme of research, development and testing began at Hatfield. The DH 108s were used to develop the power operated controls for the Comet. Airborne trials were first carried out on TG283 on 11th August 1947. Whereas the Constellation was fitted with partial power controls, the Comet was to be the first aircraft to have totally power-assisted controls. One of the advantages of using a power control system was that it could be perfected on the ground on a test rig.

As there was a certain amount of doubt over the external view which the pilots would have from the proposed windscreen which formed part of the fuselage profile, a Horsa glider was modified to take a DH 106 nose section in order to investigate visibility and the effect of rain. The Airspeed Horsa II, TL348, had been retained by de Havilland for propeller tests. It was piloted by Cunningham and towed

John Cunningham takes the final few steps into history, as he prepares to board the Comet prototype on July 27th 1949, to test the first turbine engined airliner to fly.

A view looking aft, of the 28 seat cabin, furnished in blue and grey of the BOAC Comet 1 fleet.

In serene flight above the clouds, G-ALVG sports the speedbird livery of BOAC in this early study taken on December 7th 1949.

by a Handley Page Halifax. Several flights were made in March and April, the first from Radlett as the runway at Hatfield was being rebuilt. After flights in various weather conditions, alterations were made until Cunningham was satisfied with the design and it became part of the construction programme. The nose wheel assembly was mounted on a custom built motorised chassis and tested around the airfield at Hatfield, and a pair of wheels from a wartime bomber were attached to the apparatus to prevent it from overturning.

As the Lancastrians were limited to 25,000ft, a Vampire, TG278, was modified and powered by a Ghost engine to complete the flight envelope [5]. In June, the Ghost was accorded type approval as a passenger liner power unit by the Air Registration Board, rated at 5,000lb static thrust with a 250-hour overhaul period. In anticipation of an extensive programme of production of the Comet, the floor space available to de Havilland was doubled by taking over one million square feet at the Chester factory.

Apart from the inherent simplicity of the jet engine and its own accessories, major simplification became possible in the ancillary equipment demanded by the airframe. This was no more so than with cabin pressurisation and de-icing. To pressurise the cabin, the Comet merely drew compressed air from the Ghost impellers, and the same system was used for de-icing. The greatly reduced vibration in a jet aircraft also reduced the amount of maintenance work. De Havilland had originally planned to pressurise the Comet by means of engine-driven superchargers which were designed as three stage compressors, to be driven by two engines and duplicated on both sides of the aircraft. These units were

designed, manufactured and extensively developed before the decision was taken to dispense with them altogether and to tap the main engine compressors for the required air flow. This simplified the problem and saved a considerable amount of weight but one difficulty that had to be overcome, however, was the elimination of oil leakages which would contaminate the air in the cabin.

A feature of the Comet which appealed to operators was the reduction of fire risk resulting from the use of paraffin fuel in place of gasoline. It was felt at the time that this was a powerful factor in favour of the adoption of turbine propulsion in commercial transport. The use in aircraft of large quantities of highly inflammable fuel with a low flash temperature, - 40°C as against +40°C for kerosene, was something that the aviation world was happy to discard. Insurance companies raised no objection to the Comet being refuelled overnight and parked indoors with 6,000 gallons on board.

In April 1949, de Havilland issued an introductory statement to the media headed 'First Details of the Comet'. The company thanked the British press for their co-operation in minimising public references to the aircraft during its development, and stated, inter alia, that the company's reticence was due to the need to keep design details from possible competition while the leeway lost in the war years was made up. It held that this attitude was accepted in a spirit of friendly rivalry by US manufacturers. It was also stated that, due to the complexity of modern airliners, their design and development took a number of years and if a new aircraft was given publicity in the early stages it was possible that, as time went on, the impression would be given that the type was materialising with considerable difficulty.

At 8.00 am on the misty morning of the 2nd April 1949, G-5-1 was pushed out of its hangar at Hatfield for the first time. It had grown from the size established at the end of 1946, the span increasing from 111ft to 115ft and gross weight going up to 105,000lb. The overall length remained unchanged at 93ft and with four Ghost 50 Mk 1 turbojets, it had an internal fuel capacity of 6,050 Imperial gallons. A pitot protruded from the nose to get clear air readings for the flight instruments. Although the starboard engines and certain structural components were missing, a series of engine runs were made on the port engines during the aircraft's first outing. The aircraft made its next appearance on 25th July with the following day spent completing the preflight checks, engine runs and preliminary taxiing trials.

At 8.00 am on Wednesday 27th July, Cunningham took the aircraft out to continue taxiing trials and wheel-brake checks. Then, at 9.50 am, starting with the aircraft tail almost in the hedge, Cunningham opened up all four Ghosts and after a run of about 200 yards, lifted the aircraft off for a 500-yard hop at about ten to fifteen feet. Following a repeat performance, the Comet returned to the apron for inspection. Although it was not possible to demonstrate another 'hop' to the waiting press, Cunningham took the Comet out to the runway once more, this time with the inboard engines idling. After making a number of circles at the runway intersection to demonstrate the tractable ground handling qualities, all four engines were opened up to their take-off rpm, with the aircraft held by its brakes against the 20,000lb thrust. While the Comet stood there as steady as a rock, the 200-yard plumes of dust stretching behind added emphasis to the noise in indicating the enormous power output.

Late in the evening, the Chief Inspector cleared the aircraft for flight and at 6.17 pm it took to the air for the first time, crewed by Cunningham and J W Wilson, Second Pilot, F T Reynolds, Flight Engineer, H Waters, Flight Engineer-Electrics, and A J Fairbrother, Flight Test Observer. It was Cunningham's 32nd birthday and it was also Sir Geoffrey de Havilland's birthday. During the flight, Cunningham took the aircraft to 10,000ft, tried out the general handling qualities of the aircraft over a range of low and medium speeds, and flew along the runway at 100ft in salute to several hundred members of the de Havilland technical and experimental departments. When Cunningham and his crew alighted from the aircraft, they were given a round of applause by the employees who had stayed behind to witness the event.

The press had been invited to Hatfield to witness the taxiing and high speed runs, but they had departed before the first flight. The decision to go ahead with the flight was made by Cunningham on the spur of the moment as the conditions were right, the aircraft had been cleared for take-off by the Chief Inspector and everyone was prepared. There had been no decision to exclude the press from the historic occasion but some in Fleet Street took it that way.

De Havilland were rightly proud of their achievement and confident that their design choices and working practices were heralding a great step forward in aviation. Sir Geoffrey de Havilland, in a message to the team which he headed, stated "There is much to be done, but we now know that the Comet is basically sound and its opportunities for future success are almost unlimited". De Havilland viewed the Comet as a logical step, rather than a daring stride, in their steady policy of

Comet prototype G-ALVG, sits on the tarmac at Farouk Airport, Cairo on April 24th 1950, after the record breaking flight from Hatfield, achieved in just under 5 hours 9 minutes, carrying 8,000lbs for a stage length of 2,200 miles.

Great Britain introduces
the world's first jet airliner
DE HAVILLAND

DE HAVILLAND COMET AIRCRAFT WITH DE HAVILLAND GHOST JET ENGINES

A fine shot of G-ALZK the second prototype Comet, now carrying the revised colours of BOAC, comes to rest on the hardstanding at Lusaka Airport Northern Rhodesia (now called Zambia), on another route proving flight in early 1951.

securing commercial economy by high performance. They emphasised that the Comet's wing loading was moderate and that speed had not been obtained at the sacrifice of slow flying ability. The wing loading was, in fact, less than that of some conventional airliners then in service, and the stalling speed was calculated to be correspondingly moderate. For all its advances, the aircraft was given flying characteristics that allowed it to operate from normal mainline airports used along the trunk routes.

The test flight programme for the Comet began in earnest on 4th August 1950. The upper sky belonged to the Comet where, aside from a few military jets, it was alone but on occasion, jet fighters would try to catch up with the aircraft. "He hasn't got a chance", Cunningham would say. Most of the early test-flying was over Norfolk and the Wash, north-east from Hatfield. Aircraft based at the various US bases in the area also took an interest in the Comet's activities, but most of them were also too slow to keep up. When Cunningham was asked to comment on the characteristics of the Comet, he said "It felt wonderful, right from the start and the smoothness and comfort were absolutely marvellous. It was my pleasure and enjoyment to help put it all together". Cunningham described the Comet's stall as "very gentlemanly — a big overgrown Vampire", having stalled it up to 40,000ft [6].

Everyone involved knew what the test programme was, and a weekly meeting was held to discuss the work ahead and to make sure that no avoidable cause should keep the Comet on the ground. The design team, the flight test section of the Aerodynamics Department, the Pilots' department, the Engine Company and the experimental, development and purchasing engineers all attended the meetings. The meetings were always followed by quick conferences with the workshop foremen where job schedules were discussed. While all of this was standard practice, maintaining the programme became a point of honour to all concerned and, as Rex King, Manager of the Experimental Department later wrote, "Regular working hours registered by the clock lost their significance among my boys". King was responsible for building the first aircraft and the care of it throughout the trials.

It was established at the time of the first flight that the aircraft was to be inspected and prepared for further flight immediately after it landed in the evening. This often meant working to late hours as, after dark, landings soon became commonplace, however this routine ensured that the aircraft was signed for flight by 9.00 am each morning. The maintenance crew, working under the supervision of the Chief Flight Shed Superintendent, consisted of three engine fitters, two electricians, two hydraulics engineers and three fitter riggers. At the end of a day's flying, an inspection was carried out which included a check of the engines for general tightness of joints and connections, an inspection of burner cans for cracks or leaks and the topping up of oil tanks. The electricians checked the circuits for possible faults, tested the aircraft batteries and ensured that all switches were in the 'off' position. The hydraulics engineers topped up the reservoirs as necessary and checked the system for leaks. Meanwhile, the fitter riggers were mainly engaged in adjusting the ballast load, according to the requirements of the next test programme. A chute was used on the port side of the fuselage for

This view of the second prototype demonstrates the single mainwheel housing used on the first two aircraft for test purposes, which was to give way to the standard double bogie design adopted in the service of BOAC.

convenience in removing ballast. They were also responsible for refuelling the aircraft, ready for the following day.

The evening inspection took on average two hours, but was complicated in the case of the first Comet by the amount of equipment which had been installed for performance measurement. In normal practice it was estimated that the signing out inspection would be completed in one hour. The morning routine took about one hour and included a final check by inspectors during engine runs, after which the Chief Inspector reported the aircraft ready for flight. Starting the engines was normally carried out by a petrol-engine-driven generator, although it was quite practical to use the aircraft battery. The ground starter had one connection point for all engines with a changeover switch in the cockpit, and an

outside connection to the aircraft intercommunication system was located in the nose wheel well so that the ground crew chief could remain in touch with the pilot during the engine-starting routine. This proved a great convenience and saved much awkward signalling and possible misunderstandings, especially during engine test runs. The shortness of the undercarriage legs, due to the elimination of the propeller, facilitated easy freight loading and airframe servicing, and in terms of the aircraft's design, it reduced the weight of the entire undercarriage and mounting as the loads in that part of the structure were reduced.

Early in the test programme, the design team became worried by the whine of the impeller in the front part of the cabin. After a lot of sound-proofing experiments, it was eventually found that the high-pitched noise was transmitted through the structure from the engine and it was resolved by mounting the engine on rubber. On 8th August, a Mach number above 0.8 was attained in a shallow dive and the aircraft made its first public appearance at the SBAC Display at Farnborough from the 5th ~ 12th September. As was to be expected, the Comet stole the limelight.

During a test flight under the command of the ARB's Chief Test Pilot, Dave Davies, the elevators went solid so the flight engineer and a flight observer rushed back to look at the elevator mechanism under the cabin floor. They discovered that it was jammed with bags of lead shot which were being used for centre of gravity adjustment. It transpired that the bags had lifted from the floor during negative 'g', which at the same moment had opened the floor hatch access to the elevator mechanism, and the bags had fallen in and jammed the elevator boosters, the hatch had then shut. The two men freed the elevators and averted a disaster.

As a preliminary to a test flight to Africa, Cunningham flew the Comet to London Airport on 22nd and 23rd October and carried out a series of night landings and ground control approaches in mixed weather in order to familiarise himself with the airport and the control procedure. Towards the end of this series of landings the Comet was operating in very bad visibility. On 24th October, the aircraft left Hatfield at about 21.30 and touched down at London Airport some ten minutes later. Cunningham and his crew retired to bed leaving the aircraft in the hands of the ground crew for refuelling and a final check.

At 4.00 am the weather reports were examined, navigational and radio briefings checked, and after a hasty cup of coffee to the accompaniment of flashbulb exposures, Cunningham and his crew climbed aboard. The crew were Peter Bruggé, Second Pilot, Mr E Brackstone Brown, Flight Engineer and Mr G Blackett, Navigator and Radar Operator. Bruggé was from Norway and had escaped in a fishing boat following Norway's occupation by Germany during the 1939-1945 war. He had landed at Shetland and met Cunningham not long after his arrival in Britain.

The Ministry of Civil Aviation were interested in studying traffic control problems for jet aircraft and they gave full assistance in handling the Comet at London Airport. BOAC assisted with meteorological and route information, engineering facilities and communications. Taking off at 05.33 GMT in darkness and light rain, the Comet climbed on course to its required height of 35,000ft. Eyebrows were raised at London Airport when, 27 minutes after take-off, Cunningham sent a routine message to report that he was passing through thin cloud at 31,000ft. At 08.56 the Comet touched down at Castel Benito, Tripoli, having taken 3 hours 23 minutes, representing a block-to-block speed of 440mph.

The aircraft left the ground again at 12.04 and during the homeward trip, an accurate 500 mile stretch in which light

At the conclusion of the first proving flight to Japan on July 18th 1952, G-ALYP sits on the apron at Haneda Airport Tokyo, while a long line of enthusiastic spectators file slowly through the aircraft.

This classic shot, taken in March 1951, features both prototypes and the first production Comet 1 flying in formation for the first time.

head and tailwinds alternated, the distance was covered in 61 minutes. As on the outward journey the altitude was 35,000ft, the cruising speed increased as the weight of the fuel decreased. Over the Mediterranean the winds were light and the sky almost clear but over northern Europe there was much cloud and strong crosswinds were encountered. However, at London Airport the weather improved during the morning and there was fitful sunshine with occasional showers when Cunningham circled and landed at 15.19. The return flight had been made in 3 hours 15 minutes at an average block speed of 458mph.

The Castel Benito trip was the first of a series of flights used to measure the economy of the aircraft and to ascertain the optimum cruising conditions. For the test to achieve its purpose of providing reliable operational data, the conditions of the flight were strictly controlled with preset figures for cruising altitude and engine speed, and no attempt was made to achieve spectacular times at the sacrifice of accurate data. Although the first overseas flight was a fact finding operation, it provided a glimpse of things to come with the almost total absence of vibration from the Ghost engines removing a potent source of travel fatigue, and the air-conditioning and soundproofing of the cabin meant that passengers would suffer no discomfort for the high performance which the aircraft offered.

The trip to Libya generated some observations about the Comet's performance which de Havilland felt were misleading. It had been stated that the Comet burned a great deal more fuel on the flight in October than a piston engined aircraft would have burned, and it was suggested that the difference was the equivalent in weight to some 30 passengers and luggage on a thousand mile stage. De Havilland responded that while, broadly speaking, that might be the case, the Comet could do eight trips to the current airliner's five and, although the total direct cost per hour would be more, the cost per aircraft mile and per ton mile of payload would be less, and many more ton-miles would be worked in the year.

Other critics wondered if the jet age which the Comet heralded would appeal to the general public. Might they not become bored, so high above the view? Perhaps the engines would prove too noisy? For their part, de Havilland were convinced that the passenger appeal of jet travel was sure to be high, and the strange sensation of being poised motionless in space was a new and intensely pleasurable experience. Due to the great height, the map below scarcely appeared to move and the generally stable air kept the aircraft seemingly rock steady, as if fixed in space. The lack of vibration and the absence of all sight of an engine, propeller or any moving part, made this illusion complete.

Up to the end of October, test flights were made on a medium loading corresponding to full tanks and partial payload. Gradually the loading was increased and in mid November it was near to operational weight. In other respects, the flights were fairly representative of commercial conditions except in the matter of the pressurising of the fuselage. Up to the Castel Benito flight, only about 2lb psi of pressure differential was used, higher pressures started to be employed shortly after.

During a flight on 10th November, a height of 43,000ft was reached and the 375 miles from Edinburgh to Brighton was covered in 42 minutes, averaging about 530mph, then on 14th November the Comet undertook its first long distance flight which lasted 5 hours and 35 minutes. The aircraft flew between 35~40,000ft and the 590 miles from the Shetland Isles to Hatfield were clocked in 60 minutes. During these early trials, a high degree of serviceability was attained and the aircraft averaged well over one hour of flying per day during its first 110 days. The ease of engine changing and other servicing, the quick turnaround between flights and even the simplicity of the cockpit check, were all noted.

A detailed statement of the capabilities of the Comet aircraft was delivered to major airline operators in December. De Havilland believed that the Comet could meet the requirements of the major airlines for the next fifteen years at least. The statement detailed an aircraft which cruised at 490mph at heights up to about 40,000ft, which had an all up weight of 105,000lb, and a capacity payload, as a 36 seater, of 12,000lb. With this maximum payload, operating in standard atmosphere with no wind, its Still Air Range was 3,540 statute miles. However the corresponding Still Air Range with allowances for ground running, taxiing-out, take-off, climb and descent, circuiting, approach and taxiing-in was 2,645 miles. While the Comet was presented as being primarily for long-haul flights, it was stated that it was quite suitable for short-haul operations including inter-city stages of less than 1,000 miles. De Havilland also promoted the virtues of the Ghost which, they pointed out, benefited from the extensive operating experience which had been obtained with the smaller Goblin.

De Havilland also released details of the Comet's design features and the proposed interior layouts. In a typical arrangement, accommodation was to be provided in two cabins for 36 passengers with an eight seat compartment located forward of the frontspar structural bulkhead, equipped with facing pairs of fixed seats and fixed tables. The main cabin aft of the bulkhead would hold 28 passengers in fully adjustable seats at 45in pitch in seven rows of four, two abreast on either side of a central gangway. After a flight in a Nene Viking, the designers had become worried about noise in the passenger compartment so they decided to move two rows of passengers from the back of the cabin to the front to get away from the jet-pipe noise.

Hat Racks were to be fitted in each cabin with a minimum head clearance of 5ft above the floor. A wardrobe for passengers' coats would be provided at the vestibule by the main entry door and ample stowage for light luggage up to 200 cubic feet was provided adjacent to the wardrobe.

In August 1951 at Johannesburg, G-ALZK sits in the company of a South African Airways DC4, during route proving trials.

Seen from any angle, the simplicity of the Comet's lines give it a timeless appearance.

Gangway lights at floor level were provided in the main cabin, and smoking was permitted during flight throughout the passenger and crew's quarters. Separate lavatories were to be provided for ladies and gentlemen and there was a separate washroom for gentlemen and a powder room for ladies.

The control cabin, as the flight deck was then referred to, was designed for a flight crew of four, with full dual control for pilots. The accommodation comprised the Captain's station on the port side with conventional flying and engine control layout and nose wheel steering control on the control column. The First Officer's station on the starboard side was also equipped with conventional flying and engine control layout. Both pilots' stations were equipped with full flight and radio instrumentation, with a central engine instrument panel, incorporating all engine instruments, which was visible to both pilots. The engineering control panel was located on the outboard side of the First Officer, comprising pressurising controls and instrumentation, fuel jettison and pump controls, fuel system instrumentation, electrical system control switches and instrumentation and de-icing system controls. The seats at both pilots' stations were designed to provide vertical adjustment, sixteen-inches fore and aft travel and 360 degrees swivelling. The sliding and swivelling adjustment allowed the pilots to assume alternative positions for engineering or navigational duties. A direct vision panel was incorporated in the windscreen, and windscreen wipers were fitted for both pilots. Stowage for the crew's coats, hats and briefcases was provided between the radio station and the galley.

The radio station was located behind the First Officer's station in the starboard side and included a swivelling seat facing aft, a table, stowage space and racking for all communications and other radio equipment except that under the navigator's control. The navigation station was located behind the Captain's station on the port side and was fitted with a seat and chart table facing outboard. The seat could swivel and slide inboard to the centre of the cabin and was thus convenient for engineering duties or supervising flight crews under training. Provision was made at this station for the following equipment; Loran, DME indicator, ADF indicator, ILS, VOR indicator, a compass master indicator, high range radio altimeter, ADF and DME controllers. Stowages were provided for navigation loose equipment, maps, logbooks and brief cases. A periscope sextant housing was fitted adjacent to the seat approximately on the centreline of the aircraft.

An emergency oxygen system was proposed to supply sufficient oxygen for the crew at the maximum rate of descent from the operational ceiling of 40,000ft down to 15,000ft. Four portable oxygen sets were to be carried, each of 75 litres capacity. Provision was made for the carriage of two fifteen seat dinghies, radio and emergency rations in automatic blowout stowages in the top surface of the wing between the engine tailpipes. While structural provision for the dinghy stowage would be made on all aircraft, the weight allowance for the dinghy, rations and emergency radio was made for the Atlantic route only. Lifejackets were stowed under each passenger chair and, for the crew, adjacent to the rear entry door. The first aid roll would be carried in the galley and a first aid kit would be stowed in the rear cabin. An axe would also be stowed near the crew and passenger door.

No external projecting aerials were fitted, they were all suppressed into the structure. The H.F. aerial was located in the tail with the V.H.F. aerial on top of the tail fin, the I.L.S/VOR aerials on the tailplane tips, and the A.D.F. loop aerials on top of the fuselage. ADF sense aerials were fitted in the nose wheelwell doors, and the Marker, Radio Altimeter and D.M.E. were fitted in the underside wing-root fillet. All aerials were under dielelectric panels

The main electrical system operated at 24 volts (nominal) DC. Electrical power was provided by four engine-driven alternators providing AC which was converted into DC by selenium rectifiers. This DC was fed through voltage regulators to supply a constant output of 28 volts DC. The voltage regulators were located adjacent to the rectifiers and mounted in the wings between the engines, ram air from leading edge intakes was used to cool the units. There were six 28 volt batteries located in the forward fuselage under the floor access from an external panel under the fuselage. AC voltage was provided by DC motor-driven inverters supplying 115 volts 3-phase 400 cycles and 26 volts single phase 400 cycles. Fuses and circuit breakers were in the control cabin on a bulkhead next to the navigator's station and were accessible in flight.

The flying controls were power operated by completely duplicated hydraulic boosters with a duplicated source of power through two entirely separate systems. The Smith's S.E.P. I automatic pilot was fitted with split flaps fitted over the inboard section of the wing and plain flaps outboard. Flap control was by means of a pre-selective lever on the control pedestal. Air brakes were fitted to facilitate deceleration, to provide a high rate of descent without high indicated speed in emergency.

For the production aircraft, the tricycle undercarriage was fitted with twin nose wheels and had a four-wheeled bogie unit on each main leg. There were two separate hydraulic power systems for retracting and lowering the undercarriage, backed up further by a hand pump for emergency lowering only. The nose wheel was steered by the Captain through a wheel on the control column. Provision was also made to prevent inadvertent retraction of the undercarriage on the ground and this could be overridden for deliberate retraction in emergency. Four separate power hydraulic pressure systems were fitted as follows:

1. Main hydraulic system with two engine driven pumps (E.D.P.s) supplying nose undercarriage, main undercarriage, flaps, steering, air brakes, wheel brakes and secondary flying controls.

2. Booster system with two engine-driven pumps supplying the main flying-control boosters only.

3. A standby system for an electrically driven pump supplying reserve wheel-brakes and emergency undercarriage and flaps. Twin hand-pumps were fitted to provide a second emergency method of lowering the undercarriage.

4. An electrical pump to supply secondary flying-control boosters only.

A rare colour portrait of Comet 1 G-ALYS, taken in 1952 at an unknown location.

All fuel was carried in the wing. Bag tanks were fitted in the centre section and the outboard tanks were integral. The fuel system was designed for pressure refuelling at a rate of 150 gallons per minute and for normal over-wing refuelling. Drip-sticks were fitted in the underside of the tanks for a visual capacity check on the ground. Normal fuel feed was by immersed booster-pump pressure. Two pumps were fitted in each tank and provision was made for suction feed from each tank in case of booster-pump failure. Each pump could be removed from the under surface of the wing without draining the tanks. Air for venting the tanks was drawn from a leading-edge intake and fuel could be jettisoned from the centre-section tank and the two inboard tanks on either side.

The engine mountings were specially designed for rapid engine changing and the complete under surface of the engines was in the form of hinged panels which, when opened up, exposed the whole installation. A mechanical 'wipe-off' lever was fitted to the underside of the engine cowling, this being the lowest part of the aircraft which would, when operated, cut off fuel supply at all four engines, operate the fire-extinguishing system and cut off electric power in the event of a wheels-up landing.

The cabin pressurisation system was designed to give a maximum cabin altitude of 8,000ft. When the aircraft was flying at 40,000ft, the fresh air supply for the cabin was tapped from the compressors of each of the four main engines, passed through coolers and, when necessary, through a refrigerator before entering the fuselage. Air from two engines was normally used and the other two engines acted as standby sources. Most of the pressurisation equipment was housed in a self contained pressurisation pack at the rear keel of the aircraft with a standby pack in the forward keel. Control of

The Ghost engines fitted the Comet's wing root with little room to spare. Access was by large doors under the wing.

cabin pressure was automatic, cabin altitude being governed by aircraft altitude. All that the crew needed to do was to select, on an airport altitude selector, the height at which pressure control was to begin or end. The air-conditioning system was not designed for use on the ground and provision was made for the connection of a conditioned air supply from an external source, this supply being fed into the main cabin distribution system. The ventilation of the galley, lavatories and luggage compartments was designed to prevent odours from these compartments entering the cabin.

World interest in the aircraft was focused on the trans-atlantic possibilities, where the headwind at height on the westerly crossing was an important factor. It was estimated that the Comet, as it was then, could carry a payload of 8,750lb on the difficult Prestwick~Gander crossing of 2,116 miles with a 50% regularity, depending on the winds.

While the Comet had never been considered as a non-stop London ~ New York airliner, it was suggested that it could have become one at the time with the aid of flight refuelling. The Comet in fact stood to benefit more from flight refuelling than any other aeroplane because of its high speed. It was estimated that the Comet could cut the time between London and New York from eighteen hours to twelve hours westbound and from twelve and a half hours to nine hours eastbound, even with the halts at Prestwick on the flight east and Gander on the flight west. In-flight refuelling would have reduced these times to about nine and a half hours westbound and seven and a half hours eastbound. Some trials were carried out on the prototype in May 1952 when a dummy probe was fitted to the prototype and it flew on a test flight with a Lancaster tanker. It was found that the Comet was not steady enough at low speeds in the slipstream of the Lancaster and the trials were discontinued [7].

For two weeks in December, the prototype aircraft was fitted with the new bogie undercarriage. The first flight was on 18th December and the bogies functioned well on tests involving some 56 landings. Apart from the initial balancing of the four brakes on each bogie and the adjustment of the dampers, it required no attention whatsoever during the trials. Although the new undercarriage was heavier, the advantages were immediate in braking, taxiing and general handling. The bogie undercarriage increased safety in the event of a burst tyre and the larger 'footprint' also decreased the amount of stress applied to runway surfaces, however, at the end of the tests the single-wheel legs were put back in place because the bogie would not retract into the original wheel bay.

The basic price of the Comet, fully equipped and furnished but without radio, was then put at approximately £450,000. Following an exhaustive technical study of the aircraft and its Ghost engines, including in-flight trials over the British Isles,

Newly manufactured, G-ALYS the third production Comet 1 for BOAC, is prepared for its first flight on 8th of September 1951 at Hatfield.

Canadian Pacific Airlines announced an order for two 44-seater Comets on 15th December. The aircraft, designated the Comet Series 1A, was a version produced for export orders placed by CPA, Union Aéromaritime de Transport and Air France. The Comet 1A had a reinforced structure and a MTOW of 110,000lb, which was later increased to 115,000lb. Additional fuel was carried in the outer (or extension) wing as bag tanks and the passenger load was increased from 36 to 44. The Series 1As were equipped with Ghost engines with water-methanol injection and the fuel capacity was increased to 7,000 Imperial gallons. With the use of watermethanol injection, the dry thrust of the Ghost engine was increased by 10% under ICAN conditions and at higher temperatures the proportion rose to approximately 12%. Compared with the piston engine, the gas turbine was more sensitive to changes of air temperature and pressure and, as a consequence, the take-off performance of jet aircraft was more critical in tropical conditions and on high-altitude airfields. The extra fuel in the Series 1A enabled the aircraft to operate over stage lengths some 20% longer than the Series 1. The order from CPA was a fitting end to the aircraft's first year.

The rate of progress established in 1949 was just as rapid the following year. The prototype's single-wheel undercarriage was re-fitted and air-tested on 11th February and the following day it flew using full pressurisation. On 16th March a noteworthy flight was made to Rome. The Pilots were John Cunningham and Peter Bruggé, Navigator/Radio Operator was George Blackett, Flight Engineer Blackstone Brown and Flight Instrument Engineer J.A. Marshall.

Sixteen passengers shared the cabin space with recording equipment and test gear. On board were one Permanent Secretary to the Ministry of Supply, an Air Marshall, an Under Secretary, three aviation press editors and four directors from de Havilland. They enjoyed a record-breaking flight of 2 hours 2 minutes and 52 seconds from Hatfield to Ciampino. The previous record was 2 hours 31 minutes and 51 seconds.

In the forward cabin, there was an array of instruments which included a waterballast tank used for centre of gravity tests by transferring water between front and rear tanks. The cabin conditioning system was still under development and the carpeting and furnishing was sparse. Fifteen minutes after take-off, the aircraft flew over the shore of Dungeness at 21,500ft then, fifteen minutes later, the aircraft was at its cruising altitude of 35,000ft. For reasons of passenger comfort, with the cabin pressurisation as it was then, the aircraft flew some 6~8,000ft below the most economical level. On arrival at Rome large crowds of people gathered to welcome the aircraft.

After an enthusiastic reception, the passengers were driven to an official luncheon at the Italian Air Force Club at which the Italian Under Secretary of State for Air, Signor Malintoppi, said that he welcomed "Friends from England and especially those of the de Havilland Enterprise who permit us to admire the Comet today using Italian skies". In his reply the British Ambassador noted that the English were not given to boasting but Italians had shown faith in British aviation by ordering the Vampire. Signor Malintoppi, together with three de Havilland pilots who had previously flown Vampires to Cairo, joined the

The water spray test-rig fitted to the Comet 2 prototype, for Avon engine icing trials.

Comet for the return flight. Less than 30 minutes after taking off, the aircraft was cruising at 32,700ft. and arrived in Hatfield in 2 hours 14 minutes and 4 seconds.

During the first five months of flight development, G-5-1 flew 200 hours and when it reached the 250-hour mark, Rex King reviewed the records he had kept of the maintenance programme. He had never experienced so little trouble in the first few months of prototype development, all the more remarkable when one considered the big advance which the Comet represented in both performance and in design. With the piston engined types in service at the time, it was accepted that more than 40% of the cost of each hour of operation

was spent on maintenance. It was becoming very clear that the maintenance cost of the Comet and its Ghost engines would be markedly less than for airliners in operation at that time. King also noted that the window that had endured two years of continuous testing was still fully serviceable.

Engines were changed by three men within the hour but this time could not always be achieved on the prototype because of special test equipment and connections which were installed for performance measurement. The air intakes on the Comet were over seven feet from the ground and it was possible to walk below them in perfect safety whilst the engines were running. The height of the intakes from the ground, coupled with the robustness of the centrifugal impeller, made the use of intake guards unnecessary for ground running, although wire mesh screens were normally used while the aircraft was in the hangar to prevent tools, cats or other objects being left in the intakes.

During the Comet's first 250 hours of operations, there were twelve engine changes caused by eight different faults. The fact that the Ghost engines were operated at a relatively high percentage of the available power output under cruising conditions, brought into question the performance of the aircraft on three engines. While the inherent simplicity of the jet engine made for a high degree of reliability as compared with contemporary piston engines, the possible failure of a jet engine in flight, however improbable, had to be taken into account. In the case of the Comet, it was found that the effect of shutting down one engine was not as serious as might have been expected, particularly after the point-of-no-return when the fuel load was greatly reduced.

During the period 1949 to 1951, aircraft designers and users began to realise that the life of the essential structure of

To improve the take-off performance of the aircraft at hot and high airfields, the prototype Comet was fitted with D H Sprite rocket motors. Although successful, the power unit was never used in commercial service.

De Havilland for a while promoted the Comet 2 and 3 as a complementary pair for sale to the world's airlines. However, the promotion was cut short by the grounding of the aircraft after the disastrous series of crashes which ended the Comet's service career until the advent of the Comet 4.

an aircraft was not unlimited. Consequently, repeated loading tests of the wings of transport aircraft became accepted as necessary. Tests of the Comet's wing were made in close cooperation with the RAE. The issue of fatigue to the pressurised cabin was not raised until the following year.

The aircraft was heavily flapped and on the ground it could be held tail down in a position of maximum drag until the speed was reduced to about 60mph. The wheelbrake operating system was duplicated throughout and extensive experience with the prototype showed that it was necessary to use the brakes only lightly on the 2,000 yard runway at Hatfield, even in conditions of no wind. The Comet could taxi slow or fast and manoeuvre on the ground in the same manner as propeller-driven aircraft. It could, if desired, be taxied on two engines and the normal speed was about 30mph. Starting the Comet's engines on the apron caused no inconvenience in practice and it was established that one 150ft clearance was sufficient for following aircraft. It was also noted that the concrete apron and the runway at Hatfield showed no sign of deterioration from the effects of jet blast.

From the 24th April to the 11th May, the prototype was in Africa for tropical trials. Before the aircraft left, it went into the shops for an inspection and the resulting 'snag sheet' contained ten items for attention; one was a loose

rivet, one was a defective bolt needing renewal, and three referred to accumulations of oil needing the attention of a cleaning rag. During the trials, about 40 hours were spent in the air and a great deal of valuable information was accumulated regarding performance at high altitudes and in high temperatures. A strong passenger list representing many of the technical departments of de Havilland accompanied the Comet and the aircraft's reliability made it possible for the projected tasks to be completed in only seventeen days. Apart from a delay in Khartoum while a small undercarriage part was flown out by BOAC, the trip was faultless. Aside from a routine daily inspection, the Ghost engines required under three hours of maintenance and oil consumption worked out at between 1,000 and 1,500 miles per gallon for all four engines during the 160 engine-hours on the trip.

At Nairobi's Eastleigh airport, the aircraft attracted large crowds and two of the principal de Havilland personnel on board so impressed the crowd that they were given Swahili names — Sir Geoffrey de Havilland became Numasa, the Silent One, while C T Wilkins, the Assistant Chief Designer, became Kiberiti, the Matchstick. During the tests from Nairobi's exacting high altitude airport, 90 miles south of the Equator and 5,370ft above sea level, the day temperature was equivalent to the ICAN standard plus 19°C, equal to 34°C at sea level. Later the Comet flew to Khartoum for tests in higher temperatures, then on 11th May it flew from Cairo to Hatfield in 5 hours and 39 minutes where the crew and passengers, in a variety of tropical headgear, disembarked under the supervision of HM Customs and Immigration officials.

From the outset, it was evident that the many novel characteristics of the Comet would call for a new approach to the problems of Air Traffic Control. One concern stemmed from the fact that the jet engine offered its best operating economy at high altitudes and the Comet's most economical cruising altitude was between 30,000 to 40,000ft, so that a decision to divert to an alternative airport should be made before the aircraft had descended to a low level. If traffic congestion required a further delay, the Comet could circle in the holding pattern at 20,000ft above the clouds and the stacking zones of propeller aircraft. It was generally accepted that the Comet would present little difficulty except at really congested airports where fast and slow aircraft had to be handled together, and it was proposed that the precise time of arrival of a Comet should be agreed by Air Traffic Control before the take-off.

Although scarcely heard of before the advent of the Comet, 'jet streams' had in fact been a subject of study for some years. Meteorologists were confident that such high altitude currents of air could be fairly accurately forecast up to 24 hours ahead, thus enabling the captain of a jet aircraft to adjust the flight plan to minimise the effect of an unfavourable jet stream or to take advantage of a favourable one. The Comet I's responses to gusts affecting the wings and tail were calculated by slide-rule. Little was known about gusts at cruising heights, nor about the flexibility of the large swept wing which changed as it responded to gusts, shedding lift off the outer wing as it did so.

Another meteorological factor that required attention was the variation in upper air temperature. This ranked in equal importance with the wind factor, inasmuch as a temperature error of 5°C at a cruising altitude of 40,000ft over a long stage might exact a penalty of over 2% in terms of miles per gallon consumption, which was approximately equivalent to an error of 10mph in wind speed. It was soon noticed that the Comet left a trail at high altitude and the upper air temperatures were among the lowest recorded over Khartoum during flight tests.

The total hours flown by the prototype reached 324 by the 15th June 1950, with no major modifications being called for. This represented a degree of flight test reliability that was unheard of in those days, with no serious mechanical failure of the Comet's power controls being experienced. Cunningham attributed this achievement to all the preparatory work on the flying controls and the Ghost engine.

On the high velte at Palmietfontein Airport, on the rand near Johannesburg, two Comet 1s are serviced in preparation for the return flight to London.

PRODUCTION AND ROUTE PROVING OF THE COMET 1

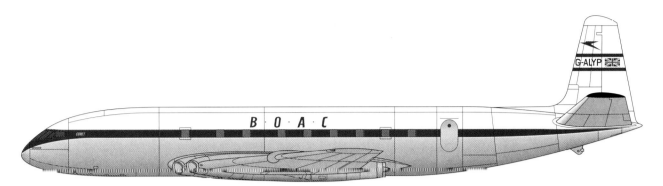

On 27th July 1950, a year to the day since G-5-1 had first flown, the second prototype, G-ALZK, made its first flight flown by Cunningham and Bruggé, with Flight Engineer Brackstone Brown and K G Rendle monitoring the test instrumentation. The flight lasted 28 minutes and like the first prototype, the aircraft had the single wheel main undercarriage units. G-ALZK was used for aircraft systems testing whereas the first prototype was used mainly for aerodynamic problems. In September, BOAC formed a Comet Unit under Captain M R Alderson, consisting of two pilots and an engineer, who spent an increasing amount of time flying in the Comets at Hatfield in anticipation of the delivery of the first BOAC Comet the following year.

Also in September, G-ALVG landed for the first time on Scottish soil when it touched down at Leuchars for the trial installation of Ferranti Distance Measuring Equipment. The apparatus was installed in the Comet, air tested and then removed and the Comet then returned to Hatfield in the evening. On the following day the two Comets flew in company on a comparative test, non-stop from Hatfield to mid Scotland and back, when both aircraft flew at 40,000ft at a constant power setting and the results of the tests were in close agreement with estimates. By 28th November G-ALVG and G-ALZK had flown 425 hours and 81 hours respectively. Tests on the second Comet were concerned mainly with thermal de-icing and the suppressed radio aerials. Preliminary air flow tests of the thermal de-icing system had proved satisfactory and the next stage entailed tests under actual icing conditions.

The first of fourteen production Comet 1s for BOAC, G-ALYP, made its maiden flight on 9th January 1951. It was expected that delivery of the Comets to BOAC would begin in the Summer and that they would start regular commercial services early in 1952. In anticipation of this, G-ALZK was flown to London Airport on 2nd April and handed over on loan to BOAC for development flying by the Comet Unit. During the first eight weeks of operation by the airline, the aircraft flew 147 hours. The preliminary flight trials were concerned largely with performance measurements for the purpose of producing a BOAC Cruise Control Manual, with proving flights also conducted to investigate thoroughly the runway conditions, radio, meteorological and traffic control services from the Comet's perspective. G-ALZK was not fully sound-proofed or furnished during the trials and the undercarriage was of the single-wheel type.

For start-up and taxiing, BOAC decided that their pilots should request clearance to take-off before starting the engines. This cut down on fuel consumption as the idling consumption was relatively high. It was found that the most economical way to taxi a jet was to keep it moving fairly fast, stops and starts led to increased fuel consumption and increased noise.

The time spent from entering the runway to starting the take-off was less than a minute. For take-off, the technique used was to line up the aircraft on the runway, open the engines up to full rpm against the brakes, check the engine limitations, release the brakes and allow the aircraft to accelerate to the take-off safety speed, which was 15% above the stall. The undercarriage was then retracted and the rpm reduced to climb rating, with the speed allowed to build gradually to the best climbing figure.

It was found that the Comet's take-off performance was different to that of piston-engined aircraft in three respects. Firstly, its performance seemed more consistent and a greater uniformity between similar take-offs was achieved. Secondly, under limiting conditions, the take-off performance was more seriously affected by high-altitude and high-temperature. Thirdly, the penalising effect of taking off at high weight against an uphill gradient — particularly under high altitude and temperature conditions — was much more severe than for piston-engined aircraft.

As far as engine failures on take-off were concerned, they were found to be less severe than on piston-engined aircraft. This was due to the close spacing of the engines to the plane of symmetry and the absence of drag normally caused by a windmilling propeller. For an engine failure in flight, the Comet Unit devised an operation that they termed 'drift-down', by which the aircraft was allowed to descend steadily to an altitude at which it could cruise comfortably on three engines.

With regard to navigation, it was found that the key to success lay in rapid fixing. It was found that as the aircraft was travelling at around seven nautical miles per minute, it was often preferable to fix a position to within ten miles if this could be done more quickly than a fix that offered higher accuracy. On the meteorological side, it was found that the crew benefited greatly from prompt notification of any deterioration in the forecast conditions at the destination airfield. In the event that a diversion was necessary, this was best done at altitude in order to save fuel. In flight, pilots found that they were seeing cloud far higher than forecast.

For landing, it was found that the approach and touch-down speeds were considerably lower than for many contemporary piston-engined aircraft and, in addition, the landing run required was quite modest. In the course of development flying, BOAC took the Comet to over 30 airfields around the world. At nearly all of these, no new arrangements were made to handle the Comet and no difficulties were experienced. The most serious criticisms levelled at the Comet concerned engine run-ups carried out near other aircraft and terminal buildings; they effectively brought all other work to a standstill. Pilots were advised to exercise caution and to carry out such checks only when necessary and for as short a time as possible.

One general effect of the rate at which the Comet operated was the need to speed up airport procedures and in order to make a prompt departure, the co-operation and efficiency of the ground staff was essential. In his concluding remarks on the Comet Unit's early experience with the Comet, Captain Majendie wrote "Having once experienced their operation, I would be very loath to have to return to a piston-engined type. Probably the single most attractive advantage in flying with turbines is the absence of vibration. On some of the long flights with the Comet, we have flown for about fifteen hours or more straight off, and yet one steps off the aircraft almost as fresh as if one had spent the time on the ground."

In May 1951, in an atmosphere worthy of a military project, G-ALVG was used to flight test the de Havilland Sprite rocket, an assisted take-off system that had been designed for the Comet by the de Havilland Engine Company. Two compact, stored liquid rocket motors of 5,000lb thrust were installed

between the jet pipes on each side to increase take-off thrust in hot or high conditions. This was thought to be of possible value to some potential operators of the Comet but was never used commercially as the take-off thrust was found to be sufficient without them.

In the same month Union Aéromaritime de Transport (UAT) ordered two Comet 1s for services from Paris to Africa and Indochina. On 24th May G-ALZK left for the first BOAC development flight to Cairo. The seventeenth overseas proving flight of the Comet was the first trip that the aircraft made to Johannesburg which took place on 17th and 18th of July and represented something of a milestone. It was the first of BOAC's trials with the Comet on an old established route, from terminal to terminal, and provided a foretaste of the service which the Comet was to give in scheduled commercial operation, marking the completion of two years since the first flight of the first Comet, during which time de Havilland and BOAC had completed a total of more than 1,000 hours of development and proving flying. Several senior pilots, radio officers, engineering officers and navigators were on board and the journey of 6,212 miles was completed in 17 hours and 33 minutes with stops at Cairo and Entebbe. During the Comet's trip to Africa, landings were made at Pietersburg — where the hard earth runway was considered a satisfactory alternative to Johannesburg — Lusaka, Livingstone, Entebbe, Khartoum, Cairo and Rome.

The eighth proving flight took place during the week of the 10th to 15th August when the Comet flew to Cairo, Baghdad and Basra, and by the end of the trip, the aircraft had flown 52,000 miles in the hands of BOAC crews. There were then four Comets flying; the two development aircraft and the first two of the fourteen on order for BOAC. By then it had been

The tables in Comet 1 forward cabin were large enough to permit covers to be laid and meals to be served as in a restaurant, a far cry from the cramped conditions of the 1990s.

In the early afternoon at Palmietfontein Airport Johannesburg, at the completion of another Comet flight
from London, passengers disembark into bright spring sunshine on May 3rd 1952.

decided that the first nine of the BOAC Comet 1s would be powered by Ghost engines and the remaining five would be powered by Rolls-Royce Avon engines, which would give them a considerably longer range.

At the end of the month, on 28th July, the second production Comet, G-ALYR, took to the air for the first time. The tenth BOAC overseas proving flight was to Pakistan and India when G-ALZK flew from London to Karachi on 31st August, a flight of 4,545 miles and the elapsed time was 12 hours and 13 minutes with a 59 minute stop in Cairo. Although not an officially timed flight, it beat the existing capital-to-capital record, held by a single-seat fighter, by over three hours. On 8th September, the third production Comet, G-ALYS, had its first flight then, on 23rd of the month the final BOAC ATC trials were completed with night flights in normal airline conditions from London Airport.

From the 10th to 19th of October, BOAC carried out its twelfth and final development flight. The route took the aircraft to Singapore and Djakarta, and on its return the aircraft had completed 470 hours flying with BOAC. During

the next five weeks de Havilland received further orders for the Comet; Union Aéromaritime de Transport (UAT) increased its order for Comet 1s to three, with options on Comet 2s, the Royal Canadian Air Force ordered two Comet 1s and Air France ordered three Comet 1s. On 13th December, the fourth production Comet, G-ALYU, made its first flight and BOAC took delivery of its first Comet, G-ALYS. Four production Comets made their first flights in 1951, and by the turn of the year they and the two prototypes had completed well over 1,500 hours.

On 22nd January 1952, the Certificate of Airworthiness for the Comet was signed by Mr Maclay, the Minister of Civil Aviation, and formally presented to R E Bishop. A few days later, on 4th February, BOAC signed for and took delivery of the first of their Comet 1s, G-ALYS. This was six months ahead of the contract date and the aircraft had already undergone acceptance trials by BOAC. Three months later, history was made when on 2nd May BOAC Comet G-ALYP inaugurated the world's first jetliner service. In August, total Comet orders reached 49 and de Havilland announced that they had made an agreement with Short Brothers and Harland in Belfast to make use of its factory.

The successes of the early part of 1952 were marred when G-ALYZ failed to get airborne at Rome on 26th October 1952. Fortunately the 42 passengers and crew were unhurt, but the aircraft was damaged beyond repair. It was just before seven in the evening when Captain Foote had taxied to the end of the runway in the dark. As the aircraft travelled down the runway he lifted the nose wheel off between 75 and 80 knots but as he did so the aircraft began a swing to starboard which he corrected. Then at 112 knots the Comet left the runway and the pilot called for the undercarriage to be raised. No sooner had this been done when he had to correct a swing to port realising that the speed was not building for the climb, suddenly a strong judder shook the plane. A stall had occurred which the pilot tried to correct by easing the control column forward twice. Unfortunately the aircraft then sank onto the runway and bounced, after which the pilot abandoned the take-off and the aircraft came to rest ten yards from the airfield boundary. The official report attributed the accident to an error of judgement on Captain Foote's part in the excessive nose-up angle adopted at take-off when the aircraft's tail had scraped the runway for about 650 yards. Captain Foote was transferred to York freighters although he remained convinced that he was not to blame.

Cunningham scraped the tail of the other Canadian Pacific Comet 1A along the Hatfield runway in order to explore the ground stall. The Comet had a symmetrical aerofoil for best Mach number and the avoidance of a positive deck angle in flight. The prototype was fitted with leading-edge tip slats as an insurance against wingdrop at the stall. However, they made little difference to stalling speed and they were dispensed with early in flight trials. It was suggested that the leading-edge slats, originally in place on the prototype, might have prevented the ground stall if they had been given a more acute angle. Bishop decided to droop the aerofoil leading-edge to maintain lift should the wing be taken too high. To determine how much droop was required, he used a soft pencil to sketch a new leading edge and said "It wants to be like this". At the same time, bag tanks were inserted as an interim measure on the Comet 1As. Five bag tanks, with cells made of rubberised fabric, were located well away from the wing tips, between the spars and the ribs, to avoid the risk of a lightning strike.

The year ended on a high note with the delivery of the first Comet 1A. The aircraft, 06015, registered F-BGSA, was received by UAT on 11th December and scheduled services commenced when the second aircraft arrived on 19th February 1953. In July that year, UAT showed its approval of the aircraft by ordering three Comet 2s. Panair do Brasil had shown an interest in the aircraft in 1951 and, in early 1953, the airline placed an order for four Comet 2s with two options on the Comet 3. However on 3rd March 1953 a 1A of CPA crashed on take-off at Karachi, killing all on board including five CPA staff and six de Havilland technicians. The aircraft, registered CF-CUN and named Empress

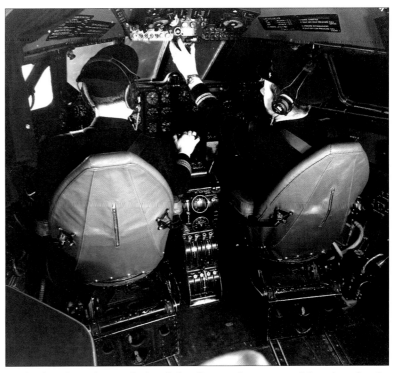

For its day, the cockpit of the Comet 1 was considered a simple and functional design, although it looks rather dated by the standards of the late 20th century.

The design of the Comet 1 interior was considered in the early 1950s to be the most advanced of its day, with ample leg room for all passengers based on a seat pitch of 45 inches.

At Livingston Airport Southern Rhodesia, the Comet makes a morning call to refuel on the southward journey to South Africa.

Ground staff at Livingstone replenish food and supplies in a quaint style of dress long gone.

of Hawaii, was on a delivery flight to Australia to open CPA's Sydney to Honolulu service and was making a maximum weight take-off in hot air from Karachi's airport. The plane taxied out just before dawn, under the command of Captain Pentland, CPA's Director of Flight Operations. On take-off, the pilot pulled back on the control column too early causing the aircraft to stall, the high drag preventing acceleration and the inlet angle reducing thrust. It failed to leave the ground and careered through a fence at the end of the runway, during which the fuel tanks were ruptured as the aircraft skidded 80 yards into a 22-foot high embankment where it burst into flames.

Both Captain Foote — at Rome — and Captain Pentland had attempted take-offs in the dark, when there was no horizon visible outside and it was harder to judge the angle of attack. They did not have any instruments to tell them that they had over-rotated and the hydraulic controls made it harder to feel precisely how the plane was behaving. This combination of factors counted against them and Captain Foote was justified in his belief that he was not to blame for the crash at Rome.

In the early days of Comet flying, the pilot was given an unstick speed. How he arrived at the unstick speed was up to his judgement. Some pilots raised the nose of the aircraft early and held it off the ground. At an angle of between 4° and 5° the wing, which was designed for high speed flight, could stall. Early in 1953, a series of tests showed that the stalling speed at ground level in the take-off attitude was several knots higher than the airborne stalling speed in the same attitude. To avoid this ground stall on take-off, an extended and drooped leading edge was installed retrospectively on all Comet 2s. With this modification it was found to be impossible to stall the aircraft on the ground, and take-offs could be made at full weight with the tail bumper dragging along the runway. This modification made a negligible difference to the cruise drag and a procedure for using a pre-determined Vr was introduced at the same time.

At 14.00 hours GMT on 2nd May, BOAC completed the first year of jet airliner operation. However just two hours before the anniversary a homeward bound Comet, G-ALYV, carrying a crew of six and 36 passengers, crashed shortly after take-off from Calcutta after flying into extreme turbulence at 10,000ft. The last radio transmission from Captain M Haddon was received six minutes after take-off. When the aircraft was overdue at Delhi, ground and air searches were instigated and the following morning the crew of a BOAC York freighter spotted the wreckage 25 miles west of Calcutta. Wreckage was strewn over an eight square mile area and an eye witness reported having seen a wingless aircraft in flames, descending through a rainstorm. There were no survivors. Comet services were suspended for a time and CPA's second Comet was diverted to BOAC.

An inquiry was directed by the Central Government of India and was held under Rule 75 of the Indian Aircraft Rules 1937. The Court reported on 26th May and concluded that the accident had been caused by structural failure of the airframe during flight through a thundersquall. Much of G-ALYV's wreckage was recovered and flown to Farnborough where it was reassembled, as far as possible, for examination. It was found that the tailplane had failed due to excessive down-loading and this had caused the wings to fail due to an ensuing excessive, negative g-force. Following the investigation, weather radar was fitted to Comets to avoid a repeat accident, and the tragedy also led to stricter rough air speeds and the introduction of Q feel, so that stick forces would be proportional to control loads, the Comet was the first aircraft to have this. It protected the pilot from over controlling the aircraft and the original Comet control column was pushed or pulled against a spring, feeling the same to the pilot at all speeds.

Until the middle of 1952 it had not been realised that the fatigue resistance properties of a pressure cabin demanded further precautions, either in design or by test, than were provided by the static strength requirements of the day. The matter first came to de Havilland's notice through studies being conducted on RAF Transport Aircraft. A paper published in October 1952 called for more stringent tests and, on 19th June, the ARB issued proposals which similarly called for changes in the test procedure where civil aircraft were concerned. The paper also suggested that certain structural parts, such as riveted joints and door and window frames, might have to be re-designed to meet these requirements.

As a result of these developments, de Havilland reconsidered the position of the Comet's cabin in July 1953. Up to that time no Comet had exceeded 2,500 hours flying, the equivalent of around 800 pressurised flights. In order to satisfy themselves of its safety, and also to discover its probable safe working life, they carried out repeated loading tests of the test section of the forward part of the cabin, applying the working pressure 'P' about 16,000 times. By September 1953 this specimen had withstood 18,000 applications of 'P'. These tests were ended by a failure of the skin in fatigue at the corner of a window, originating at a small defect in the skin. The number of pressurisations sustained was so large that, in conjunction with numerous other tests, it was regarded as establishing the safety of the Comet's cabin with an ample margin.

On the 10th January 1954, G-ALYP crashed off Elba. There were two BOAC aircraft due to leave Ciampino airport that morning; a Canadian-built C4 Argonaut, G-ALHJ, and the Comet. The Comet took off twelve minutes after the Argonaut, with 29 passengers and a crew of six on board on the last leg of a flight from Singapore to London. Prior to take-off, Captain

Comets were dry leased from BOAC by South African Airways, for service on the 'Springbok' route.

Gibson agreed to tell the Argonaut's pilot what the cloud tops were like as he passed them. At 10.50, nineteen minutes after take-off, Captain Gibson reported breaking through the cloud tops at 26,000ft over the Orbetello radio beacon. He was leaving the Italian coast and climbing to the planned cruising altitude of 36,000ft. He then radioed the Argonaut. "George How Jig from George Yoke Peter, did you get my…" was as far as the message got.

Some Italian fishermen sailing south of Elba heard three explosions. Giovanni di Marco, the fisherman who first reported the crash to the island authorities, said "I was fishing just south of the island when I heard the whine of a plane above me. It was above the clouds. I could not see it. Then I heard three explosions, very quickly, one after the other. For a moment all was quiet. Then, several miles away, I

Ground staff load fresh supplies on to the Comet at Entebbe Uganda, under the watchful eyes of the aircraft crew.

Two Comet 1 aircraft receive final servicing at Hatfield in preparation for delivery to BOAC in 1952.

saw a silver thing flash out of the clouds, smoke came from it and it hit the sea. There was a great cloud of water and by the time I got there all was still again. There were some bodies in the water which we began to pick up, but there was nothing else we could do."

The fishermen reported to the carabinieri at Porto Ferrajo, whence the report was relayed to Pisa and Italian search aircraft were airborne by 12.30 from La Spezia and Pisa. The bodies of fifteen passengers were taken to Port Azzuro by local fishermen accompanied by a priest to the quayside where he gave a benediction as the bodies, laid on planks, were transferred ashore and taken to the cemetery chapel where a temporary mortuary had been arranged. The fishing boats also brought in some wreckage, including a mail bag, some coats, a handbag and two life jackets. The Comet had been carrying mail from Bangkok, Karachi, Kuwait, and Rangoon.

Three Italian warships, using searchlights, patrolled the area of the crash that night. Search by aircraft of the waters between the islands of Elba and Monte Cristo was abandoned on the morning of the 12th January, but an Italian corvette remained in the vicinity, however its under-water detection apparatus was not working and it was clear that there were no survivors. Among the passengers was Mr Chester Wilmot, a well known war correspondent. Ten children were also on board, flying to school in Britain after having visited parents in the East during the Christmas holidays. Captain Gibson, DFC, was 31 and had flown 1,300 hours with the Comet and 4,267 with BOAC.

Recovering the wreckage was a difficult and slow process. The Favilla, one of two ships of the Anglo-Mediterranean Sea Recovery Company, reported late on the night of the 21st of January, that she had probably located the main part of the fuselage of the aircraft. In the first week of February an Italian motor trawler, the Sirio, located a large object with its nets which was thought to be the fuselage of the aircraft. Then, on 16th February, underwater television on board the frigate HMS Wakeful sighted a large piece of the body of the Comet. By the 21st February, part of the aircraft, along with some clothing, was recovered by the RFA Sea Salvor after the items had been spotted 67 fathoms below with an underwater camera. Next the engines were recovered and sent by air to de Havilland on 21st March, then later the wing centre section was received on 5th April followed by the front part of the cabin on 15th April. On 27th May, the complete tail section of the aircraft was recovered from the sea and shipped to Rome, where a BOAC Hermes collected it and flew it to England. The salvage operation which had been going on for just over four months was completed with the discovery of the tail section which was found 600 yards from where the engines and a large section of fuselage had previously been recovered.

On receiving news of the accident, BOAC decided to suspend their normal Comet passenger services in order to carry out a detailed examination of the aircraft of the Comet operational fleet in collaboration with the Air Registration Board and de Havilland. BOAC's Comets all returned to London Airport, without passengers, for a thorough inspection. At the time of the accident the aircraft had completed 3,681 flying hours in 1,290 flights, a fraction of that endured by components tested during the aircraft's development. The investigating parties came to the view that possible main causes of the accident included the flutter of control surfaces, primary structural failure, a malfunction of one or some of the flying controls, fatigue of the structure, especially of the wing, an explosive decompression of the pressure cabin or an engine fire.

As a result, a number of modifications were made and it was concluded that fire was the most likely cause of the accident. The parties concerned indicated to the Minister of Transport that they saw no reason for not resuming Comet services following the modifications and flights began again on 23rd March 1954. Meanwhile, BOAC did not lose faith in the Comet and the airline reached a decision to order five Comet 3s for the trans-atlantic route, with options on further aircraft. The contract was signed on 1st February 1954 but a further misfortune befell de Havilland before the prototype Comet 3 took to the air for the first time on 19th July.

On 8th April 1954, Comet Aircraft G-ALYY, which was on charter to South African Airways, crashed near Naples while on a flight from Rome to Cairo. The accident occurred at approximately the same height and after approximately the same lapse of time after departure from Rome as in the case of Yoke Peter. G-ALYY had departed on 7th April from London to Rome on the first leg of the journey to Johannesburg as flight number SA201.

The aircraft, commanded by Captain W Mostert, took off for the second leg of the flight from Rome on Thursday, 8th April at 18.32 hours GMT with fourteen passengers and seven crew members on board. The flight proceeded as normal climbing to a cruising height of 35,000ft, during which time the crew reported in over the Ostia beacon, again at the Island of Ponziane, with a third report made when they passed Naples. The final transmission made was received by Cairo, reporting an estimated arrival time of 21.20 hours GMT. However, the aircraft crashed into the Tyrrhenian Sea with no survivors. Two Royal Navy ships were sent to the area; a destroyer, HMS Darling, and the aircraft carrier, HMS Eagle. HMS Eagle recovered five bodies from the ocean on 9th April 1954 and a sixth body was found washed ashore, but the aircraft was never recovered.

On receiving news of the accident, BOAC decided immediately to suspend all Comet services until more was known. On 12th April, the Certificate of Airworthiness was withdrawn for the Comet and a Court of Inquiry was convened. The Court sat in London between 19th October and the 24th November, 1954.

Shortly after the Naples accident, the Minister of Supply instructed the RAE to undertake a complete investigation of the whole problem presented by the accidents. The RAE decided that a repeated loading test of the whole cabin ought to be made in a water tank and the tests, which were to last six weeks, began early in June on aircraft G-ALYU, or Yoke Uncle, as it became known to the Inquiry. A water tank with a capacity of a quarter of a million gallons was built at Farnborough, into which a Comet could fit, with its wings protruding either side through water-tight rubber seals. The cabin and wings were repeatedly subjected to a cycle of loading as far as possible equivalent to that experienced in the period between take-off and landing. Each five-minute cycle was the equivalent to a three-hour flight. The wings were subjected to simulated flight and gust loads by hydraulic jacks in order to simulate gusts.

While the water tests were underway, other tests were also carried out. Models were made of the Comet to try and work out where wreckage would have fallen into the sea. The wreckage which had been recovered was pieced together on a wooden frame at Farnborough, and dummies were dropped from the air at various altitudes to compare them with the medical evidence gathered from the bodies that had been recovered. Comets were flown at speed at high altitudes, with the pilots using oxygen, to check for pilot error. Much of this work was carried out on the first Comet 1A, number 06013, registered as G-ANAV whilst a Canberra was used to keep a photographic record, but the trials proved inconclusive. Two other Comets, G-ALYR and G-ALYS, were tested for fatigue in ground tests.

Yoke Uncle had made 1,230 pressurised flights before the test and, after the equivalent of a further 1,830 such flights making a total of 3,060, the cabin structure failed, the starting point of the failure being the corner of one of the cabin windows. Examination of the failure provided evidence of fatigue at the point where the crack would be most likely to start, namely near the edge of the skin at the corner of the window. While many possible sources of trouble were continually investigated during the whole of the summer, the problem of fatigue in the structure of the cabin began to dominate all others. The inference that the primary failure of Yoke Peter was the bursting of the pressure cabin was confirmed by a close examination of the wreckage and by further experiments in the water tank, after the first failure had been repaired by de Havilland. It now seemed probable that the stress near the corners of the windows was higher than had been expected by the designers.

In the light of known properties of the aluminium alloys DTD 546 and 746, of which the skin was made, the Inquiry accepted the conclusion of the RAE that this was sufficient explanation for the failure of the cabin skin of Yoke Uncle by fatigue after a small number, namely 3,060 cycles of pressurisation. At the time of the Elba accident, Yoke Peter had made 1,290 pressurised flights and at the time of the Naples accident, Yoke Yoke had made 900 pressurised flights. It was stated that the cabin of Yoke Peter had reached a point in its life when it could be said to be in danger of failure from fatigue, and that the cabin of Yoke Yoke would also be in danger.

As a result of further salvage near Elba, in mid-August the RAE received a piece of cabin skin which had been found by an Italian fishing boat. It was identified as coming from the centre of the top of the cabin approximately over the front spar of the wing, and it

At London's Heathrow Airport, the second prototype Comet 1 G-ALZK is serviced during the route proving trials with BOAC on 28th June 1951.

A dream of effortless flight come true

contained the two windows in which lay the aerials which were part of the ADF equipment. At the same time, the RAE received a part of the aileron of the port wing and a part of the boundary fence fitted to the leading edge of the port wing not far from the tip. The latter parts provided important evidence about the bursting of the cabin. There were marks on them which were identified as made by pieces from the cabin itself. Taken together with the paint mark on the leading edge of the centre section, not far from where the outer wing broke off, (which was identified as being caused by the piece of the cabin wall containing the first window - which was also the escape hatch), they established that the cabin burst catastrophically in the neighbourhood of the front spar of the wing when the aircraft was flying substantially normally. By examination of the piece containing the ADF windows and the adjacent pieces, it was established that it was here that the first fracture of the cabin structure of Yoke Peter occurred. In general terms, it took the form of a split along the top centre of the cabin, along a line approximately fore and aft, passing through corners of the ADF windows. The direction in which the fracture spread was determined by examination of the lines of separation of the material. The Inquiry could not establish with certainty the point at which the disruption of the skin first began, but considered it probable that it started near the starboard aft corner of the rear ADF window, at the edge of the countersunk hole through which a bolt passed. The only alternative point suggested was the opposite — port forward — corner of the same window, where the fracture passed through a small crack in the reinforcing plate, about 0.2in long, made accidentally during the building of the aircraft.

The centre section of the wing of Yoke Peter, which had been recovered from the sea on 15th March, was severely damaged by fire and by impact with the water. It contained the four Ghost engines substantially intact with the exception that the turbine disc of No. 2 engine was missing. The shaft on which it had been mounted had broken near the hub to which it was bolted and it had escaped through a large gash in the exhaust cone.

The disc was not recovered. Dr Moult, Chief Engineer of the de Havilland Engine Company Limited, said in evidence that there were no signs consistent with seizure of any engine, or of any excessive internal heat, or of any failure having occurred before the break-up of the aircraft. The extensive fire damage was all external to the engines. The Inquiry concluded that the fire which damaged the engines externally was subsequent to the disintegration of the aircraft and not a cause of it.

The RAE Report, which was part of the evidence before the Court, stated that it had formed the opinion that the accident at Elba was caused by structural failure of the pressure cabin, brought about by fatigue. Owing to the absence of wreckage from the accident near Naples, the RAE were unable to form a definite opinion on the cause but suggested that the explanation was likely to be the same. The medical evidence from the bodies recovered was consistent with that conclusion. The findings also raised some doubts as to whether the tragedy that befell G-ALYV near Calcutta was solely due to turbulence [8].

The Findings of the Report were issued on 12th February 1955. In a covering letter, it was stated that all three Assessors agreed with the findings and that de Havilland, BOAC and the ARB had offered every possible assistance, in a genuine desire to arrive at the true cause of the accidents and so enable a redesigned Comet aircraft to take to the air once more. The Report blamed pressure cabin fatigue and included a de Havilland statement on the future action proposed in Comet development. Measures would be taken in conjunction with the ARB to deal with the fatigue problem, involving thicker gauge materials which would be used for the pressure cabin and windows, and cut-outs would be redesigned so that local stress concentrations at rivets, bolt holes or manufacturing cracks would not lead to fatigue difficulties. The wing structure would be redesigned in fatigue prone areas to reduce the stress level, and the fuel system would be modified to prevent fuel venting during take-off and the possibility of structural damage during refuelling.

Few of the Comet 1s survived after the crash investigations and for many months the whole Comet project hung in the balance. The crashes almost broke de Havilland, spiritually as well as financially. "We discovered metal fatigue and paid the price" was how one former employee put it. The remaining UAT Comets were withdrawn from use and scrapped and the assembly lines at Belfast and Chester were closed down. All export orders were terminated and all Comet 1As were returned, except for those of the RCAF which, without fuss, were suitably modified with stronger skins and oval cut-outs and served with No. 412 Squadron until late 1964. The other Comet 1s and Comet 1As were used up in test programmes or simply scrapped. A total of four Comet 1As were upgraded to 1XB standard which had a reinforced structure and oval windows. The total cycles of those upgraded Comets was however limited.

THE COMET 2

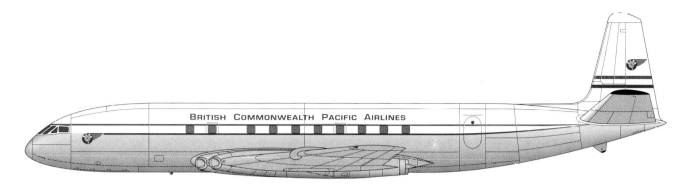

The sixth Comet 1, 06006, which was jointly owned by de Havilland and the MoS, became the Comet 2 prototype and was designated Comet 2X. Registered as G-ALYT, it was the only Comet 2X and was used to test the Rolls-Royce axial-flow turbo-jet Avon engines which were intended to power the Comet 2. G-ALYT first flew on 16th of February 1952, the flight lasting 1 hour and 53 minutes achieving a height of 25,000ft. The aircraft was initially powered by four Avon RA9 Mk 501 engines, with a sea level static rating of 6,500lb, later improved Avon RA9 Mk 502 engines were fitted. The production Comet 2 had a three-foot longer fuselage, modified drooped leading edges and four Avon RA25 Mk 503 or Mk 504 engines with 7,300lb s.t. The maximum take-off weight was 120,000lbs, the fuel capacity was identical to the Comet 1As and the aircraft had an increased range of about 2,200 miles with a full payload. There was a 185cuft underfloor hold behind the wing, supplemented by two holds forward above the floor, totalling an additional 246cuft. The first production model first flew on 27th August 1953, but the Comet 2 was never used in commercial operation following the Comet 1 disasters. Of the twenty-two Comet 2s manufactured, five were scrapped, three went into storage and the rest were converted to become other Comet versions.

BOAC confirmed that it would require eleven Comet 2s, and British Commonwealth Pacific Airlines became the second

In this serene study, the first production Comet Series 2 fitted with Rolls-Royce Avon engines, is caught on the occasion of the first flight from Hatfield on August 27th 1953, with John Cunningham at the controls.

This artist's impression of the Comet 2 in Panair do Brasil's livery, was produced
for presentation to the Airline on delivery of their first Comet.

customer, early in 1952, with an order for six. Japan Air Lines signed up for two Comet 2s in July 1952, then LAV for two in August, followed by orders and options placed by CPA, UAT, Air France and Panair do Brasil. On 16th November, CPA announced an order for three Comet 2s, with an option on a fourth, for operation on their trans-Pacific service linking Vancouver with Sydney, a distance of some 7,500 miles.

There were four variants of the Comet 2, namely the Comet C2, the Comet T2, the Comet 2R and the Comet 2E. The fuselage and cabin floor of the Comet C2 were reinforced and the aircraft was fitted with oval windows. The MTOW was 127,600lbs and it was powered by four Avon Mk117/118. Eight C2s were used by the RAF and each aircraft was allowed to operate 8000 cycles.

The Comet T2 was identical to the C2 but without the reinforced floor and, later both Comet T2s were upgraded to the C2 standard. The fuselage of the Comet 2R was unpressurised and had square windows. It was powered by Avon Mk117 and was the first production Comet 2. The Comet 2E was a C2 fitted with two Avon RA29 Mk524 engines in the outer positions and two RA9 Mk504 engines in the inner positions. The Avon RA29 Mk524 was the engine later used by the Comet 4.

When the Comet 2 was announced, it was anticipated that initial deliveries would be cleared for operation at the RA9 rating. This was referred to as the first stage of development and a higher rating was expected to become available after approximately one year of active operation. The standard accommodation configuration on the Comet 2 was 44 passengers in reclining double chairs, with a capacity payload of 13,500lbs. De Havilland felt that this layout offered the best compromise between high density and comfort, but other arrangements were possible. In the first stage of development, a range of cruising speeds between 460mph and 500mph was available and in this speed range, the fuel consumption was relatively insensitive to speed. The fuel capacity was 6,900 Imperial gallons.

The second stage of development on the Comet 2 was based on projected engine developments which Rolls-Royce anticipated. They expected to be able to provide an increase of take-off rpm, an increase of maximum continuous rpm and an increase of maximum cruising rpm to 7,350. The use of the higher take-off rating would initially be restricted to the higher aerodrome temperatures where it was of most value and the MTOW and other characteristics remained unchanged. The higher take-off thrust increased the payload by about 2,700lbs, while the higher cruising thrust further reduced the sensitivity of payload to speed, raising the lower limit to about 480mph. The cruise rating was set such as to give satisfactory life to the engine and its individual components without falling far below maximum continuous rating, thus affecting the aircraft's performance and fuel consumption. In the case of the Comet 2, this was set at 7,250 rpm with an overhaul period of 500 hours. The maximum operating altitude was 42,000ft. The engines could be slightly throttled with reduction in weight as fuel was used.

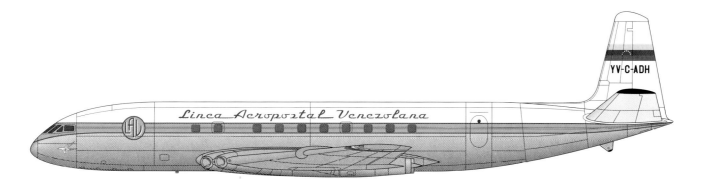

One of the most important changes made, following the commencement of the design work, was the development of a modified wing section. This feature was tried out on the prototype Comet 1 in 1952 and there was therefore time to incorporate the alteration in the production stage of the Comet 2. The new wing section gave an improved C L max and was also in part responsible for a better take-off performance. It also improved the slow flying characteristics, reduced the landing speed and made it impossible for the wing to be stalled during the take-off run. The Comet 2's range was adequate for all but the very longest trunk route stages of the world, and the cruising speed of 480-500mph was higher than that of any transport aeroplane likely to be offered for sale for some time to come.

The prototype made its maiden flight at Hatfield at 3.24 pm on Saturday, 16th February 1952. Cunningham flew the aircraft for 1 hour and 54 minutes at heights up to 25,000ft and landed as dusk gathered. By the end of the month, de Havilland had orders for 45 Comets, 24 of which were Comet 2s. On 27th August 1953, the first Comet 2 production aircraft, G-AMXA, flew for the first time and soon joined G-ALYT in the test programme. During one development flight the Inspector General of the Comets, Air Chief Marshal Sir Ralph Cochrane, was in the right hand seat. As the Comet was descending for Hatfield it flew overhead Bassingbourne, south of Cambridge, where a squadron of Meteors was based. When the aircraft was flying at 200 knots at about 8,000ft, Cunningham noticed out of the corner of his right eye a Meteor just off the starboard wing. "The pilot was very happy, raising two fingers! I looked at Cochrane, I don't think he saw it. I prayed he had not seen it as the RAF had given instructions to its pilots not to formate on civil aircraft." Back on terra firma, Cunningham phoned the officer-in-charge of the Meteor squadron and passed on the aircraft's registration in order to alert the ambitious pilot to the possibility of a repercussion.

In the early stages of test flying, the prototype was used for extensive tests on the ice protection system on the engines and the intakes. The experimental department at de Havilland installed an RA29 Mk 523 engine and a Comet 2 production type air intake to the starboard outboard position of G-ALYT. A grid was mounted forward of the air intake to spray water at the required concentration onto the air intake and engine inlet guide vanes, and to provide maximum icing. Distilled water from two 96-gallon Vampire fuel tanks, situated in the main passenger compartment, was supplied to the rig, and temperatures down to − 30°C provided the most severe icing conditions. The control panel for the system was situated to the left of the crew entrance door and it occupied the former galley position. Water was delivered to the panel by the tanks' booster pumps while a converted fuel heater, using hot air from the port engines and fed to the spray grid, heated the water as required, the temperature being maintained by running hot air and water pipes together inside a lagged fairing. Both hot air and water were released through finely calibrated nozzles on the spray grid, preventing any tendency of the water to freeze prematurely.

A periscope mounted at the control panel station enabled the physical process of ice accumulation and removal to be observed. The wing leading edge adjacent to the engine intake, the intake itself and the front portions of the engine, could all be seen. Two electrically-operated Robot miniature cameras were used to record these conditions. One was mounted in a heated box on the spray grid structure, facing aft towards the engine and covered the leading edge, intake and part of the engine. The other, also in a heated box, was mounted on the side of the intake and operated through perspex windows covering the intake and the lower part of the engine on a larger scale.

To photograph the engine and intake, extra lighting was used which consisted of three electronic flash tubes spaced around the intake. The windows in the intake were fitted with infra-red filters and the cameras were loaded with infra-red sensitive film. Experience had shown that infra-red penetration of the spray was much better than in normal photographic light.

To assess the efficiency of each method of de-icing and the effect on engine performance, it was necessary to obtain comprehensive data on pressures, temperatures and valve positions relative to outside conditions of altitude, speed, temperature and water concentration. To achieve this, the observer's panel containing 60 instruments was photographed, and a continuous trace recorder was used for selected transient conditions.

G-AMXD, the first of two Comet 2Es, was used for tropical trials in Africa visiting Khartoum for take-off trials in hot weather and Entebbe, situated at 3,760ft, for similar trials at high altitude. These tropical trials formed part of the programme for obtaining a full civil C of A for the Comet 2 and confirmed the Comet 2's performance with the improved Rolls-Royce Avon engines. During the trials, the aircraft was flown by Cunningham and Buggé. On the outward journey on 30th September, the Comet flew from Hatfield to Athens, a distance of about 1,530 statute miles, in 3 hours 25 minutes, and from Athens to Khartoum, 1,633 statute miles, in 3 hours 40 minutes. At Khartoum the weather was ideal for the purpose of the hot-weather tests and was indeed unusually hot for the time of year, the air temperature being 43°C. After completing take-off tests at Khartoum, the Comet flew to Entebbe on 4th of October, covering 1,074 miles in 2 hours 30 minutes. The aircraft then left Entebbe on 6th of October, stopping at Khartoum after a flight of 2 hours 25 minutes and then flew non-stop to Rome, 2,171 miles in 5 hours 20 minutes. The final leg from Rome to Hatfield, approximately 930 miles, was completed in 2 hours 35 minutes. On all the sectors the Comet carried a full capacity payload of 13,000lb, largely made up of lead ballast. G-AMXD returned to Hatfield on the 7th of October 1954 after completing the trials, which supplemented similar tests carried out in January and February 1954 when G-AMXA, fitted with an earlier type of Rolls-Royce Avon engine, visited Khartoum and Johannesburg.

By October 1952, it appeared to de Havilland that the Comet was in danger of becoming, to some degree, a victim of its own success, at least in terms of the company's marketing plans. At the time, twenty-one of the Comet 1s and 1As were under construction, larger sales of the Comet 1s were not expected as production of the Comet 2 was under way and operators were confident that further, improved versions, were likely to be available at a relatively early date. With their confidence in the merits of jet propulsion growing all the time, operators were faced with the problem of whether to purchase the Comet 2, due for delivery in 1954, or to wait for the recently announced 58-76 passenger Comet 3 in 1957. Furthermore, operators were aware that de Havilland's developments would not stop with the Comet 3.

At the time of the Comet groundings in April 1954, three Comet 2s had taken to the air and twenty others were under construction at Hatfield, Belfast and Chester. The first three Comet 2s, and twelve of those constructed at Chester, were eventually completed and went into service. Three of the

Comet 2E G-AMXD was one of two aircraft used for Comet 4 development. The outboard Ghost engines were replaced with the Avon RA29, the cabin was strengthened and oval windows fitted allowing the aircraft to be operated on BOAC route proving flights.

On 16th of February 1952, the Comet 2 prototype took to the air for the first time, when this classic shot was taken with the aircraft wearing a new grey, white and blue livery, replacing the natural metal finish used on the Comet 1s.

Comet 2s entered service with the RAF's 51 Squadron at Wyton for special electronic reconnaissance duties. They were not modified and operated with their cabin pressurisation systems deactivated.

A further ten Comet 2s were modified to become Comet C2s to serve with 216 Squadron RAF, from June 1956 until April 1967. The first two of the batch of ten Comet C2s were delivered to the RAF on 7th and 8th June 1956 and they were the first jet-engined aircraft ever to be operated by the Royal Air Force Transport Command. They were also the first military aircraft to enter service with a full civil passenger carrying C of A. The C2s joined 216 Squadron at RAF Lyneham in Wiltshire, with the first operational flight of a C2 in squadron service taking place on Saturday, 23rd June when a British Minister and staff were conveyed to Moscow. It was the first British jet-engined aircraft ever to visit Russia's capital. A second Comet of Transport Command flew to Moscow on 3rd July and, while in Moscow, the opportunity was taken to give a group of Russian officials a flight in the aircraft. This was to have taken place during the first Comet's visit but was postponed due to a fault in one of the aircraft's batteries.

Two other Comet 2 airframes were completed as Comet 2Es to serve as Avon engine test beds leading to the introduction of the Avon 524 in the Comet 4. The engine development programme was by BOAC's Comet Flight, under the management of Captain T B Stoney and his deputy, Captain R E Millichap. The Flight was equipped with two Comet 2Es, G-AMXK, owned by BOAC, and G-AMXD, owned by the MoS. Each aircraft was fitted with two Rolls-Royce Avon RA29s of 10,500lb s.t. in the outboard nacelles and two RA9 engines of 7,300lb s.t. in the inboard nacelles. The inboard engines were standard on the Comet 2 and the air intakes were unchanged. But the RA29 engines required an enlarged air intake.

The programme started on 16th September 1957 and ended on 31st May 1958. The aim was to achieve 7,000 engine hours and in order to reproduce realistic airline operating conditions, the aircraft, for the most part, flew from London Airport to Beirut and back within a day, a round trip of some 4,500 miles. During the first six weeks, the schedule was six return flights to Beirut each week but during the following fortnight some time was spent on the training of an additional crew and the flights were reduced to four each week. From 10th November onwards, the number of flights to Beirut was stepped up to eleven per week, with occasionally twelve flights if the programme fell behind because of weather delays. During April a number of flights were made to Nairobi and, on 5th May, daily return flights to Gander, Newfoundland, were started.

Throughout the programme, plans were made so as to ensure that the maximum flying time was achieved during each sortie. For this reason a lowspeed cruise technique was adopted so that the flying time from London to Beirut and back was rather more than eleven hours. With the RA29 engines installed, the Comet 2 was naturally overpowered and in order to remain within airframe limitations, the inboard Avons were throttled back so that the RA29s in the outboard positions were working at the normal cruising revolutions. When necessary, other delaying tactics were used such as flying holding patterns and making practice approaches at terminal airfields en route. If wind conditions were such that the return flight to Beirut could not be completed within the statutory tour of duty of an individual crew because a refuelling stop at Rome was called for, a different flight plan was adopted. The alternative was usually two flights in the day from London to overhead Brindisi and back. The aircrews were keen to accumulate flying hours and they often prolonged their flights beyond the original plan if an opportunity presented itself. For instance, a Captain Kelly, finding himself with fuel to spare at the end of his routine flight, elected to add more hours by flying from London Airport to Geneva and back, thus, incidentally, keeping his Comet in the air continuously for more than eight hours, longer than any Comet had ever flown before.

Although nothing was allowed to interfere with the main objective of collecting hours, other development work was fitted in during Comet flights and the opportunity was taken to try out some Comet 4 components. Among these were fuel heater control valves and the latest jet-pipe temperature servo potentiometer. The flights also provided useful opportunities for trying out operational techniques and one such study, on behalf of the Ministry of Transport and Civil Aviation, was concerned with the use of Decca in connection with airport control. One of the Comets was fitted with Decca and it was found that the Decca coverage of the Orkney Islands area had characteristics similar to those in the vicinity of London Airport. Thus the Orkneys provided a most useful experimental area where Decca holding and approach techniques, which were applicable to London, could be tried out at will. It would have been extremely difficult to have carried out the tests in the crowded air of the London Control Zone. For their part, de Havilland were able to use some of the flights to give flightdeck experience to members of the Design Department and to the Servicing School instructors who were to train airline engineers for the Comet 4 and the Comet 4B.

The Comet 2E flights started operations with six crews and one spare pilot, with a seventh complete crew later joining the programme, all pilots having had previous Comet experience. From the start of the programme to the 10th of May, the two Comets had accomplished 3,344 flying hours at an average of more than fourteen hours per day. Throughout this period there was only one unscheduled engine change following the failure of an auxiliary unit. The tests were based on a pool of eight engines, four in the two aircraft and four either in store or undergoing an inspection strip. The standard Comet 2 Avon engines in the inboard positions caused no trouble whatsoever.

When the Comet 2Es were delivered to BOAC in September 1957, the approved life of the Avon RA29 engine stood at 250 hours. This figure had been determined largely as a result of engine hours built up in the Comet 3 development aircraft at Hatfield and in a Canberra operated by Rolls-Royce. According to schedule, the first Avon RA29 was removed and stripped at 247 hours and, as a result of this inspection, two engines were allotted to run up to 500 hours and the life was officially extended to this figure at the end of November. In February 1958, two engines started a 750 hour trial and in March this life was officially approved. Two engines then started a 1,000 hour trial which was completed without incident by the beginning of May.

Following their service with BOAC, both of the Comet 2Es were later used as test-beds. One was used for long-range radio development flying at the RAE Farnborough and one for Smith's autopilot and automatic landing research at the B.L.E.U. at R.A.E. Bedford.

One other Comet 2 modified to full C2 standard became a wing and fuselage fatigue tank test specimen, but seven other airframes, on which work had begun, were abandoned. Three had been under construction at Hatfield, four at Chester, and although Short Brothers completed a number of Comet 2 fuselages, the plan to build complete aircraft at Belfast was abandoned.

Even when the Comet C4 entered service with the RAF in 1962, the C2 continued to operate with 216 Squadron until its gradual retirement commenced towards the end of 1966, with the last Comet C2 operational flight being operated by XK698, arriving back at Lyneham on 1st April 1967. The last aircraft, XK699, was flown into retirement on 13th of June 1967 at RAF Henlow for storage and on to RAF Lyneham as a gate guardian. The Comet 2Rs with 51 Squadron continued in service until the 10th January 1975.

The Comet 2X was flown to Halton on 15th June 1959 after completing the Rolls-Royce Avon engine trials. It was given maintenance serial number 7610M and was used for instruction until the Autumn of 1966 when its engines were removed, and by the following September the airframe had been scrapped.

THE COMET 3

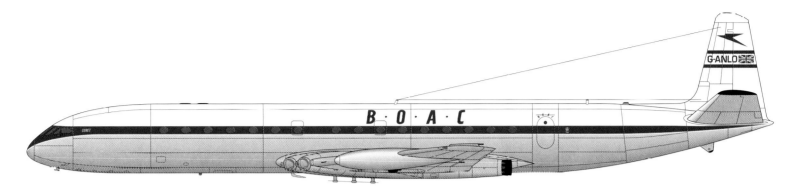

At the Farnborough Air Show in September 1952, de Havilland announced the projected Comet 3, a version with a greater capacity and range than the Comet 2. The Comet 3 was to have a maximum take-off weight of 145,000lb, passenger capacity of 58 to 76, and a maximum stage range of about 2,700 miles, approximately 60% more than that of the Comet 1. The aircraft fuselage had been stretched to 111ft 6in, oval windows were fitted, a higher fuel capacity due to pinion tanks, and Avon RA26 Mk502 engines were used, giving 10,000lb s.t. The two pinion tanks were a distinctive feature of the wing and they brought the total fuel capacity up to 10,000 Imperial gallons and the jet exhaust pipes were moved outward to reduce noise and fatigue. Orders for the Comet 3 were received from BOAC, Pan American and Air India, with a choice of 58 seat First Class passenger layout or a 76 seat Tourist Class accommodation.

In late 1952, before the Comet 3 specification was finally defined, a major modification to the wing geometry was tried on G-ALVG. This change of shape — sometimes referred to as the 'full soft-pencil' change of leading edge profile — extended well beyond the front spar and dummy wing pod tanks of 400 gallon capacity were fitted. The original Ghost engine and intakes were retained. A large wind-tunnel model was mounted in the low-speed wind-tunnel so that detailed testing of stall 'fixes' could be carried out in parallel with the full scale tests. This parallel testing rapidly achieved a high standard of free-air stall handling which carried over to the Comet 3 prototype, G-ANLO [9].

While G-ANLO was under construction, a trial installation of the pinion tanks was made on G-ALZK, the second Comet 1 prototype. The first flight of G-ANLO took place on 19th

On a fine evening on 19th of July 1954, G-ANLO the prototype Mk III, displays the extended fuselage and wing pinion tank on the occasion of its first flight.

The prototype Comet 3 in the revised colour scheme worn for the around the world record flight performed in December 1956.

July 1954 and the aircraft soon demonstrated a stall-free envelope on take-off over the full weight range. However due to the problems with the Comet 1s and 1As which had been grounded three months earlier, the Comet 3 programme was abandoned. The first production Comet 3 had been scheduled to appear late in 1956 and during 1957 the production rate was expected to average approximately four per month. De Havilland had planned to supply the Comets to prospective customers at the rate of six per month within two years. The ten airframes under construction were scrapped, apart from G-ANLO which was used for development testing to define the Comet 4. Part of the programme involved testing the larger plain flaps and modified split flaps under the centre section for the Comet 4. When G-ANLO had completed this project it was then modified to repeat the process in support of the Comet 4B proposed for BEA and was re-designated Comet 3B. For this programme the pinion tanks were removed and the wing tips were clipped to reduce the span to 108ft, with its first flight taking place on 21st August 1958 [10].

Both the Comet 2 and the Comet 3 had a bulkhead separating the cabin into two compartments, thus avoiding what was termed the 'tube effect.' This was of greater benefit in the case of the Comet 3 with its longer fuselage. Another advantage of the bulkhead, in the case of the Comet 3, was the ability to operate it as a two class aircraft. The seating capacities of the two compartments were between 26 and 34 in the front and 32 and 42 in the rear. No tourist scheme was adopted for the Comet 2, which had a standard seating layout for 44 passengers.

Both Comets were the first aircraft to employ the new de Havilland double chair, which effected a considerable weight saving as it weighed only 50lb but offered First Class comfort. Each half of the seat was individually adjustable, through a

John Cunningham and crew are given the traditional 'Hawaiian welcome' on arrival at Honolulu.

At Bombay (Santa Cruz Airport) India, during the world flight on 3rd of December 1955, the prototype Comet 3 spent 1 hour and 48 minutes replenishing food and fuel supplies in the company of an Air India Lockheed Super Constellation.

reclining angle of 26.5 degrees, and a legrest attachment could be fitted for night travel. The structure of the chair and its seatbelts were stressed to 9g forward. When it is borne in mind that no Comet normally operated stages taking longer than about five hours, the 'passenger amenity' space was generous in both the Comet 2 and the Comet 3. The washrooms, wardrobe and similar installations in the aircraft occupied some twelve feet of fuselage at full cross section. The aircraft had an additional emergency exit door on the starboard side of the fuselage, opposite the passenger entrance, and the greater length of the fuselage made available a considerable increase in freight and baggage volume. There was a 150cuft hold under the forward floor, a 240cuft hold under the rear

The crew of the Comet 3 have one last photograph taken before boarding the aircraft for the next stage to Singapore and Australia.

floor and a 155cuft hold at the extreme end of the pressure hull, which could be reached from inside the cabin and loaded via a separate door on the starboard side of the aircraft.

During its test-flight programme, G-ANLO established a number of speed records. The de Havilland Gazette detailed these events under proud headlines such as 'A Quarter Way Round The World in Thirteen Hours' and 'Fastest Airline Timetable Cut by More than Seven Hours'. Twice within eight days the Comet set new records. On 16th October 1955, piloted by Cunningham, the aircraft flew from London to Khartoum at a speed of 523mph. On the night of the 23rd to 24th October, it covered the 5,634 statute miles to Johannesburg in 12 hours 58 minutes 57 seconds, including 53 minutes on the ground at Khartoum. The flying time of about 12 hours 10 minutes and the actual distance flown, about 6,000 miles, represented a cruising speed of more than 490mph.

Much of the work carried out on the Comet 3 was concerned with the eventual certification of the projected Comet 4. The Comet 3's performance demonstrated, in a practical fashion, the commercial capabilities of the Comet 4. The hope was for a one stop Comet service from London to Johannesburg which could cut existing timetables by more than seven hours. Such a version of the Comet could pay its way with only half the seats occupied.

In December 1955 the Comet 3 flew around the world, with the purpose of the flight to study the operational performance of the Comet 3, flying strictly in accordance with

On 13th of December 1955, G-ANLO taxies in at Honolulu airport Hawaii, after the 3,220 mile stage from Nandi Fiji, which had taken 6 hours 40 minutes on the record around the world flight.

airline procedure, on representative stages of a familiar trade route around the world passing through a wide variety of climatic and other conditions. It was essentially a British Commonwealth circuit of the globe. Mr. Frank Lloyd, Commercial Sales Manager and Contracts Manager of de Havilland, was the executive in charge of the business aspects of the flight, and Cunningham and Bruggé were the pilots. The aircraft flew in BOAC colours and Captain Peter Cane, who was Head Pilot of the Comet fleet in 1952~54, accompanied the aircraft as a member of the crew throughout the tour.

En route, de Havilland and BOAC received assistance for the flight from Qantas Empire Airways, Trans Australia Airlines, Australian National Airways, Tasman Empire Airways, Canadian Pacific Air Lines, Trans Canada Airlines, the Shell Company and its associates, the Royal Air Force and the Royal Australian, New Zealand and Canadian Air Forces, with respect to ground handling, maintenance, refuelling, meteorology, radio and communications, customs, immigration and other services. Pilots from these airlines also flew as supernumerary crew members on sectors with which they were professionally familiar.

The aircraft had been due to depart from Hatfield at 05.00 GMT on Friday, 2nd December for the 30-hour flight to Sydney via Cairo, Bombay, Singapore and Darwin. Fog prevented a pre-dawn departure and as it was deemed likely that the next few mornings would be foggy, the aircraft took off at 10.54 GMT when there was a break in the weather and visibility was about 300 yards. As the crew had already been busy for about ten hours before take-off, they could not safely work the 30-hour

flight so an overnight stop was made at Cairo. The Comet thus arrived at Sydney's Kingsford Smith airport on the afternoon of Sunday, 4th December, when a vast crowd was there to meet it. Enthusiastic children led a break through onto the airfield and the Comet was asked to circle Sydney once more while the runway was safely cleared. As the aircraft came to rest, the crowd surged around it and the airport staff had to provocatively brandish a water hose in order to clear a way for the gangway, to which the crowd responded in good spirits.

As well as the supernumerary crews, the aircraft also carried a team of flight observers including a senior aerodynamicist from Hatfield. The performance, fuel consumption and all-round economics of the Comet, on every stage of the world flight, were found to be within very close tolerances of the flight planning data. In exterior form and drag, the Comet 3 was identical with the Comet 4 then going into production except that the Comet 4 was to have slightly smaller nacelle tanks. One aspect of operation which the flight bore out was the small effect of winds upon the punctuality of a jet liner. However, the weather forecasts were more realistic due to the shorter period of forecast.

Where possible, the Comet was flown strictly in accordance with airline technique, however, some sectors were concerned almost as much with public relations. On the sector from Sydney to Melbourne, the aircraft circled Canberra then, on the way to Perth it circled Adelaide. During a stopover at Auckland at midday on 13th December, the Comet took 50 people on a flight around North Island which was followed by a formal reception in one of the hangars. The

One of the tasks performed by G-ANLO was Comet 4B development flying, during which the aircraft was fitted with the 4B wing and painted in the then current BEA livery. Here seen in a fly-by at Farnborough Air Show.

aircraft then flew to Fiji where the passengers were showered with leis as they disembarked at Nandi. The aircraft then flew on across the International Date Line to Honolulu where the following day many of those on board had a swim at Waikiki before a dawn take-off for Vancouver, arriving in time for lunch on Sunday, the 18th. There was a hard frost on the ground when the aircraft touched down at Downsview beside the new de Havilland factory outside Toronto, to be greeted by a gathering of de Havilland people. When the aircraft reached Montreal on 20th December, the temperature was -15°F. At the end of the Montreal to London stage on 28th December, a distance of 3,350 miles, enough fuel remained in the tanks to circle London for an hour at low level and then, if diverted, to fly to Prestwick, 330 miles away, and there safely circuit and land.

During its circuit of the globe, a great many people were able to fly in the Comet. Local flights of 60 to 90 minutes were flown from Sydney, Melbourne, Perth, Auckland, Honolulu, Vancouver, Montreal and Hatfield. Parties were also carried from Sydney to Melbourne and from Toronto to Montreal. In all, approximately 600 people were given passenger rides.

In the 27,000 miles of route flying from London to Montreal, plus a few thousand miles of local demonstration flights, there were no flight snags and no hold ups whatsoever. In the course of the inspections, the normal schedule of which was strictly adhered to, all that had to be done was to change a fuel pipe seal which was seeping slightly due to having been cut on assembly, and to change a refuelling actuator. Each engine used two pints of lubricant in some 72 hours and 35,000 miles. Aside from the fog in London on 2nd December which had set the programme back by just one day, as far as Montreal no

departure had to be made from a schedule which had been drawn up before leaving Hatfield. A technical fault, to do with the attachment of the jet pipe of No.3 engine, prevented an eastbound flight across the Atlantic on the night of 21st December. The fault was rectified without recourse to any of the spare parts which, as a precaution, had been sent from England.

The crew on the flight had been surprised to find that in some parts of the world, notably Hawaii, the public and even the aviation community seriously thought that a jet airliner would need a long runway, would climb at a flattish gradient over the city of departure causing a noise nuisance, would circuit, approach and land rather fast and would be unbearably noisy when standing and manoeuvring in front of the terminal building, perhaps even scorching the paving. In Honolulu the ground staff thought that special regulations might be needed to keep people a considerable distance away from the jet engine intakes and effluxes during ground running. One local newspaper referred to the efflux as "a blast as hot as a blow torch", and said that "the danger point behind a jet engine is 100 yards". For their part, de Havilland had always stated that the Comet was designed to use runways and airport facilities as they existed, and that a low wing loading was specified so as to be sure of a short take-off and steep climb and a low landing speed with a short landing run. The Comet landed on the short runway at Honolulu, which was 7,000ft, pulled up within 3,000ft and turned off at the intersection, much to the amazement of observers from the Hawaiian Aeronautics Commission. They were equally surprised to see ground staff standing and walking quite close behind the aircraft's tail, while all four engines were running fast enough for the aircraft to start taxiing.

On 21st June 1961, the Comet 3 joined the Blind Landing Experimental Unit at the Royal Aircraft Establishment Bedford as XP915 and from then on was used on the development of 'autoland' equipment.

During tests conducted in connection with the proposed Comet 4, the measured take-off performance of the Comet 3 proved to be slightly better than originally estimated, whilst the cruising Mach number of 0.74 was attained at some 30 rpm below the recommended engine speed. The cruising economy was also close to the estimate. There was no sign of a ground stall during take-off at the maximum ground angle, with the tail bumper rubbing the runway, at the full all-up weight of 150,000lb. The Comet 3 was flown up to a true Mach number of 0.81. Following its career as a civilian prototype, G-ANLO was given serial number XP915 and delivered to the B.L.E.U. at

Bedford on 21st June 1961 for work on autoland testing. However the aircraft was damaged on 19th April 1971 when it was hit by a BEA Trident 3, G-AWZA, which was on a crew-training exercise and was making an approach to land. XP915 had been waiting to turn onto the runway to take-off and the impact knocked its fin off and wrinkled the fuselage. It is understood that no accident report was ever published. It was repaired using a fin from a Comet 2 and finally retired in 1972. In 1973 it was used for non-flying foam arrester trials, at the end of which it was dismantled and the fuselage was taken to Woodford to be used as a Nimrod mock-up.

The Comet 3 comes to a halt in a bed of urea formaldehyde foam, in a trial programme on the use of permanent arrester beds to halt aircraft in the event of an overrun.

THE COMET 4

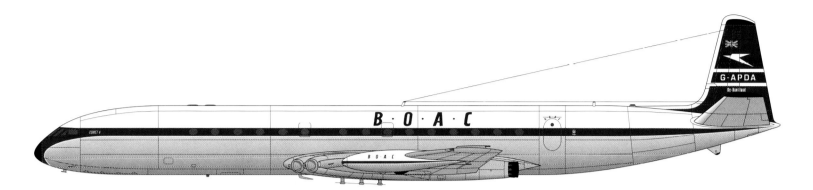

Production of the Comet 3 was deferred pending the Inquiry of 1954. As a result, it was possible for de Havilland to bring forward the introduction of the more advanced formula, namely the Comet 4, which could then be made available earlier than would otherwise have been the case. De Havilland announced their plan to develop the Comet 4 on 17th March 1955, and deliveries of the aircraft were expected to begin in the latter part of 1958. The aircraft was referred to by the manufacturer as the Intercontinental Comet 4. After the Report of the Court of Inquiry, BOAC announced their intention to order nineteen Comet 4s.

The Comet 4 took off from Hatfield on its 83-minute maiden flight at 6.13 pm on Sunday, 27th April 1958 under the command of Cunningham. The aircraft was G-APDA, the first for BOAC. The Comet 4 was extensively modified, with realistic fuel reserves which included allowances for a 30 minute standoff at 1,000ft, followed by a diversion of 200 miles from sea level. A reduction of about 9% in cruising specific fuel consumption was achieved compared with the existing RA26 engine on the Comet 3. The usable fuel capacity was increased to a total of 8,750 Imperial gallons and the MTOW was increased to 152,000lb. A total of 28 Comet 4s were built.

A number of Comet versions were planned. The concept of a Comet 4A was launched in June 1956, and this was to be a short range version of the Comet 4 with the fuselage stretched by 40in and the wing span reduced by 7ft. The fuselage stretch allowed for a layout which would seat 92 tourist passengers in five abreast seating, the rear fuselage and tail were reinforced to permit higher cruising speeds at lower altitudes and the MTOW was increased to 152,500lb. The optimum altitude for maximum cruising speed of the Comet 4A was 23,500ft and at this height the true air speed attainable at Mach 0.75 was 522mph on a standard day. Airlines would probably plan to use a cruising altitude of 23,500ft for short stages but would fly higher over the longer sectors. Increasing the cruising altitude, while still flying at the normal operating limit Mach Number of 0.75, was a way of gaining increases in payload or range at the expense of a small reduction in true air speed. The payload of the Comet 4A was well suited to the US domestic network and was also convenient in relation to existing passenger handling facilities being conducive to short turn-around times. On 24th July, Capital Airlines ordered ten Comet 4As for delivery from mid 1959, but ten months later the airline had to defer the order due to financial difficulties and it was subsequently cancelled. The project was shelved and as a result no Comet 4A was built.

In May 1957, de Havilland announced the Comet 4B which they also termed the Continental Comet 4B. This was intended specifically for short-range operations such as on BEA's longer routes. It had a reduced wingspan of 7ft 2ins in comparison to the Comet 4, the pinion tanks were removed, thus reducing drag and improving operating costs which, in turn, reduced the fuel capacity to 7,800 gallons. The fuselage was 6.5ft longer than that of the Comet 4, the rear fuselage and tail were strengthened, the MTOW was 158,000lb and four Avon RA29 Mk525 were used. It cruised faster than the Comet 4 and at lower altitude, carrying up to 100 passengers over stage distances between 300 and 1,500 miles. The optimum altitude was 23,000ft and the payload was 22,200lb which represented 102 Tourist Class passengers. A Comet 4 reverse thrust was fitted to the outer engines and the engine noise was also reduced with silencing nozzles. In August 1957, BEA stated their intention to order six Comet 4Bs, later increased to fourteen for their trunk routes and the contract was signed in March 1958. The first Comet 4B, G-APMA, came off the Hatfield production line on 15th June 1959 in the new BEA colours of a white roof, black cheat line and red wings, making its first flight on 27th June. G-APMB made its public debut at Farnborough in September and the first two BEA Comet 4Bs, G-APMB and G-APMC, were handed over at Hatfield on 16th November ready for route familiarisation flights throughout Europe. Full Comet schedules commenced on 1st April 1960

The first production Comet 4 takes to the air for the first time at Hatfield on 27th April 1958, with John Cunningham in command.

G-APDA is prepared for engine test runs prior to the first flight in April 1958.

with five aircraft. In August 1959, Olympic Airways ordered two Comet 4Bs, later increasing this to four. A total of eighteen Comet 4Bs were built.

In November 1957 de Havilland announced the Comet 4C, also known as the Intermediate Comet 4C. The aircraft had the fuselage and engine configuration of the Comet 4B and the wings of the Comet 4. A total of 23 Comet 4Cs were built and the first flight took place on 31st October 1959. Misrair, subsequently to become United Arab Airlines, ordered three Comet 4Cs in December 1959, later increasing this in steps to nine and In March 1960, Middle East Airlines confirmed their order for four Comet 4Cs. The first Comet 4C to be handed over, XA-NAS, (ex G-AOVV), was delivered to Mexicana on the 14th January 1960 and entered service with the airline six months later on 4th July. Comet 4Cs entered service with United Arab Airlines later in July and with Middle East Airlines in January 1961. In August 1961 a Comet 4C, with an executive suite at the front of the aircraft and seats for 50 people in the aft cabin, was ordered for the personal use of King Saud bin Abdul Aziz al Saud of Saudi Arabia. In March 1962, Aerolineas Argentinas ordered a Comet 4C and took delivery the following month of the aircraft that had first flown the previous August in MEA colours, registered G-AROV, in anticipation of MEA's option on a fifth being confirmed. Sudan Airways signed a contract for two Comet 4Cs in May 1962, and started services in December 1962. In August 1962 Kuwait Airways ordered one Comet 4C which later increased to two, starting services with their own aircraft in January 1963.

The MoD ordered a Comet 4C, XS235, for use at Boscombe Down for research into long range navigation and instrumentation. The aircraft had a bulbous radome under the forward fuselage and flew to many parts of the world in order to gain information from all environments on the operation of the equipment on board. Two final Comet 4Cs were built at Chester but remained unsold until they were allocated to the Nimrod programme as prototypes. 23 Comet 4Cs were built, eighteen of them at Chester, bringing total production of all Comets to 113, with the Comet 4C being the most successful model.

In September 1960 a military version, the Comet C4, was ordered by the RAF Transport Command, for service with 216 Squadron at RAF Lyneham who had operated Comet C2s and Comet T2s since 1956. The Comet C4s were fitted with 94 rearward facing seats and could be converted for ambulance duties to accommodate twelve stretchers, forty-seven sitting patients and six attendants. They could also be operated as VIP transports. On the retirement of the Comet C2s in March 1967, the five Comet C4s were allocated solely to VIP duties.

In its genesis, the Comet 4 was a logical development of the Comet 3. Test flying with the Comet 3 prototype had continued without interruption. The take-off and stalling characteristics were examined and the performance throughout the complete range of speeds and altitudes was measured. De Havilland were thus confident that the estimated performance figures for the Comet 4 could, even at an early stage in the project, be accepted with some confidence as realistic minima. The Comet 4's airfield requirements were notable when compared with the take-off and landing performance of many contemporary aircraft. During the test flying of the Comet 4, hundreds of payload take-offs were made at all times of the year from the runway at Hatfield, which measured exactly 6,000ft. The take-offs were made with plenty of runway to spare.

Due to the increase in thrust of the Comet 4 and in spite of the greater MTOW, the take-off distance was somewhat better than that of the Comet 3. At sea level and at standard atmospheric conditions, the take-off length for the Comet 4 was reduced by almost 2% compared with the Comet 3. The wing flaps of the Comet 4 were of greater area than those on the Comet 1 and for landing they could be lowered to 80° compared with 60° on the earlier aircraft. This increased both the lift and the drag on landing. The stalling speed of the Comet 4, in its landing configuration, was only 96 knots. A yaw damper was incorporated in the rudder circuit, making it possible for the fin and rudder size of the aircraft to remain unchanged.

The projected overall journey times for the Comet 4, calculated from the Comet 3 prototypes world flight, were impressive. From London to Tokyo, with four stops, the journey time was 22 hours and 3 minutes, and to Sydney, with four stops, the time was 27 hours and 37 minutes. There were two routes for the journey from London to Johannesburg, one via Tripoli and Brazzaville taking 14 hours and 40 minutes, and one via Cairo and Nairobi in 15 hours and 23 minutes. The flight from London to Rio de Janeiro took 13 hours and 58 minutes, with one stop, and from London to New York, the flight took 9 hours and 30 minutes with one stop.

The trans-continental route across the United States was another natural application of the Comet 4. The non-stop flight from New York to San Francisco could be made in 6.5 hours and the tourist capacity payload of 19,300lb could be carried with a regularity of more than 85%. On shorter routes within the US, the aircraft offered savings in time, for it was designed for stage lengths up to 3,000 miles, and nowhere on earth was more than 36 hours away from a point of departure.

The Comet 4 incorporated all the developments accumulated since the first flight of the Comet 1 prototype in 1949, including those resulting from the practical experience gained in some 30,000 hours of airline operation, together with findings from the exhaustive investigation of 1954 which was without precedent in aeronautical engineering.

Prior to delivery to BOAC, G-APDA received a change of livery when the blue cheatline was extended through the nose to the nose wheel door housing.

Advances in the knowledge of metal fatigue were heeded and a great deal of repeated load testing was carried out on full-scale components. In particular the stress level in the fuselage seam joints and cutouts was kept low so that local damage would not affect the safety of the structure. De Havilland were confident that the integrity of the new structure would be beyond question. They conducted literally thousands of fatigue and strength tests on the Comet 4 to satisfy the airworthiness requirements of fatigue life and static strength.

The fatigue properties of the wing were greatly improved by producing wing tension members and skins with copper bearing alloy. Tougher aluminium copper alloys were used in place of the higher strength but brittle aluminium zinc alloys for tension applications. Although this involved a weight penalty, the fatigue life was greatly increased and safe fatigue lives for the main spar booms were shown by full-size tests to exceed 80,000 hours.

Fifty test panels, some incorporating windows and an escape hatch, were tested in water tanks at Hatfield and a full-scale nose section was water tested to the equivalent of twenty years of intensive airline flying. A full-scale rear portion of the fuselage, incorporating the passenger entry doors, the luggage doors, windows and the rear pressure dome, was tested to the equivalent of 360,000 flying hours and the equivalent of more than two and three quarter million gust loads were applied. In a further test, a three-inch crack was deliberately introduced and, when further tests followed, the equivalent of six thousand flying hours were completed before the crack began to grow significantly [11].

The aim was to design for a safe life of at least 30,000 hours, equivalent to ten years of operation at 3,000 hours per year, during which time the aircraft would have flown some fifteen million miles. Assuming a flight duration of three hours, this meant that the fuselage would be pressurised 10,000 times. De Havilland had bought a computer, named Pegasus, to help with the development of the Comet 2, 3 and 4 which was particularly helpful for calculating the response of the wing and tail to gusts and manoeuvres.

Fatigue tests were not confined to the pressure cabin; wingspar components and complete wings and tailplanes were also tested. The test programme for the fuselage was designed to demonstrate that no cracks would occur in the specimens before 60,000 reversals, equivalent to 180,000 hours of flying, and that any cracks occurring later would not extend seriously before another 60,000 cabin pressure reversals. These tests were made to six times the operating life of 30,000 hours to allow for any scatter in fatigue life. Water tank tests were made to prove that the structure bettered these limits. Certain tests were made with wing loads applied to the specimen. The centre portion of the fuselage, with the wing centre section, was subjected to 120,000 pressurisations, and 2,880,000 wing gusts, equivalent to 360,000 flying hours, without any major structural failure occurring. Finally a complete fuselage and wing fatigue test was conducted in a similar manner to the G-ALYU Farnborough water tank test.

The flying control system of the Comet 4 was fully duplicated mechanically and triplicated hydraulically. There was spring-feel on all flying control circuits and dynamic pressure, or Q feel, on the elevator control. The high control breakout forces which were criticised on the Comet 1 were reduced. The breakout force required for initiating movement of the control column was set below that used on the Comet 1.

There were two gear ratios on the elevator control and the pilot selected the changeover from the coarse to the fine control at 170 to 200 knots IAS. An automatic trim control, which applied a nose up trim change at Mach 0.78 indicated, was added to counteract the nose down trim change that the aircraft experienced at this Mach number, and a warning horn sounded at Mach 0.77 indicated. Stall warning was given by a stickshaker at about 10 knots above the stall.

Electric power for the Comet was generated as AC and rectified to DC. On the Comet 4, alternator capacity was increased from 4 x 250 to 4 x 350 amps to cope with the greater power requirements. Electric and hydraulic equipment was housed in separate underfloor bays separated by the main cargo compartment to avoid explosion risk. Any electrical equipment installed in the airframe which was likely to come into contact with hydraulic fluid had been explosion tested.

Another change which affected the structure was the redesign of the engine jet pipes to avoid pressure wave buffeting on the fuselage structure. These changes formed the basis of the structural design of the Comet 4. The basic policy adopted was to establish a safe life, but fail safe features were also incorporated in the design. Stress levels were kept to a low value so that cracks were unlikely to develop in service, and if they did they would spread slowly. The fuselage skin was increased to a minimum thickness of 19 SWG compared with 22 SWG on the Comet 1, and as a result the working stress was only 22% of the ultimate.

On the Comet 4, thermal de-icing was used for the leading edges of the wing, tail and engine intakes, and control cabin windows were de-misted by Triplex electrically heated goldfilm glass. Only the windscreen panels immediately in front of each pilot were continuously de-iced. All fuel tanks were integral except in the centre section where bag tanks were used and each engine was normally fed independently. The fuel tank vents were at the wing trailing edge and the blow off valves of the underwing pressure refuelling system were redesigned to avoid over pressurising the tanks during refuelling.

Extremely thorough systems testing was a feature of Comet 4 development. Tests were made with a full-scale flying

The first production Comet 4, G-APDA is towed to the runway at Hatfield to continue route proving flights in the summer of 1958.

The view from the Comet 4, during trials in-flight over Greece.

control and hydraulic test rig representative of the Comet 4 system. Similar tests were made of the electric, air-conditioning and fuel systems. Results of tests with these rigs no doubt played an important part in the rapid airworthiness certification of the Comet 4. Following functional tests with the rigs and the simulation of various failures, the rigs were engaged on endurance tests. This thorough background of testing, both of systems and structure, combined with thousands of hours of flight experience, gave the Comet 4 an unprecedented development background as it entered service over the North Atlantic.

The question on de Havilland's mind was whether they could ever succeed in selling a completely redesigned derivative of the Comet 3, or whether the image was so damaged that the Comet had become unsaleable to the airlines and to the public. The answer came in February 1955 when BOAC announced it would buy nineteen Comet 4s, similar to the Series 3 (which from the start had oval windows) but with even greater fuel capacity and range, with a weight up to 70762 kg (156,000lb), which later grew to 73483 kg (162,000lb).

The Comet 4 could carry its capacity payload of 16,850lb with 85% regularity or better over the great majority of the important trunk routes of the world. The payload capacity of the Comet 4 was planned to meet the need for a mainline aircraft to serve the trunk routes between Europe and the Far East, South Africa and South America and across the continents and the Pacific Ocean. Its size and capacity were calculated so as to be large enough to cater for the growing traffic on these routes during the following five to ten years and it represented an unrivalled combination of speed and capacity over these routes. However, it did not have the range to operate a non-stop westbound trans-atlantic service.

The Comet was launched in an age when the general public were becoming concerned about 'noise pollution'. Work on jet noise and on methods of reducing it was largely sponsored by the Ministry of Supply and began in the early 1950s. Models were tested by researchers at Cranfield and Southampton, and the results were developed into full-scale hardware by Rolls-Royce. Similar research was also being carried out in the US and literally hundreds of different nozzle shapes were tried out. In Britain, the ones that were then developed were a variant of the 'corrugated' type which was introduced on the Comet 4. While a good idea of the relative merits of various silencing nozzles could be obtained from model tests and from static tests on engines running on the ground, the actual amount of silencing achieved by any nozzle in flight could be measured only by means of a direct flight test. Rolls-Royce carried out a large amount of carefully controlled flight testing, measuring on the ground the noise from the aircraft flying overhead when fitted with various nozzles. The overall noise from the aircraft, flying on one engine at 500ft over the measuring point, was plotted against the relative velocity of the jet to the surrounding air, both for a standard nozzle and for the Comet silencing nozzle.

A US company who specialised in acoustical engineering, Bolt, Beranek and Newman Inc, of Cambridge, Massachusetts, carried out noise measurements on the Comet at New York on 11th August 1958. What were then referred to as 'shake-down trials' were conducted by G-APDA in the autumn of 1958. The ARB required that one aircraft be used for these flights before allowing the type into public service. The aircraft flew from Hatfield to New York on 10th August and returned on the 12th.

The Port of New York Authority granted noise approval on 3rd October. The ruling stated that the Comet had to adhere to a preferential runway system, its take-off weight and technique had to be such that a height of 1,200ft was reached over the nearest residential area and power had to be reduced before overflying built up areas. The Authority concluded that the noise of the Comet, as it flew over the airfield boundary, was about 8 or 9 db lower than that of a DC7 or a Constellation. However, as people find higher frequencies more disturbing, and a jet's noise has more of its energy in the high frequencies, the noise from the Comet was judged to be effectively about 3 or 4 db quieter than that from a DC7 or Super Constellation. If the person was listening from inside a building, where the walls and windows cut out the higher frequencies, the result was around 6 db.

Bolt, Beranek and Newman Inc also conducted a series of measurements of the Comet's jet engines at Hatfield from the 18th to the 26th November. Their report was based on measurements at Hatfield of the Comet and four engine propeller driven aircraft. Recordings were made from

The Comet's size fits the available traffic

The Comet's capability fits the runway conditions

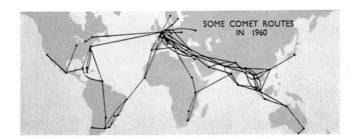

SOME COMET ROUTES IN 1960

DE HAVILLAND
COMET
(Rolls-Royce Avon Jet Engines)

observation positions on the ground ranging from 2.2 to 3.5 miles from the start of the take-off roll. The engineers analysed the sounds recorded during these observations in terms of three principal characteristics of noise which must be considered in community reaction to noise of aircraft, namely; relative noise levels, duration of the noise, and frequency distribution of the noise.

The operating characteristics of the Comet 4 were such that it offered a better noise rating than most large aircraft of the day. The technique for reducing noise in the areas beneath the flight path was to climb as steeply as possible on full power until the aircraft reached the populated areas, and then to reduce power while passing over them. As the aircraft noise diminished, a height advantage achieved before passing over the built up areas paid a big dividend in noise reduction. In a typical case where the first community was around 2.5 miles from the start of the take-off run, the Comet reached 1,000ft while heavier aircraft were at about 350ft and the noise they produced was much more objectionable.

The second production Comet 4, 06402, was used for tests in the water tank at Hatfield which began towards the end of June 1958. By the beginning of March 1959, it passed the equivalent of 100,000 hours of flying, corresponding to some 33 years of normal commercial operation. Every 21 minutes spent on test represented a typical four hour flight, during which the aircraft structure was subjected to twelve damaging gust loads in order to represent the cumulative effect of all gusts experienced in flight. The actual cycle of loading was first the application of ground to level flight loads representing the take-off, followed by the application of the

loads arising from twelve 13ft/sec positive and negative gusts, during which sequence the fuselage was pressurised and depressurised. The application of landing loads to the whole structure completed the cycle. Testing was halted every 2,000 'flying' hours for a thorough inspection of the whole aircraft structure which called for the draining and refilling of a quarter of a million gallons of water before testing could begin again.

G-APDA's shake-down trials also took the aircraft to Hong Kong, Canada and Central and South America, completing the flights on 27th September. Fifteen local demonstration flights were made in the course of the tour of the Americas, including landings at Guadalajara, from Mexico City, and Montevideo, from Buenos Aires. There was no mechanical or other hitches whatsoever. All the flights were made without any spare-parts backing along the routes flown and there were no delays in schedules that had been strictly laid down in advance.

The Comet showed its low speed docility at Bombay on 10th September during a demonstration to Air India officials when a monsoon shower lowered the already poor weather conditions to 350ft and one mile of visibility. A visual circuit was nevertheless made in these conditions, a task which was rendered more difficult by the presence of a large hill on the extended centreline of the runway. The final roll-out onto the QDM of the runway was made at 100ft, a tribute to the powerful ailerons and low wingloading of the Comet.

G-APDA had been loaned to BOAC, in advance of the formal deliveries, in order to assist with the conversion of pilots. Pilots with Comet 2E experience were converted to the Comet 4 in about eight hours, pilots with Comet 1 experience took ten hours, and pilots without jet airliner experience took twelve hours. Circuits were flown on four, three and two engines, and engine failures were simulated at just above critical speed (V1). Flapless landings called for an increase of only 10 knots above the Comet's normal approach speed of 120 knots at maximum landing weight. Re-lighting the Avon engine presented no problem but was practiced nonetheless. One senior captain said that the Comet marked the first cutback in approach speeds in 25 years of airliner development. Another noted that the take-off from Kai Tak's 7,730ft runway with a full payload, heralded the boon of jet travel to branch-line centres as well as national capitals. Another noted that the approach and short landing stop at Bombay, in a monsoon and under a minimum cloud base, could not have been accomplished by the latest piston-engined aircraft.

The Comet was the first jet airliner to land at Hong Kong's Kai Tak airport and, during the visit, the aircraft carried the Governor of Hong Kong, Sir Robert Black, on an inaugural fly-past as he had just declared the airport's new runway open. The Governor was accompanied by 50 guests and on the gangway of the aircraft were the Chinese

COMET 4

Rolls-Royce Avon Jet Engines

The right airliner

DE HAVILLAND

For all too brief a period, until the introduction of the Boeing 707 fleet in the late 1950s the sleek Comet 4 became the flagship of the fleet of BOAC.

characters for 'Happy Flight'. On the return flight from Hong Kong on 14th September, Basil Smallpiece, the Managing Director of BOAC, was accompanied by 30 other passengers on what was to become the fastest long flight in airliner history. Leaving Hong Kong after an early breakfast, they lunched over the Arabian Sea and were in London in time for dinner. The aircraft made the 7,925-mile journey from the China Sea to Britain in daylight in 16 hours 16 minutes flying time, averaging 487mph. Two fuelling stops were made, one of an hour in Bombay and the other of 66 minutes in Cairo. On a scheduled flight the stops would have been shorter, indeed the aircraft was refuelled at Bombay in twelve minutes. The overall time was thus 18 hours 22 minutes and the overall speed, including stops, was 432mph.

A good practical illustration of the Comet's capabilities at high altitude was Mexico City Airport, situated at 7,350ft above sea level. Here the Comet could take-off at its MTOW without restriction, in temperatures up to 18°C and land at its maximum landing weight in temperatures of up to 30°C. Other typical heavyweight jets had to sacrifice more than one fifth of their MTOW and nearly one fifth of their landing weight. Lima Airfield was another test of the aircraft's capabilities as the airfield had hills of 2,500ft in the circuit and the runways were very short, the longest being 6,200ft. Under instrument flight rules, which often applied by reason of

the frequent low stratus cloud, the pilot was committed to land in one direction which could be downwind, but the Comet was able to accept these conditions. Similarly, the 7,300ft runway at Rio de Janeiro, Galeao, was entirely adequate for the Comet at gross weight at the highest air temperatures. On Thursday, 25th September the Comet, fully loaded for a flight of 2,830 miles to Caracas, took off in zero wind at midday and passed over the runway end at 300ft, having already reduced to climb power in the usual way.

During a Comet 4 training flight from Hatfield to Gibraltar, a series of small errors led to an incident worthy of mention. During the flight the Radio Officer leant across the Flight Engineer's panel to re-select something on the First Officer's panel. At the same instant a fire warning was given for the No. 1 engine and Captain Pat Fillingham shut down the engine and operated the fire extinguishers. It transpired that the Radio Officer's headset had caught one of the Fire Warning Test switches at the top of the Flight Engineer's panel, thus triggering the alarm. The Comet continued the flight to Gibraltar on three engines, with the Flight Engineer constantly monitoring and balancing the fuel. The aircraft was delayed at Gibraltar as it had to await the arrival of new fire bottles from Hatfield [12].

The maiden flight to Hatfield of the first Chester built Comet, G-APDE, took place on 20th September 1958. It was

G-APDA served with BOAC for nearly 6 years before onward sale to Malaysian Airways as 9M-AOA in December 1965.

the third Comet 4 to fly. On Monday, 29th September the Air Registration Board issued the airliner's C of A and the following day BOAC took delivery of its first Comet 4, G-APDB. The hand-over took place on the day specified in the contract signed three and a half years earlier. A second Comet 4, G-APDC, was handed-over on the same day and a third, G-APDE, was delivered two days later. The first flight carrying farepaying passengers was on Saturday, 4th October 1958, when G-APDC inaugurated the first commercial trans-atlantic scheduled jet service. The Comet 4 had entered service ahead of Pan American's Boeing 707s.

Aerolineas Argentinas ordered six Comet 4s which started services in April 1959, and EAA ordered two, putting theirs into service in September 1960. In August 1961, following an increase in the recommended cruising rpm of the Rolls-Royce Avon 525B, the ARB ruled that the Comet 4C could increase its cruising speed by twenty mph. The ARB ruled that the limiting Mach number be increased by Mach 0.03 to 0.79 and, in September 1962, this ruling was also applied to the Comet 4B.

It was estimated that de Havilland, which had by then become the de Havilland Division of Hawker Siddeley Aviation, broke even when 67 Comet 4s had been sold. Throughout the entire Comet 4 programme, deliveries were made on or before the contract dates. A total of 74 Comets of all the 4 series were manufactured. Of this total, 34 were manufactured at Hatfield and 40 at Chester.

In April 1961, the US Federal Aviation Authority certified the Comet 4C. It had not been customary to obtain American certification for an aircraft type until an American carrier intended to operate it, but it was negotiated in this case at the request of Latin American operators of the Comet. The US assessment method permitted the Comet slightly higher take-off and landing weights than did the British and a few

modifications were introduced, mainly of a minor nature to suit American operating procedures.

Whereas the Comet 1s were the only commercial jet aircraft in service, the Comet 4s faced severe competition from other jet airliners, ranging from large intercontinental aircraft such as the Boeing 707 and DC8, to short and medium haul jets such as the Caravelle. As Comet operators steadily retired their Comets, Dan-Air acquired many of the second-hand Comets and, at one time, the Gatwick-based holiday-charter airline was operating Comet 4s, Comets 4Bs and Comet 4Cs. When the Comet 4s started to enter service, de Havilland were confident that there was no justification for an aircraft of greater capacity than the Comet for at least the next ten years. They formed their view on the assumption that the aircraft of the day were the right size for the traffic of the day. One mixed-class Comet 4 could produce 100 million seat-miles per year and a Comet 4B could produce more than 125 million. The Comet was not the largest airliner in operation but it offered greater flexibility and was better suited to most of the traffic streams of the world.

This flexibility was particularly so with the Comet 4B and could be achieved by the use of alternative methods of cruising the aircraft. The aircraft could cruise at speeds of between 520mph and 545mph, depending on temperature, at its optimum altitude of 23,000ft. With this operating procedure the Comet 4B could carry a capacity payload of 20,000lb, representing 84 First Class passengers and freight, over stages of up to 2,000 miles. The alternative method of cruising, in which the aircraft climbed to 38,000ft and cruised at 490 to 500mph, extended the range to about 2,600 miles with a capacity payload of 20,000lb.

One Comet 4C has been preserved at Seattle, where the Boeing company has restored a Mexicana aircraft and painted it in BOAC colours, colours never carried in service. The Comet 5 existed only as a project to counter the success of the DC8 and the Boeing 707. It incorporated major design changes - in particular the fitting of Conway turbofan engines which were being developed at the time and offered better fuel economy — but the risk was evaluated as being too high.

During production of the Comet, the number of employees at Hatfield ranged from six to eight thousand. One former employee reflected on those days and stated "The atmosphere was electric, like a great big family. It is a huge thing still to this day". There are a number of clubs and associations in the Hatfield area open to those who worked for de Havilland or who have a keen interest in the de Havilland aircraft, including the Comet.

IN SERVICE WITH BRITISH OVERSEAS AIRWAYS CORPORATION

On 2nd April 1951, G-ALZK landed at London Airport prior to being handed over on loan to BOAC, to be operated by the BOAC Comet Unit. Several BOAC crews converted to the Comet and all the maintenance and servicing work on the aircraft was undertaken by BOAC engineers, with only advisory help from de Havilland. During the first eight weeks of operation by BOAC, G-ALZK flew 147 hours. After preliminary flight trials in Britain, which were concerned largely with performance measurements for the purpose of producing a BOAC Cruising Control Manual, experimental flights without passengers were made to Cairo and Calcutta. The passenger cabin was not fully soundproofed or furnished and the undercarriage was of the singlewheel type.

In March 1952, BOAC took delivery of two further Comets, G-ALYU on 6th March, and G-ALYP on 11th March. The fifth production aircraft, G-ALYV, took to the air for the first time on 9th April then, on 23rd April, BOAC took delivery of its fourth Comet, G-ALYV.

BOAC inaugurated the world's first passenger jet airliner service on 2nd May 1952 when, at 3.00 pm, G-ALYP took off from London Airport bound for Johannesburg. The Comet was under the command of Captain A M Majendie and it was grey and cloudy when a single coach conveyed the 36 passengers to the aircraft. Among them was a Mr A Henshaw of Mablethorpe, Lincolnshire, who, eighteen months

BOAC took delivery of its first Comet 1 on 4th February 1952, on a typical rainy day at Heathrow Airport.

Camels of the Sudan Camel Corps move across the tarmac at Khartoum Airfield at midday in June 1953. With shade temperatures of over 110° F, the Comet schedules were arranged so that take-off was made during the cool hours of darkness.

previously, had reserved a place to became the world's first commercial jet passenger. Of the 36 passengers who boarded the Comet, 34 were business men. Of the two women on board, one was Miss Avril Coleridge Taylor, daughter of the poet. She intended to sketch out the first music ever written during a jet liner flight called 'The Comet Prelude'. The other woman was a Railway Policewoman, heading for a holiday with her brother in South Africa.

The departure went like clockwork. At 2.45pm the last passenger embarked, the door was closed and at 2.58pm the engine-starting routine commenced. At 3.00pm the Comet moved off from the apron and taxied direct to the duty runway, a distance of nearly three miles. At 3.10pm the aircraft was lined up on the runway and at exactly 3.12pm the Comet was airborne en route for Rome. As the aircraft crossed the English coast it received a message of best wishes on behalf of de Havilland, passed on by radio from another Comet which was airborne from Hatfield. During the flight a passenger was photographed demonstrating the smoothness of the aircraft by balancing pencils, coins and cigarettes on a table top. G-ALYP landed at Palmietfontein Airport, Johannesburg, at 3.37pm on 3rd May, three minutes ahead of schedule, after a flight of 6,724 miles. The journey had taken 23 hours and 37 minutes. The Comet then departed on the first northbound service at 9.00pm on 5th May, arriving at London Airport two minutes early at 7.48am on the morning of the 6th May.

During May 1952 the Comet service operated once per week in each direction, leaving London on a Friday and Johannesburg on a Monday, making it possible for Londoners to spend a weekend in Johannesburg, leaving London after lunch on Friday and returning on Tuesday morning. By the end of the month, demand for seats led to the introduction of a twice-weekly flight and in June the rate was increased to three per week. BOAC showed a profit on Comet operations of £3,000 during the month of May on the Johannesburg route. The actual flying time of the Comet service was 18 hours and 40 minutes southbound and 18 hours and 55 minutes northbound but, in due course, the journey time was reduced. Once the upheaval of the Suez Crisis had subsided, the service was routed through Cairo instead of Beirut which reduced the distance by 450 miles and cut nearly an hour off the schedule time. Jan Smuts airport was nearing completion and it soon became the terminal point of the service from London.

The layout accommodated 36 passengers; eight were accommodated in the forward cabin and 28 in the main cabin — fitted with adjustable dark blue and grey 'slumberseats' providing a high degree of comfort. The Comet service operated on the Springbok route in conjunction with the Constellation services of BOAC's partners, South African Airways. BOAC's Hermes services, operating three times per week between London and Johannesburg, were progressively withdrawn as the Comet frequencies were increased. The entry of the Comet into passenger service was a tonic to the nation. Britain had endured seven years of post-War rationing and also the death of King George VI in February 1952. The Comet heralded the prospect of better times to come.

The travelling public's approval of the Comet was matched by the sense of satisfaction felt amongst the employees at BOAC. One public relations officer later wrote "The joy of being with BOAC at this very exciting era, The Jet Age, was so thrilling … there was such a buzz in the corporation. Britain was showing the world we had talent, knowledge and the ability to be top of the world in every sense, in spite of food rationing and the lack of luxuries". [13] The introduction of the Comet into service with BOAC coincided with the appointment of Sir Miles Thomas as Chairman. He was credited with lifting BOAC out of the doldrums and he did this by recruiting a team of younger employees, some of whom joined at the age of eighteen.

BOAC planned to start a Comet service between London and Singapore and a series of proving flights on this route commenced on 15th May 1952. On 11th August G-ALYU left London for Colombo, inaugurating the first eastward route in BOAC's network of Comet routes. The distance of 5,925 miles was made in 18 hours and 35 minutes flying time, with stops at Rome, Beirut, Bahrain, Karachi and Bombay. During the stop-over in Bombay, the Maharajah of Baroda made a request for the Comet to be chartered to take his family and a few friends for a flight around Bombay, including an overflight of

his palace. It transpired that 70 passengers were to make the flight so the Comet had to perform two flights on the same day. Once the aircraft was safely away from 'dry' Bombay, champagne was served and glowing reports were later received by the airline [14]. On the return flight to London, the Comet had to be diverted from London Airport due to fog as visibility was down to 120 yards. As similar conditions prevailed at Blackbushe and Hurn, the Comet diverted to Prestwick, some 320 miles north of London.

After a series of seventeen proving flights, the service to Singapore was inaugurated on 14th October. The route was via Rome, Beirut, Bahrain, Karachi, Calcutta, Rangoon and Bangkok, with a stop at Delhi on the return flight. The elapsed time between London and Singapore was 27 hours 30 minutes and on the return journey it was 34 hours. By the end of the month the service had increased to twice per week and BOAC Comets were flying 80,000 miles per week. On one flight to Rangoon, Captain Dyer remarked to his Co-Pilot "We're a bit heavy" whereupon it was discovered that an engine had cut-out without the crew noticing.

The seventh Comet, G-ALYX, was handed over to BOAC at London Airport on 23rd July 1952. G-ALYY was later delivered on 29th September and the last Comet 1, G-ALYZ, was handed over to BOAC on 30th September. Within a month, however, the Comet fleet was down to eight when, on 26th October, an unfortunate mishap occurred at Rome when G-ALYZ was damaged beyond economic repair.

The old and the new. A Comet of BOAC's fleet is serviced at Livingstone Airport, Northern Rhodesia before leaving on the last lap of the journey to Johannesburg, under the watchful eye of an Eagle Aviation York used on the African freight run.

On 4th August 1962, Comet 4 G-APDO follows the glidepath to another landing at London's Heathrow Airport.

During May 1952, the total utilisation of the Comet 1 was in the order of three hours per day, of which just over one hour was revenue earning. With the gradual introduction of new services and the stepping up of service frequencies, the rate of utilisation steadily improved. By October 1952, this total had reached four and a half hours then, with the start of the service to Tokyo, five hours. The increase in the Tokyo schedule to two services per week, ten days later, raised it to six and a half hours per day.

Mechanical delays were fairly prevalent at the start of the Comet service and, during the first month, the average arrival time at the terminals was behind schedule to an amount equal to nearly 40% of the journey time. One of the most serious faults and one which nearly led to the temporary grounding of the fleet was the misting of the windscreen which, without any previous warning, suddenly started to occur in June when the aircraft were on the final approach to Beirut and Khartoum airfields. This phenomenon occurred only in certain conditions of temperature and humidity and the cure was to increase the flow of warm air across the inner face of the screen. While simple enough in principle, the cure required a fair amount of engineering but the modification was incorporated in every aircraft within a very short period.

Trouble was also encountered with the early type of windscreen wiper which, having worked satisfactorily during the test flying period, proved to be unequal to the job in service. After a considerable amount of development work, the original wiper was replaced by a more satisfactory, hydraulically-driven type. There was also some evidence of cracking in the elevator skin which called for its replacement in certain areas by a heavier gauge of metal.

The Ghost engine developed two main faults. After some months of trouble free running, cracks began to appear in the centrifugal compressors, the cause of which was finally traced to high-frequency vibration. These cracks had not caused any noticeable effect on the running of the engine and were only discovered upon inspection. The cure was to crop the impeller blades by a small amount, not enough to affect the efficiency but sufficient to shift the frequency nodes outside the critical range. The need to incorporate these modifications into the Comet fleet increased the hours required for maintenance beyond the original estimate. These were based on the proving trials with the preproduction aircraft G-ALZK. The yearly average of maintenance hours consumed for a major Check 4 routine inspection were still lower than for the best of the four engined piston aircraft in the BOAC fleet. By way of comparison, with regard to operating characteristics, the Comets were between 100 and 150mph faster than propeller turbine aircraft. The Comet's Check 4 was progressively extended from every 200 hours to every 1,040 hours.

By August, the ground organisation on the route was beginning to run so smoothly that at Khartoum and Livingstone the transit time was cut from one hour to 40 minutes. It was the first time in history that a BOAC aircraft had been scheduled for so brief a stop. This reduction in ground time and the re-routing of the flight through Cairo, enabled the elapsed time for the journey between London and South Africa to be reduced from 23 hours and 40 minutes to 21 hours and 20 minutes. The delivery of the sixth and seventh aircraft by July was followed on 11th August by the introduction of the service between London and Ceylon to be flown weekly. The distance of 5,961 statute miles was flown in 20 hours and 35 minutes. Until April 1953, this service worked under a severe handicap as the Government of Ceylon refused permission to uplift passengers from Colombo, which made it necessary for the homeward bound aircraft to fly empty as far as Bombay

During the first six months of scheduled operations, 71% of Comet flights arrived on time. Seven engine-related delays amounted to only nineteen hours and seven minutes out of the total loss of 100 scheduled hours. Of the seven, five concerned fire extinguishers and two involved engine instrument transmitters. Within eleven months of the inauguration of the first ever jet service, Comets were flying 122,000 miles per week on a network of routes with an unduplicated mileage of 20,780. During the year, the Comets flew 9,443 revenue hours and carried nearly 28,000 passengers, thus achieving 104,600,000 revenue passenger miles.

As was to be expected, the early services were fully booked for months ahead and bookings for the first service itself were being received by BOAC over a year before the start and before the applicants knew where the inaugural flight was to be routed. While BOAC were aware that there was always

a large number of people anxious to be 'first', it was recognised that the novelty factor which led to the heavy bookings during the first weeks of operation could not be considered as necessarily representative of the normal demand. In the event, however, there was no detectable falling off in the high load factors in the first twelve months of service and the Comet became firmly established as a favourite medium of travel with the public.

In common with all major airlines, BOAC provided each passenger with forms on which they were invited to make comments about the quality of the service. On the Comet, the vast majority of passengers who turned in comments were full of praise for the comforts of jet travel. However, one point of criticism was that passengers seated towards the centre of the aircraft suffered from cold feet. This was due to the fuel tanks underneath which became very cold, so electrically heated floor matting was laid down to help overcome the problem.

As in any such exercise, there were a number of notable submissions. One American stated that he could detect no improvement in noise and vibration, and one woman wrote that, from her own experience, she was able to assure BOAC that there was no truth in the rumour that the high cruising altitude disintegrated nylon stockings and underwear. The distribution of the sexes on the Comet was a cause for minor concern. With passenger loads which were predominantly male, the equal provision of toilets for both sexes inevitably led to congestion in the men's room, particularly at shaving time. BOAC could only hope that the British male traveller would become more continental in his outlook.

On a winters day at Heathrow on 2nd January 1962, Comet 4 G-APDF takes a brief rest from BOAC service. This aircraft was one of the few Comet 4s to survive into the 1990s, under the guise of XV814, flying for the RAE/DRA at Farnborough.

One Stewardess, who had joined the Comet 1 after a year on the Handley Page Hermes, was amazed to see how many passengers kept themselves occupied during flights by gauging the vibration of the aircraft with the use of tumblers of liquid and up-ended pencils, cigarettes and coins. The passengers were also thrilled to be able to converse in a normal voice anywhere in the cabin during flight.

Before taking a Comet on regular service, each BOAC Captain had completed at least 60 hours of flying on the aircraft, about ten hours of which consisted of local flying followed by at least two trips under supervision over the route that he was to operate. In addition, all Pilots had to undergo a nine week course of instruction covering the technicalities of the airframe, the engine and the theory of cruise control. Under Captain Rodley, who was in charge of Comet flying training, five of the fleet captains were qualified as instructors and after qualification, each Captain had a check flight of two hours or more every six months. The training syllabus of First Officers, Flight Engineers and Radio Operators and the cabin crew varied in detail according to their duties but was equally thorough. First Officers and Flight Engineers had to complete at least three route trips before qualification.

BOAC spent nine months proving the Comet route to Tokyo. Between 4th July 1952 and 9th March 1953, eleven trial flights were made between Bangkok, on their twice weekly line to Singapore and Tokyo, and many crews were thus familiarised with every feature of the natural and the contrived

aids on the last three legs. Hong Kong, served by the Argonauts, was not available for the Comets because of the lack of a suitable alternative airport, so the aircraft flew from Bangkok to Manila and then to Okinawa and Tokyo.

Okinawa, 70 miles long and home to 600,000 inhabitants, was occupied by US forces who had constructed two air bases; Naha for civil operations and Kadena for military operations. Both were comprehensively equipped. US bomber crews and their wives, as well as jean-clad juniors in bright Cadillacs, turned out to view the Comet, expending record footage of Kodachrome as they did so. The Comet was processed by the ATC within the heavy air traffic, which consisted of jet fighters, transports and bombers. There were similar scenes at Tokyo, where the military and civil air traffic accounted for up to 600 movements per day. There were tremendous winds in this region, 180 and 200 knots at Comet height, and it was found that the velocities off the Asiatic seaboard at high latitudes were the greatest in the world, sometimes up to 400 knots. With experience, it was found that balancing fuel reserves and frequent fixes, with a readiness to take advantage of every favourable element, was the best way to operate.

The service to Tokyo was inaugurated on the 2nd April and among the VIPs on board were a group of Japanese businessmen connected with the aeronautical industry. During the flight they produced large notebooks and proceeded to sketch detailed diagrams of the wing structure and anything else that could be viewed from the window. They also

Under murky skies on 4th June 1959, G-APDM taxies to the runway at Hong Kong for the return flight to the UK. This aircraft had the distinction of flying the last Comet service for BOAC in November 1965.

requested many trips to the flight deck, following which they returned to their notebooks [15]. From 13th April the service to Tokyo operated twice per week and, even with the Comet 1 working relatively short stages, it was able to cut the timetable on this route from the 86 hours taken by the Argonaut service to 36 hours. The Argonaut service included two night stops and was continued after the introduction of the Comet. Travelling eastbound, the Comet left London at 9.00 am and flew against the sun, passing the first short night between Beirut and Karachi and the second between Bangkok and Tokyo, by way of Manila and Okinawa, reaching Tokyo for breakfast. Westbound, with the sun, the Comet took off from Haneda Airport on Tokyo Bay at about midnight and after a long day flight between Manila and Karachi, arrived in London for an early breakfast the next morning. The Comet was appreciated in Japan and Japan Airlines planned to base its fast overseas operations on the Comet 2, starting in 1955.

Operating figures for the first year showed that the eight Comet 1s made sufficient profit during the period to cover the interest on the capital expenditure. The fleet had been operating at an overall load factor of nearly 80% and it was found that an average load factor of 75% showed a profit. Both BOAC and de Havilland were pleased with the performance of the Comet during its first year and de Havilland noted, in an edition of its Gazette, that "They [BOAC] have shown the world that the spirit of the British merchant adventurer is vigorously alive today ... they have gained a lead that their competitors will be hard put to recover".

On 30th June 1953, the Queen Mother and Princess Margaret left London Airport in G-ALYW on a flight to Salisbury, Southern Rhodesia, to attend the Rhodes Centenary Celebration. Stops were made at Rome, Beirut, Khartoum and Entebbe, where the Queen Mother and Princess Margaret stayed for two hours to take breakfast at Government House. The aircraft arrived at Salisbury at 9.52 GMT and the door was opened at precisely 10.00 am. The journey home took three hours longer and the Royal Party slept in the Comet at Rome during a four-hour stop. The Comet landed at London Airport at 09.00 am on 17th July, exactly on time.

They were not, however, the first Royals to board a Comet. One day, whilst a Comet 1 was awaiting clearance following a short delay, a large limousine drew up at the steps and the station master asked the stewardess, Diana Furness, if she would show a visitor around the aircraft. Princess Alexandra, who happened to be waiting for the arrival of an incoming aircraft, alighted for a tour of the Comet. She had a coffee on board and departed saying that she was thrilled to be the first member of her 'family' to view the wonderful, new aircraft [16].

As a first step towards the opening of a service to South America, a proving flight to Rio de Janeiro was carried out in

A view of the first class cabin of the BOAC Comet 4 gives some idea of the leg room and luxury aboard the aircraft.

September 1953 using the Comet 2 prototype, G-ALYT. The aircraft was flown by BOAC crews headed by Captain A P W Cain and Captain Majendie, and among the nine passengers were Sir Miles Thomas, Chairman of BOAC and Dr Paulo Sampaio, President of Panair do Brasil, which also planned to operate Comet 2s between Brazil and Europe.

G-ALYT left London Airport on Sunday, 13th September at 17.29 GMT. Flying via Lisbon, Dakar and Recife, the aircraft arrived at Rio de Janeiro at 14.35 GMT on 14th September, an elapsed time of 21 hours and 6 minutes. The flying time for the 5,850 miles journey was 15 hours and 49 minutes which may be compared with the normal BOAC piston engined airliner schedule of 30 hours and 45 minutes. The return flight commenced at 15.57 GMT on 17th September and routed via Natal, Dakar, Casablanca and Madrid, a distance of 5,910 miles. The flying time to Madrid was 15 hours and 51 minutes. After a 24 hour stop-over at Madrid, the aircraft arrived back at London Airport at 14.37 GMT on 19th September after a flight lasting 2 hours and 10 minutes.

In a shot taken at Heathrow in the last days of Comet 4 service in September 1965, G-APDN displays the final BOAC livery carried.

Throughout the tour, tremendous interest was displayed, especially at those places where the Comet was appearing for the first time, namely Madrid, Recife, Natal and Rio de Janeiro. At Natal, the military were called out to disperse the crowds thronging around the Comet and at Rio similar scenes of enthusiasm were witnessed. Before landing at Rio's Galedo Airport the Comet flew several times around the town, finishing up with a low flypast along the famous Copacabana beach. Although it was the first time a jet airliner had flown to South America, no attempt was made to break records. Long ground stops were planned in advance, due to the unfamiliarity with the Comet of the ground staff and refuelling crews. On many of the stages, practice approaches were made and, in some cases, short demonstration flights were given before landing. The tour coincided with the publication of a book entitled 'Comet Highway' by BOAC's Chief Photographer, Henry Hensser, which contained many high-altitude views taken along the Comet routes [17].

The cruise technique adopted by BOAC's Comet 1s consisted of flying at a constant angle of incidence, which was achieved in practice by flying at an IAS selected in relation to the weight. Alterations in speed were made at half-hourly intervals as the weight decreased which resulted in a gradual climb. Depending on load and the length of the stage, and to some extent on the ambient temperature, the cruising height would vary from about 35,000ft to 42,000ft. During the development period of the Comet 2, a fundamental question that had to be

resolved for the operation of the Comet 4 across the Atlantic, was whether a drift-up cruise rather than a stepped-climb procedure could be permitted by ATC. All of the airlines were held back by the requirement to use stepped-climb techniques, with steps of 2,000ft, or even 4,000ft, as well as the standards of separation of the day. Another concern was the large amount of US military traffic that had to be accommodated in the ATC system. The military authorities tended to block a complete series of flight levels, for example from 35,000 to 40,000ft, thus forcing the Comet to fly at uneconomic levels in certain areas and for quite long periods of time.

Profitable operation of the Comet was continued by BOAC until the 10th January 1954, when the Elba accident occurred and BOAC's Comets were withdrawn from service for thorough inspection. They were reintroduced ten weeks later after some precautionary modifications but, in April 1954, another Comet crashed off Naples and the type was grounded indefinitely.

From 1954 until 1958 when BOAC took delivery of its first Comet 4s, the airline had little involvement with the Comet. As already detailed, two Comet 2Es, G-AMXK and G-AMXD, served as Avon engine test beds with BOAC's Comet Flight from 16th September 1957 to 31st May 1958. Also in the interim, the Chairman, the Deputy Chairman of BOAC, and executives of the airline, made a one hour flight around East Anglia, the French Channel ports and Southern England in the Comet 3, G-ANLO, which continued to fulfil the requirements of the

Comet development programme. Both Mr d'Erlanger and Sir George Cribbett handled the controls of the aircraft.

G-APDC, a Comet 4, inaugurated the world's first trans-atlantic jet flight on 4th October 1958. The Port of New York Authority had announced the previous evening that the Comet was cleared to land at New York's Idlewild Airport. Overnight, bookings that had been made, in some case years beforehand, were confirmed and the aircraft left London Airport for New York on time. Under the command of Captain R E Millichap, G-APDC took off for New York at 9.55 BST. The flight took 10 hours and 20 minutes, including a 70 minute refuelling stop at Gander. Meanwhile, G-APDB, under the command of Captain T B Stoney, the Comet Flight Manager, left New York for London at 07.00 local time. The flight was made non-stop in a recordbreaking time of 6 hours and 12 minutes. The Comet was capable of flying non-stop from New York to London in approximately seven hours, with a high regularity and this was some three hours quicker than the non-stop services flown by piston-engined aircraft.

BOAC's Comet 4 fleet required a total of 261 Pilots and 130 crews, many of whom had previously served in BOAC's Comet 1 fleet. This generous scale allowed the extensive use of slip crews throughout the airline's network [18]. All airline crews were fascinated by the Comet's contrails, learning to tell outside temperature from their characteristics, reading the upper air and its hitherto mysterious gusts and jet streams.

G-APDR was modified to have reverse thrust on all four engines and, on 22nd September 1959, the aircraft was flown by Captain Perry to demonstrate the reverse thrust operation. It was

Passengers boarding G-APDC for the first ever jet airliner service across the North Atlantic on 4th October 1958, to New York.

The crew of the first BOAC Comet 4 Atlantic crossing to New York Left to right: Capt. E E Rodley, Capt. T B Stoney, Capt. C Farndell, Steward J Miller, Steward A C J McCormack, Stewardess Barbara Jubb and Stewardess Peggy Thorne.

then deemed safer, from the crew's point of view, to have reverse thrust fitted on all the engines of the Comet 4 fleet. The following week Perry flew G-APMA to Australia on a proving flight. On 3rd November G-APDL flew the first passenger-carrying flight to Sydney then, on 28th November 1959, BOAC announced that Comet services were to be extended to the Caribbean. The services were inaugurated on 30th January 1960, operating from New York, flying six services per week to and from Montego Bay, Jamaica. Three of the services were direct and three were with intermediate stops at Nassau. BOAC Comet's were, by then, operating across both the North and South Atlantic, to the Caribbean, South Africa and the Far East. The Comet had become the principal express airliner of the BOAC system. On 2nd December, Comet 4s had taken over the London to South Africa service and the 5,650 mile route was covered in around 17 hours 30 minutes with stops at Rome, Khartoum, Nairobi and Salisbury. Dar-es-Salaam was the alternative airport to Nairobi. There were four weekly services each way to Johannesburg and one which terminated at Salisbury.

Initially, BOAC decided that Captains and First Officers with route experience with the Comet 1 should fly the Comet 4s but, for the first time, BOAC was in a situation in which a new trans-atlantic aircraft was being captained by newcomers with experience of the aircraft rather than of the route. It was held that there was an almost fundamental difference, amounting to a new philosophy, in the thinking of those who were responsible for conducting turbojet flights, with regard to the shorter timescale. There was the need for the crews to be continually conscious of the fuel position, the different cruise control methods at high Mach numbers, rapidly changing weight as fuel was burnt, and the subtle differences in handling techniques.

Supreme jet comfort!

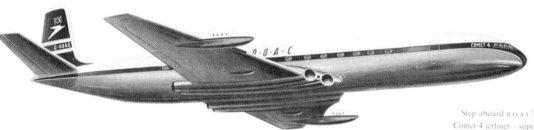

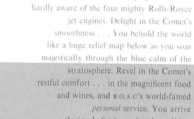

Step aboard B.O.A.C's incomparable new Comet 4 jetliner – supreme in the skies for super-fast, super-smooth, vibration-free travel. With the introduction of the B.O.A.C. Comet 4, distance shrinks and time takes on new meaning!

Step aboard . . . Marvel at the Comet's vibration-free flying . . . You're hardly aware of the four mighty Rolls-Royce jet engines. Delight in the Comet's smoothness . . . You behold the world like a huge relief map below as you soar majestically through the blue calm of the stratosphere. Revel in the Comet's restful comfort . . . in the magnificent food and wines, and B.O.A.C's world-famed *personal* service. You arrive gloriously fresh . . . barely realising you've travelled at all!

B·O·A·C COMET 4 JETLINER

The North Atlantic schedules assumed one refuelling stop westbound, generally at Gander, and a non-stop flight eastbound on 85% of occasions during the year. Normally, at least during this early period of Atlantic operation, a full fuel load was taken on for the more critical sectors, such as the stages from London to Gander and from Keflavik to New York.

BOAC, through the Comet Flight Manager Captain T B Stoney, proposed to simplify the methods of flight planning and to leave much more to the decision of the Captain. It was held that the Captain's sole object was, after all, to reach the destination at either end as safely, quickly and economically as possible. The Captain had several alternatives for use and was free to fly to any one of them according to the particular situation facing him hour by hour. In addition, simple formulae were provided for the quick assessment of the penalties involved in any alteration of the flight plan, and a standard graph was available for use on the flight deck from which could be derived the ranges which were possible with various fuel loads from different cruising or descent altitudes. The Comet 4's navigational and communication equipment were all duplicated, removing the need for a specialist Radio Officer. During the Comet 1 operations five

years before, a Radio Officer had been a crucial member of the flight deck team because HF/RT facilities were not available on the eastern runs.

Another item of equipment which came into use at the time and which was standard in the Comet 4, was Selcal (or selective calling system) whereby the crew of a particular aircraft was alerted only when a message was intended for that aircraft. There was no longer any need for the crew to listen out continuously. Selcal ground equipment had been in use at Shannon for some time and later became available at London Airport, Gander and Keflavik.

Experience gained from the earlier Comet era using the Comet 2Es for engine development and training, meant that crews who were already experienced on Comets were able to convert quickly. Training was mainly at the RAE aerodrome at Thurleigh, near Bedford which had an adequate runway, the full range of navigation aids and little traffic. The Comets used London Airport in the morning and at midday were flown to Bedford, where ILS approaches, overshoots and other exercises were completed. There was still enough fuel for three to four hours of flying before returning to London Airport.

Airways and approach pattern practice and training, which was particularly necessary for crews who had not previously flown in the New York area, was completed on the Stratocruiser simulator which had been designed for this purpose. It was upgraded for the task and fitted with the Smiths Flight System, and the electronics and other devices were also adjusted to offer a performance similar to that of the Comet 4. These included rates of descent of up to 4,000ft/min. The real Comet simulator, designed and manufactured by Redifon, did not come into use until 1959.

The Comet 4's take-off and climb profile were impressive. At a speed 10 knots less than V2, the nosewheel was lifted and the Comet rocketed into a steep take-off attitude which was maintained at V2 plus 15 knots, to a minimum height of 1,200ft. There the revolutions were brought back from 8,000 to 7,350 and the speed was allowed to build up to that required for the most efficient climb to initial operating height. To the passengers who remembered the technique with the

Comet 1, the behaviour of the new Comet was exhilarating. From a normal runway and climbing at about 3,000ft/min, the Comet was at 1,000ft over or soon after crossing the reciprocal threshold. It was thought advisable for the steep angle to be explained to new passengers before the aircraft left the apron as it was not unknown for curtains to fly back and trolleys to roll around.

Passengers in the rear compartment were informed that there would be a sudden increase of noise as the power was reduced for descent and the engine bleed valves were opened. From BOAC's seventh Comet, thrust reversers were fitted and the earlier aircraft were then retrospectively modified. The earlier aircraft had the emergency oxygen equipment and masks under the seat, to be used on instruction from the crew. All BOAC Comets were soon fitted with an automatic oxygen supply system which provided masks from the overhead racks and a supply of oxygen in case the cabin pressure fell to the equivalent of that at 14,000ft.

Comet 4 G-APDR demonstrates the ample wing area which gave it the superb flying characteristics enjoyed by many thousands of passengers while in the service of BOAC.

B·O·A·C **COMET 4** JETLINER

FIRST EVER ATLANTIC JET SERVICE!

Supreme in the skies!

BOAC were *first* across the Atlantic with a "pure jet" passenger service. Why? Because *Comet 4* jetliners were delivered ahead of schedule ... because the *Comet 4* which made this historic first flight is the most tested airliner the world has ever known ... and because BOAC has years more experience with jets than any other airline.

CONSIDER THE RECORD ...

One hundred and twenty BOAC pilots have logged a total of 15 million *Comet* flying miles. This year alone, BOAC *Comets* have logged 3,700 flying hours and made some 50 more transatlantic jet crossings than any other commercial jet airliner. Months and months of careful, patient and prolonged testing, proving and training flights lie behind this great achievement.

Now BOAC invites you to fly *Comet 4*. Your flight is swift, serene and undisturbed as four mighty Rolls-Royce Avon engines multiply your speed, and search radar ensures fair weather flying all the way.

Book now by *Comet 4* and enjoy the superlative comfort of First Class or de Luxe "Monarch" services. *Consult your local BOAC Appointed Travel Agent or any BOAC office.*

BRITISH OVERSEAS AIRWAYS CORPORATION

There was an exceptionally high incidence of fog in London from October 1958 through to the end of February 1959. During this period, London Airport was closed on many occasions, sometimes for days at a time, with a consequent disruption of all air services. In general, rather than subject passengers to the inconvenience of being landed in Scotland when they wanted to go to London, it was preferable to hold the Comet in Rome until the weather cleared at London Airport. This procedure was made more acceptable because the high speed of the Comet reduced the overall delay which would be involved in the case of a slower aircraft.

For a modern jet aircraft the Comet 4 had a low first cost, little more than half that of the largest American jets. In addition, the low number of passengers required to break-even gave increased profits from the same traffic. The Comet 4 carried twice as many passengers on stages twice as long as did the Comet 1. The routes south and east out of Europe had much less total traffic than that carried over the North Atlantic. They were routes on which sector traffic was much heavier than end-to-end traffic. The Comet fitted this kind of operation admirably and such conditions were typical of many other parts of the world.

At the time, BOAC considered the possibility of using their nineteen Comets throughout their network, which by then exceeded 65,000 unduplicated statute miles. This option followed on the decision to disband the Stratocruiser, Constellation and older Argonaut fleets, leaving Comets, Britannias and DC7s to operate over the routes until such time as the Boeing 707-436s took over the North Atlantic service. Any Comet used on the North Atlantic could then be redeployed on the airline's trunk routes.

The overall load factor during the first few weeks of daily North Atlantic Comet services was 90%. The service to Canada started on 19th December and the first crossing from Montreal to London was made in record time, less than six and a half hours from take-off to touchdown. Some 4,000 passengers crossed the Atlantic between London and New York and London and Montreal by the 31st December. A Mrs Charles James Shuckburgh, 91, had the distinction of being the oldest passenger to cross the Atlantic by Comet, and Stephanie Schofield was the first child to cross alone by Comet 4. A Comet promotion tour was flown at the close of the year, visiting New York, Baltimore, Boston, Chicago and Detroit creating a great deal of interest at each stop.

In a New Year announcement BOAC's Chairman, Sir Gerard d'Erlanger, outlined a joint Comet-Britannia round the world service starting in April. Comet 4 deliveries were up to two months ahead of schedule and BOAC were confident that they were in a good position to both attract traffic and to retain it.

An engineering labour difficulty delayed the BOAC crew training programme by a short while. This interfered with the intended weekly frequency from 4th October to 14th November so that westbound services were flown on 4th and 10th October and eastbound services on 6th and 12th October.

A series of six Tokyo route familiarisation flights for BOAC crews started on 21st January 1959 and all expectations were fulfilled from that first flight onward. The route spanned climatic extremes and a 10,000 mile network of some twenty airports and as many diversion fields, serving cities large and variously equipped with aids and amenities. Excepting only Kuwait, Colombo and Kuala Lumpur, the Comet 4 could operate throughout with scarcely any restrictions. The service from London to Tokyo was increased to four flights per week from April, and the flight linked up with westbound Britannias from London, offering round the world flights.

The Comet 4's ability to use the airfields of the day was further enhanced by the fitting of Rolls-Royce thrust reversers to the outboard engines. This optional equipment reduced runway length requirements for landing by 81% and actual ground run on a wet runway by approximately 12%.

On the North Atlantic route, some jet airliners were forced to fly at uneconomical lower altitudes, for example when the air temperature was such that the higher altitude for which clearance had been obtained could not be reached because of lack of thrust. This was never the case with the Comet as the thrust available was always ample. A Comet's flight procedure could thus be planned irrespective of en route temperatures.

The high position of the engines relative to the ground, and the fact that they were buried in the wing, proved to be a considerable operational advantage both from the ingestion point of view and because there were no pods to scrape along the runway. There was no need for special precautions with regard to debris. One Comet ingested a seagull without difficulty and the crew were unaware of anything amiss and completed their flight without incident.

The Comet 4's passenger break-even load factor was between 43 and 47% — the variation being due to route, seat arrangement and season. The break-even point allowed for interest on capital, training and route-proving costs, spread over the life of the aircraft.

After a year in service, BOAC referred to the Comet 4 as 'The Money Spinning Comet' as the statistics were impressive. From the first jet service across the Atlantic on 4th October 1958 (when BOAC had only three aircraft), Comet weekly services and route mileage grew to 26 return services per week out of London. They had a route mileage of 70,000 miles, flying almost 400,000 aircraft miles per week by the end of 1959. By then, eighteen aircraft had been delivered.

Due to the Comet's popularity, BOAC made dramatic strides towards reducing the dominating lead which Pan American Airways had held for many years. BOAC was the only airline using Comets and it had made traffic gains far in excess of those of all its competitors. This was particularly impressive as it was during the season when Pan American introduced the 111-seat Boeing 707-120.

A major factor contributing to the reliability of the Comet was the excellent record of the Rolls-Royce Avon Mark 524. Approved overhaul life for the engines had soon risen to 1,600 hours, a unique record, and trials to increase this life were in progress by the end of 1959. In the first twelve months there was a total of 32 unscheduled engine removals. Ten were caused by ingestion while airborne, two were caused by ingestion from runways, five were as a result of generator defects, thirteen were due to minor defects in the engine ancillaries and accessories, and only two were as a result of basic engine defects. The incidents involving airborne ingestion consisted mainly of birds but there was one case involving two engines, caused by trees, and four cases caused by ice from the aircraft's forward toilet.

As planned in 1958, the Comet 4 was withdrawn from the Atlantic route from the 16th October 1960 to be replaced by the larger Boeing 707. For twenty months the Comet had been BOAC's sole jet aircraft on the route. All of the BOAC Comet 4s were then working the routes for which they had been chosen in 1955, linking London with South America, South Africa, the Orient up to Japan and down to Australia. The Comet 4 was never intended as a North Atlantic aircraft, having been designed for trunkroutes involving stages of up to about 2,500 miles. Traffic was heavy and due to time difference between London and North America, departures tended to be concentrated upon certain periods of the day. A greater frequency of service had no particular attraction and did not yield a further traffic growth. Due to the fact that the stage was exceptionally long and because of the strong westerly winds, an airliner with a somewhat longer range than the Comet was required. The Comet 4 had, however, served the route as it proved to have a substantially better performance than had been expected. Early BOAC proving flights had demonstrated that it would be capable of operating profitably on the route.

In two years of operation across the North Atlantic, from the 4th October 1958 to 16th October 1960, the Comet made 2,304 crossings, an average of just over three each day. Over the first year, the frequency of the trans-atlantic services increased from one per week to a summer peak of two services per day. During this period, 73% of the London to New York flights arrived within fifteen minutes of the advertised time and 89% arrived within an hour. In those first twelve months, there was not a single case of an engine failure in-flight. There was one case of an engine shut down and that was due to problems with a fuel control unit. At the end of the first year the Managing Director of BOAC, Mr Basil Smallpiece, announced that the Comet had been mainly responsible for a 40% increase in BOAC's trans-atlantic passenger traffic.

While on the trans-atlantic route, the Comet operated services from London to New York, Montreal, Toronto and Boston. It carried a total of 94,000 passengers and achieved an overall passenger load factor of 74%. On the eastbound services, more than 92% of flights were accomplished non-stop and on the westbound flights, against the strong prevailing Atlantic winds, more than 100 flights were made without a halt.

Perry became the Chief Pilot on the BOAC Comet 4s. Prior to making the Comet proving flight to Mauritius, he flew to the island as a supernumerary crew member on board a Britannia. The talk at the time was that the island's runway was too short for jet aircraft and Air France had already decided that it was not possible to fly their Boeing 707s there. When he made the proving flight, by using full reverse thrust, he was able to bring the aircraft to a halt only half way down the runway. "It was a bloody nose for Air France. They had given everyone the impression that it was unsafe for jets. They had continued using Réunion." [19]

The aircraft was known as the 'pocket rocket', a nickname that has been applied to other jet aircraft at various times. A somewhat buccaneering spirit evolved on the fleet and this led to what was described as 'a nasty crop of incidents'. In one incident a Pilot hit a tree on the approach to Dum Dum airport and overshot the runway. He hit the same tree again on the second approach. Another incident concerned a Pilot who made an approach to land on a road in the Nairobi game reserve, some miles short of the main runway at Nairobi airport. One Pilot damaged a Comet's flaps whilst landing in Khartoum and another hit a ridge on an approach to Madrid. The CAA responded to this spate of incidents by introducing an extra simulator check and an extra route check, thus bringing to an end the exuberant period. "We were serious, but many had no idea of jet problems" one Captain later remarked.

Chester built Comet 4 G-APDM, which was delivered to BOAC on 16th April 1959 and first flew on 21st March 1959, operated the final BOAC Comet service on 24th November 1965, from New Zealand via Australia and Singapore [20].

IN SERVICE WITH CANADIAN PACIFIC AIRLINES

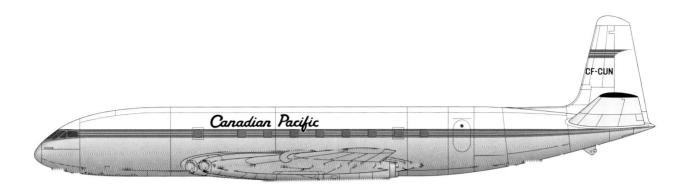

CPA was formed in the period from 1933 onwards by the organisation of the northern and western services of Canadian Airways Ltd and a number of independently developed bush operations under the flag of the Canadian Pacific Railway, a process which was consolidated by 1942. In 1948 the airline carried 7,309,633lb of freight, 145,891 passengers and 1,882,034lb of airmail over a distance of 4,952,614 miles. After BOAC, CPA was the second airline to order the Comet.

On 15th December 1949, the first export order for the Comet was announced by CPA. It was for two aircraft in the 48 seat layout to operate from Vancouver to Hong Kong. This plan was later changed so that the Comets would cover the Sydney to Honolulu route with a connecting flight by DC6 over the last long leg to Vancouver. The route was across one of the remotest quarters of the globe and the Comets were, therefore, to be based in Sydney. The decision to use the Comet was taken after an exhaustive technical study of the

Pictured at Hatfield prior to the first flight in December 1952, CF-CUN was destined never to serve Canadian Pacific Airlines as the aircraft crashed while on delivery at Karachi on 3rd March 1953, and was written-off.

This view of 'Empress of Hawaii' displays the streamlined contours of the Comet 1 nose.

aircraft and its Ghost engines at the de Havilland factories and in flight over the British Isles. The appraisal of the aircraft was personally supervised by Mr G W G McConachie, the President of CPA.

More light was thrown on the economy and technique of Comet operations by Mr W G Townley, Operations Manager of CPA, in a paper he read before the American Society of Mechanical Engineers. He noted that the Comet was comparable in size and capacity to a Douglas DC4 and one Comet could do the work of two DC4s. He also noted that as the Comet would reach its destination in half the time, the necessity for providing meals, refreshments and other services was consequently reduced. This would represent not only a substantial initial cost saving but also a continuing operational saving.

One issue that concerned CPA was the fact that accurate meteorological data, observed over an appreciable period, was only available for the North Atlantic, Northern Europe and, to a more limited extent, North America. The Pacific was not catered for and the ICAO was looking into the development of additional weather stations. At the same time, the Canadian Government stationed a weather ship, 'Peter', in the Pacific Ocean at latitude 50° North and longitude 145° West. Of particular concern to Comet operations was the possibility of turbulence or sharp gusts

at 30,000ft. It was anticipated that the swept wing of the Comet would alleviate most of the severe gusts and not pass the effect on to the passengers.

At the time of the Comet 1A orders, CPA was operating approximately 10,000 miles of routes in Canada, mainly feeder services to Trans Canadian Airlines and the trans-continental railroads of Canadian National Railway and Canadian Pacific Railway. Its air services ran from Edmonton to Aklavik in the Arctic North West Territory, and from Winnipeg to Churchill on Hudson Bay, as well as to distant mining areas of northern Quebec. The internal fleet comprised seventeen DC3s, nine Lodestars, four Cansos and six Ansons. From the Spring of 1949, CPA had been using Canadair 4s with Rolls-Royce Merlin engines and on 13th July that year, operations with Canadairs started between Vancouver and Sydney via Honolulu. Charter operations on the northern route to the Orient led to the opening of a regular weekly service from Vancouver to Tokyo and Hong Kong by way of Anchorage and Shemya on 19th September. Four Canadairs worked these services. On the route to Australia the stages were Vancouver to San Francisco, a distance of 801 statute miles, then to Honolulu, a distance of 2,395 miles, Canton Island, 1,907 miles, Fiji, 1,271 miles and finally, Sydney, 1,966 miles. The total distance was 8,340 miles and on this run CPA divided the traffic with Pan American and British Commonwealth Pacific Airlines. On the Orient service which ran from Minneapolis via Edmonton and Anchorage to Tokyo, Shanghai and thence to Manila, it shared part of the route

The tail design changed very little over the production life of the Comet.

On 10th August 1952, CF-CUM of Canadian Pacific Airlines was the first of the series 1A Comets to fly.

with North Western Airlines. NWA also ran a service from Seattle, which linked up with the main Orient route at Anchorage. According to Great Circle calculations, the four stages between Vancouver and Hong Kong total 5,725 nautical miles or 6,590 statute miles and the flown track was about 6,800 or 6,900 statute miles. The Canadair C4s were covering this with three halts westbound in 45 hours and eastbound in 38 hours. The Comets would cut the journey down to about 20 hours westbound, including three one hour halts, and 15 hours or so eastbound.

The second Comet 1A ordered by CPA was c/n 06014, registered CF-CUN and first flown on 24th December 1952. The aircraft was named The Empress of Hawaii. It left the United Kingdom on 2nd March 1953 on a delivery flight to Sydney but crashed at Karachi the following day killing all eleven people on board. As with the accident on 26th October 1952 at Ciampino Airport, Rome, the official report attributed the accident to an error of judgement by the captain in not appreciating the excessive nose-up attitude of the aircraft during the take-off.

The first Comet 1A ordered by CPA was c/n 06013, registered CF-CUM and first flown on 10th August 1952. Following the accident to CF-CUN, the aircraft was sold to BOAC in August 1953 and registered G-ANAV. Then, on 24th May 1954, the aircraft was flown to the RAE at Farnborough and used for strain gauge testing during August and September of that year. The aircraft, which never flew for CPA, was scrapped the following year and its nose section was donated to the Science Museum.

On 16th November 1953, CPA ordered three Comet 2s with an option on a fourth. The airline planned to use the Comet 2s initially on a trans-Pacific service linking Vancouver with Sydney, cutting the flying time by about one third. This was a development of the original programme for a jet service between Australia and Honolulu based on the Comet 1A, which was withheld because of the accident with the first aircraft in March 1953. The route between Sydney and Vancouver, a distance of some 7,500 statute miles, was by way of Auckland, Fiji, Canton Island and San Francisco, the longest stage being the 2,400 mile leg between Honolulu and San Francisco. However in the light of the withdrawal of the Comet's C of A in 1954, this order was cancelled.

IN SERVICE WITH UNION AÉROMARITIME DE TRANSPORT

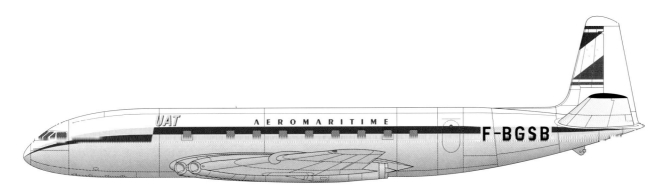

In 1935 the French shipping company Chargeurs Réunis formed an aviation division known as Aéromaritime. Five Sikorsky twin engined, 8 passenger flying boats operated between the coastal towns of French colonial Africa. When the war began in 1939, Aéromaritime was turned over to active service and subsequently dispersed, however in 1948 Chargeurs Réunis decided to revive its airline associate. At that time, the Société Aéronautique de Transports Intercontinentaux, a small airline directed by its two founders, Monsieur Roger Loubry and Monsieur Jean Combard,

respectively an airline captain and an engineer of many years experience, was operating a fleet of Liberators on general charter work to Indo China and Africa. An agreement concluded in October 1949 between Chargeurs Réunis, Air France, and SATI resulted in the formation of Union Aéromaritime de Transport, with all the crews and personnel of SATI joining the new airline. The Liberators continued to be operated until April 1951 when four DC4s were brought into service on routes to Saigon, the Far East and Francophone Africa and the fleet was soon increased with three DC3s and two DC4s.

Destined to be the first Comet 1A delivered to Union Aéromaritime de Transport, F-BGSA nears completion at Hatfield in July 1952.

F-BGSA sits on the slushy Hatfield apron on 9th of December 1952, two days before delivery to UAT.

In 1951 it was decided to order a fleet of Comet 1As for the primary routes to West and Central Africa, with an option on four Comet 2s and nine Herons to feed the Comets. The Comets were ordered for the routes to Casablanca, Dakar, Abidjan, Bamako, Duala and Brazzaville and a contract for two Comet 1As was signed on 1st May 1951, with a further one being ordered on 30th October. UAT engaged in a period of thorough technical planning and the training of selected crews and engineers and, in December 1952, the airline was ready to take delivery of its first Comet. UAT was then the largest private airline in France and it was not without some pride that the airline became the first in France and the second in the world to operate the Comet.

The first Comet 1A to be delivered, F-BGSA, took to the air for the first time at Hatfield on 13th November 1952. It was flown from Hatfield to Paris on 17th December by Monsieur Loubry who subsequently carried out all the route-proving flights. Later the aircraft was baptised at UAT's Le Bourgét base on 23rd December by Madame Jacqueline Auriol, daughter-in-law of the French President, who at the time held the Women's International Speed Record with a Vampire. It took off on 27th December on its first proving flight to Dakar.

The second captain on F-BGSA's delivery flight was Monsieur Jean Pierre Villacéque, the company's Chief Pilot. He

and four other captains had taken familiarisation courses on the Comet at Hatfield and accompanied BOAC crews on passenger services to Johannesburg and Singapore. BOAC cooperated generously with UAT, enabling the airline to call upon existing Comet airline experience for their flight planning. Fuel reserves, for example, were based upon those used by BOAC for their Comet 1s, and were strictly adhered to.

Crew training was continued in France after delivery of the first aircraft. The instruction of five captains and five first officers was carried out by Monsieur Villacéque, assisted for a time by Mr Peter Bois of de Havilland. All pilots received a minimum of fifteen hours instruction and the full training syllabus was completed in each case without difficulty. Each member of UAT's ten Comet crews was trained as a navigator, although in practice the crew member licensed and responsible for navigation was the first officer. Two senior captains attended the BOAC navigation school at Middlebank to study the Comet navigation technique then, afterwards, they undertook the training of other personnel in France. Four radio officers trained at Hatfield and returned to instruct six others. The chief flight engineer and nine others spent twelve weeks in the Comet school and similarly undertook the instruction of other engineers on their return.

A total of 90 hours of route proving flights were carried out before the start of passenger services. The Comet visited

Casablanca, Dakar, Abidjan, Algiers, Marseilles and Toulouse and during the course of these tests, the aircraft was granted formal certification for SGACC (Secrétariat Général L'Aviation Civile et Commerciale) by pilots and engineers of the Centre d'tssais en Vol and Veritas. No difficulty was experienced by UAT in the ratification by the French authorities of the ARB certificate, and the Comet aroused great interest when it first arrived at the airports which it was subsequently to serve. At Abidjan practically the whole town went to the airport to greet the Comet's first visit on 15th April 1953. 2,500 people filed through the aircraft during the day and caviar and champagne filled the spacious tables of the Customs hall. This was not altogether surprising in a country where other forms of entertainment were limited and where the airport terraces were the social meeting places. It was not that many years since the comings and goings of the local train had provided similar entertainment.

UAT quickly became more and more technically independent of de Havilland with regard to the maintenance of their Comet fleet. An office was provided for the de Havilland service representative at Le Bourgét, but the hour to hour business of maintaining the aircraft and delivering them to the crews for the next service quickly became a matter of orderly routine within the resources of the operator. UAT's engineering departments at Le Bourgét were fully equipped for complete electrical, radio, hydraulic, instrument overhaul and engine maintenance. The Comet flight hangar, known as

'Section Comet' was impressive for the quality of its equipment, much of which was specially made to UAT designs. No hangar or office building was more than two or three minutes walking distance from another. One of the permanent residents of the main Comet hangar was a dog by the name of SATI, who had been with the airline since 1949, and a cat that answered to the name of Gasket inhabited the Magasin Comet, where Comet stores were kept.

The schedule of check inspections for the Comet's airframe was drawn up in accordance with de Havilland recommendations. The Check 1 was at 60 hours, the Check 2 every 120 hours, the Check 3 at 240 hours and the Check 4 at 720 hours. In addition there were two other regular visites. One, boute de ligne (line check), was carried out the moment the aircraft returned to Paris which took about one hour unless some difficult snag was reported. It involved an examination of the main working components, in particular the turbine and compressor, accompanied by the clearing of flight snags reported by the crew in the Flight Log or Compte Rendu de Voyage. The moment a Comet arrived back from service, a mechanic sped off on a bicycle to the Arrivals apron to receive the report and, usually within half an hour of touchdown, a typed copy was with each department for scrutiny and action if necessary. Seldom was a flight snag left unattended until the next day. The visite d'escale, or the between flights inspection, was carried out by UAT mechanics stationed at the airports down the line.

The second Comet delivered to UAT, F-BGSB, gleams in the afternoon light at Paris Le Bourgét Airport in 1952, while a party of school children are given a conducted tour of the aircraft.

On 29th October 1953, F-BGSA rests on the hardstanding at Jan Smuts Airport, Johannesburg, South Africa, prior to servicing for the long journey home to Paris.

trouble free service given by the Ghost. After only three months of operation, they calculated that the hours of maintenance required per flying hour were half of those needed for well established piston engines of which they had extensive experience.

UAT inaugurated its Comet service on 19th February 1953, with the departure of F-BGSA from Le Bourgét on the first of a twice-weekly return service to Dakar by way of Casablanca. The flight, which took 3 hours to Casablanca and 6 hours and 40 minutes to Dakar, cut the existing fastest times by nearly a half. The second Comet, F-BGSB, which had first flown at Hatfield on 21st January 1953, was also delivered on 19th February 1953 and, on 14th March, an extra twice-weekly return service to Casablanca began. A month later, on 14th April, operations were extended to include two services per week to Abidjan, via Casablanca and Dakar with one of these services being an extension of the Dakar service.

The third Comet, F-BGSC, took to the air for the first time at Hatfield on 15th April and was delivered to UAT on 30th April. On the 6th May it was possible to open a once weekly service to Brazzaville, capital of French Equatorial Africa. At first the route was by way of Casablanca and Abidjan and the flying time of 11 hours and 23 minutes from Paris cut existing times by four hours. Then from the 3rd July the time was further reduced by an hour by re-routing via Tripoli and Kano. On that date, just nineteen weeks after the start of Comet services, the unduplicated route mileage was 8,615 statute miles and the aircraft were flying 37,635 statute miles each week and averaging 97 hours. This represented an annual utilisation per aircraft of 1,680 hours.

This record was achieved despite the fact that F-BGSC was damaged beyond repair after skidding off the runway at Dakar on 25th June 1953, after a little under two months in service.

The MTOW of 115,000lb was not used except on the 1,970 mile Casablanca-Abidjan stage. A limitation was imposed on the stage from Abidjan to Casablanca as temperatures at Abidjan averaged 30°C over the whole year, day and night, and midday take-offs for Casablanca from the 2,200 metre runway required the number of passengers to be limited to 34. Despite the high temperatures, it was not necessary to schedule take-offs for the cooler but inconvenient hours of the early morning.

Observers detected a special keenness among the engineers and maintenance crews of the Comet fleet, and it was not unusual to see a mechanic repainting a wheel after it had been changed. Each aircraft was polished by hand, not by buffing every 60 hours, and all personnel were issued with special shoes for walking on the airframe. A number of small improvements in design were carried out by UAT. Pitot covers were attached to long sticks to avoid the need for steps and along with the jet pipe and air intake covers, were always put in place a few seconds after the engines had stopped. A public address system was fitted to each aircraft to enable the captain or the hostess to talk to the passengers in flight and special fittings were made to enable infants' carry cots to be slung from the luggage racks.

At first a certain amount of difficulty was experienced in becoming accustomed to British standard measurements. Familiar with their own and American standards until the arrival of the Comet, UAT engineers had to quickly get used to a different currency in nuts, bolts and screws. The success of UAT's engineering organisation was due in part to its capable direction and in part to an individual engineering skill that had something of the artistic about it.

Comet operations began with the overhaul life of the Ghost 50 Mk4 set at the comparatively cautious figure of 375 hours. In July 1953, an extension to 450 hours was agreed as a result of the satisfactory condition of the engines on intermediate inspections. Major overhauls of the engines were carried out at the de Havilland Engine Company's factory at Watford in England. UAT planned to use the Ghosts with the water methanol injection system as soon as it could be fitted, and were pleased with the

UAT hoped to be able to use the Ghost's water-injection system by 1953. The system's restoration of take-off thrust in hot conditions would allow the airline to offer different services. One was the re-routing of the Brazzaville service through Algiers instead of Tripoli, with no take-off limitations for the 1,730 mile stage from Kano to Algiers. Another route in which UAT was interested was that from

Paris to Saigon on which an elapsed time of 23 hours would be achieved.

Meteorological forecasting in West and Central Africa was reliable and, as civil aviation expanded, its scope was widened by increasing the number of radiosonde installations. From Dakar southwards, on UAT's Comet routes, lay the area that experienced periodic monsoon type weather. Violent, rapidly forming cumulo nimbus clouds rose to 30,000 – 40,000ft, with 'linesqualls' at lower altitudes. For this reason, all flying at night was forbidden and the Comet schedules were planned accordingly.

Radio communication facilities, HF and VHF, were adequate at airports along the route, although the HF was affected when stormy weather was prevalent. Fogs and ground mists were uncommon, except in the early morning at Casablanca, and Comets were diverted on three occasions to the French Air Force base at Marakesh, 135 miles away.

The transporting of passengers, freight and mail between France and French colonies by both air and sea was principally generated by the lively commerce that existed between metropolitan France and its colonies. Aside from some en route to Casablanca, few of the passengers on UAT's Comets were tourists. French families living abroad generally returned to France once every two years and, in some cases, each year. Those who were inclined to turn the trip into a holiday tended to go by sea. The holiday movement homewards was at its highest in June and July, and in the return direction during September and October. All year round there was a sustained movement of businessmen and government officials. UAT also carried large quantities of perishable goods, which ensured the sustenance of the French abroad, as well as the mail.

At first, fare paying passengers were comparatively few because the seasonal peak of holiday traffic was yet to come, and the First Class fare which was charged for Comet travel, at 20% higher than competitive tourist rate fares, mitigated against the reduction in travel time offered. Moreover, since most commercial companies in Francophone Africa paid their employees' fares, it was only a minority of private businessmen who travelled First Class, as many companies had discount agreements with the airlines for carrying employees and their families.

In July 1953, UAT showed its approval of the aircraft by ordering three Comet 2s. The airline planned to use the Comet 2's better range and take-off performance for services between Dakar and Marseilles, Dakar and Paris and possibly Douala and Paris via Algiers.

Initially UAT operated three 14-seat Herons, based at Douala, on a network of internal routes. The aircraft offered both an improvement in internal communications and also fed passengers to the Comets. UAT's in-flight catering was widely held to be excellent, even by French standards, and several hundred of the Comet postcards given to passengers in flight were later addressed to the UAT office in Paris with messages of appreciation.

F-BGSA and F-BGSB were withdrawn from service on 12th April 1954 following the Comet 1 accidents. They remained at Le Bourget until they were eventually scrapped and UAT's order for Comet 2s was cancelled.

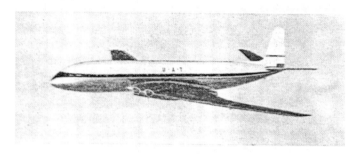

UNION AEROMARITIME DE TRANSPORT

YOU can now fly by . . .

U.A.T. COMET

from

JOHANNESBURG to PARIS

in Seventeen Hours (fourteen hours actual flying time)

Ask your agent to arrange your air journey by U.A.T. and experience incomparable COMET comfort plus a FRENCH welcome, FRENCH cuisine and FRENCH courtesy. Achieve a memorable air trip by flying to Europe by U.A.T. FRENCH AIRLINE.

F-BGNX, the first Comet delivered to Air France, poses for the camera during a final pre-delivery test flight in May 1953.

The first two Air France Comets share the tarmac at Hatfield with a de Havilland Dove, prior to delivery in May 1953.

IN SERVICE WITH AIR FRANCE

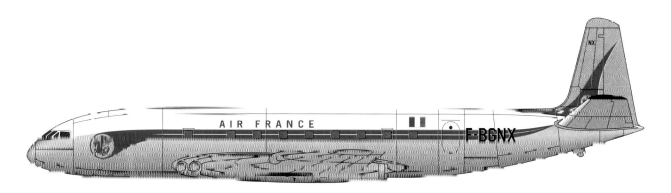

Air France came into being on 30th August 1933 when four separate airlines were merged, namely Air Union, Comagnie Générale Transports Aériens, Campagnie Internationale de Navigation Aérienne and Air Orient. The newly formed airline had 259 aircraft and the fleet composed of 32 different types. Among them were the Potez 62, the Dewotine 333 and the Dewotine 338, the CAMS 53, the Breguet Saigon, the Wibault 283, the Fokker FVIIb/3m and the Bloch 220. A

fourth regional airline, the Résau des Lignes Aériens Fransáise, was established on 12th February 1945. Later that year on 26th June, Air France was nationalised and, on 2nd June 1946, the entire air transport network in France was handed over to the new Société Nationale Air France.

The new airline retained 80 aircraft from its pre-war fleet and incorporated other acquisitions, among them Ju 52/3ms,

The first Comet 1A to wear the classic 'seahorse' livery of Air France stands virtually complete in the assembly hall at Hatfield in early 1953.

A rare colour shot of Comet 1 F-BGNX, taken on a pre-delivery test flight.

Lockheed 14s and 18s and Sikorsky S-43s. Over time the new aircraft acquired included the SE161 Languedocs, the Latécoère 631 flying boat, DC3s, DC4s, Constellations and Viscounts.

On 21st November 1951, Air France's President, Monsieur Max Hymans, announced that, subject to the formality of government approval, the airline wished to order three Comet 1As for introduction on trunk routes, to satisfy the steady rise in traffic which the airline was witnessing. At the time the order was placed, the airline intended to use the Comets on the route between Paris and Cairo and Beirut, on an express service between Paris and Saigon, and on the Paris to Dakar route. Some thought was also given to the possibility of extending the network to include Buenos Aires and Brazzaville, with the introduction of the Comet 2. These routes were then served by Constellation L749s.

On a sunny day at Hatfield in 1953, F-BGNX heads for the runway during on-going flight trials.

Air France's first Comet, F-BGNX, first flew on 6th May 1953. It was delivered to the airline on 12th June and served Air France for two years until 27th June 1956, when it was returned to Britain and allocated the registration G-AOJT before being dismantled at the RAE. It was never modified to become a Comet 1XB as it was to have been used for water tank tests. In the event, this rare fuselage now resides at the de Havilland Mosquito Museum, as one of the saddest exhibits in the world, where it is used as a storage shed for junk, while completely neglected still carrying the original and faded Air France livery.

The airline's second Comet, F-BGNY, first flew on 22nd May 1953 and was delivered to the airline on 7th July. It operated the first service from Paris to Beirut via Rome on 26th August, was eventually returned to Britain, modified to become a Comet 1XB and first registered as G-AOJU. It was later registered as XM829 and served with A&AEE at Boscombe Down for Decca/Dectra trials until its retirement to the Stansted Fire School on 20th February 1964. It was used as a training airframe for some time and became a

source of spares for another ex-Air France Comet, XM823, before it was burnt during the Autumn of 1970.

The third and final Comet for Air France was F-BGNZ which took to the air for the first time on 16th March but was not delivered to the airline until the 22nd July. The aircraft was later returned to Britain, modified to become a Comet 1XB in March 1957 and registered as G-APAS, then G-5-23, with de Havilland Propellers and, finally, XM823 with Hawker Siddeley Dynamics. Both de Havilland Propellers and Hawker Siddeley Dynamics operated XM823 on various trials at Hatfield. The aircraft was retired to Shawbury on 8th April 1968 and preserved at the Aerospace Museum at Cosford, near Shifnal in Shropshire, England. G-APAS exists as the only surviving and intact example of a de Havilland Ghost-powered Comet 1.

On 7th August 1953, following the delivery of all three Comet 1As, a contract was placed for the supply of three Comet 2s, a further three being ordered on 31st December. Subsequently, after the Comet crashes, all orders were cancelled.

IN SERVICE WITH AEROLINEAS ARGENTINAS

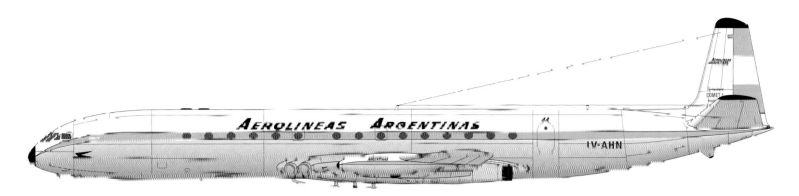

On 3rd May 1949, Argentina's President, Juan Domingo Perón, nationalised four of the country's fledgling and ailing private airlines; Aeroposta Argentina, FAMA, Zomas Oests y Norte de Aerolineas Argentinas (ZONDA) and Aviación del Litoral Fluvial Argentino (ALFA), thus forming Aerolineas Argentinas. The plurality of the name reflects the fact that the airline was created from the amalgamation of these four separate airlines. Aerolineas Argentinas became the flag carrier of the nation and it came into being on the same day as the opening of Buenos Aires' international airport, Ezeiza. On that day, a DC4 took off for Rio de Janeiro and a DC6 took off for Santiago. The airlines' operations started on 14th May that year

and the fleet consisted of twenty-two DC3s, six DC6s, five Convair 240s, five Shorts' Sandringhams and a Shorts' Sunderland. The company formally came into existence on 7th December 1949, when a government decree established the Empresa del Estado Aerolineas Argentinas and appointed its first president. International operations commenced on 21st March 1950 with a DC6 flight to New York and the airline also flew a DC6 service to Amsterdam via Rio de Janeiro, Natal, Dakar, Lisbon, Paris, London and Frankfurt.

On 19th March 1958, Aerolineas Argentinas and de Havilland signed a contract for the supply of six Comet 4s

The first Comet 4 for Aerolineas Argentinas LV-PLM 'Las Tres Marias', is towed into position for engine runs at Hatfield prior to the first flight in January 1959.

During the first flight on 27th January 1959, LV-PLM in the colours of Aerolineas Argentinas displays
the classic lines of the aircraft, in what was the first export order for the Comet 4.

with Rolls-Royce Avon RA29 engines. The contract value, including spare-parts provisioning, exceeded £9 million. A Comet 2 of the RAF, conveying the Rt Hon George Ward MP, Secretary of State for Air, landed at Buenos Aires on 27th April 1958 when the MP was detailed to represent Queen Elizabeth II at the inauguration of the new President, His Excellency Dr Arturo Frondizi. The Comet also carried the ground support party for two RAF Bomber Command Vulcans which accompanied the flight. The Comet and the Vulcans performed a formation fly-past in Buenos Aires and later visited Montevideo and Rio de Janeiro, where seven demonstration flights were made during the ten day tour and the Comet's modest runway requirements were the subject of particularly favourable comment. Some senior South American airline executives took advantage of the opportunity to fly in the aircraft and a few days later the

Argentine Government ratified the Aerolineas Argentinas contract. The airline planned to introduce the Comet to its network in early 1959 and the delivery of the Comets was expected to be completed during 1960.

The production programme at de Havilland was ahead of schedule and thus the manufacturer was able to release the seventh, ninth and tenth aircraft, originally assigned to BOAC, to Aerolineas Argentinas while still meeting the delivery dates in their contract with BOAC. At a ceremony at Hatfield on 27th February 1959, Sir Aubrey Burke, the Managing Director of de Havilland Aircraft, handed over the first of the Comets to Señor Enrique Bermudez, Technical Director of Aerolineas Argentinas. The Argentinian Ambassador to London was also present and joined the aircraft for a flight around England, the first to be made under the flag of Aerolineas Argentinas.

The first Comet, LV-PLM, c/n 6408, first flew on 27th January 1959 and was then delivered on 2nd March 1959 following a two stop flight from Hatfield to Buenos Aires. The aircraft covered the 7,000 statute miles in an overall time, to overhead Buenos Aires, of 18 hours and 23 minutes. It then circled the city before landing at five in the evening to be greeted by Dr Arturo Frondizi, President of the Republic, Comodoro Juan Jose Güiraldes, President of Aerolineas Argentinas, and an enthusiastic gathering. Comodoro J J Güiraldes, President of the airline, and his wife Señora Güiraldes, formally christened the Comet Las Tres Marias, after a star constellation in the southern hemisphere, after which the aircraft was then re-registered LV-AHN.

The second Comet, LV-PLO, c/n 6410, first flew on 25th February 1959, and left Hatfield on 18th March, making a series of demonstration flights to Paris, Frankfurt, Amsterdam, Rome, Madrid and Lisbon before arriving in Buenos Aires on 25th March. The aircraft was re-registered LV-AHO and named Cruz del Sur, Lucero de la Tarde and later named Lucero de la Tarde. The third aircraft, LV-PLP, c/n 6411, first flew on 24th March 1959 and was delivered on 2nd May. It was re-registered LV-AHP and named El Lucero del Alba.

The flight crews converted to the Comet with ease and the passenger appeal of the aircraft was unprecedented. Flight training started in Buenos Aires immediately after the arrival of the first aircraft on 2nd March 1959, with the airline being responsible for the flight training and the ground training while the early ground training had been the responsibility of the de Havilland Servicing School at Hatfield. All flight training was carried out from Buenos Aires and ten crews completed their training by August 1959. Mr Peter Wilson, a de Havilland Training Pilot, and Mr J Crowe, a Training Flight Engineer, assisted and advised over the introductory period, while two more de Havilland flight engineers accompanied the first services to help and advise where needed. Mr George Errington, former senior de Havilland test pilot, maintained continuous liaison.

Each Argentinian Comet pilot received ten hours of conversion flying and forty hours route training. All reached full capacity standards quickly and without difficulty which reflected well on the crews who lacked the extensive range of training aids available to the larger operators. The Buenos Aires-Santiago run provided a good training ground because of the topography, the weather and the characteristics of the Santiago airfield and approaches. Los Cerrillos Airport, Santiago, was frequently subjected to low stratus cloud and low visibility. Moreover, the airfield was situated close to the Andes foothills and the runway had little more than 6,000ft to offer, after a rather difficult approach. An estimated 20,000 people made their way to the airport to witness the arrival of the first Comet flight on 28th March while an even larger crowd, estimated to have been twice the size, turned out to greet the aircraft at Mendoza, the alternative airport for Santiago. The conversion programme was completed far more quickly than was the case with the previous piston engined type.

The airline introduced the Comets on four international routes of widely differing characteristics within three months of the delivery of their first aircraft. The aircraft was referred to as 'El Comet' and on 8th April 1959, flew on a proving flight from Buenos Aires to New York's Idlewild airport. The 6,100 mile flight was via Port of Spain and Rio de Janeiro and the time taken was 15 hours 30 minutes. The airline expected that its Comets would offer an annual utilisation of 3,000 hours per aircraft following the introduction of the service to New York in May. It was expected that this would increase to 3,800 hours and that by June 1960 their fleet of six Comet 4s would be covering some ten million miles per year. Following the commencement of services, the airline discovered that on the route to Europe, the passenger mileage factor increased by 36% and on the route to North America it rose by 84%. Charles Butler Associates devised the interior decor for the aircraft and the airline selected de Havilland's seats with foot rests for the First Class accommodation. The cabin arrangement was for 24 First-Class passengers forward and 43 Tourist Class passengers aft.

The Comets flew to four continents and operated five services per week between Buenos Aires and Santiago, two services per week between Europe and South America, and three services per week between New York and Buenos Aires. On the route to Europe, one service was to London via Paris, Madrid, Dakar, Recife, Rio and Buenos Aires, and the other was to London via Frankfurt, Rome, Madrid, Dakar, Recife and

In a ceremony at Hatfield on 27th February 1959, Sir Aubrey Burke, Managing Director of de Havilland, hands over the first of six Comet 4s to Aerolineas Argentinas.

LV-AHO, One of three aircraft lost in service, lies fatally wounded at Ezeiza airport, Buenos Aires on 20th February 1960.

Rio. The three services to New York called at Trinidad and Rio and one of the services made an additional stop at Havana.

Aerolineas Argentinas had well equipped workshops at Ezeiza Airport and the airline also carried out engine overhauls. Any urgent requirements were sent out by one of the regular Comet services from London, and the success of the maintenance programme resulted in an aircraft utilisation of nine hours per day. The Comets made a number of extremely fast flights in commercial service. On the Santiago to Buenos Aires route, a time of 1 hour and 17 minutes was recorded while on the New York to Buenos Aires route a time of 11 hours and 17 minutes was recorded, and across the South Atlantic from Dakar to Recife, 3 hours and 59 minutes was achieved.

An alternative view of LV-AHO, demonstrates the extent of the damage caused to the aircraft during the crash.

LV-AHP was the first of three Comets which the airline was to lose. After only three months with the airline it disappeared on 27th August 1959 near Asunción. Then, some six months later on 20th February 1960, LV-AHO was destroyed at Ezeiza airport during a crew-training exercise.

On 29th September 1960, a ceremony was held at Ezeiza airport to christen two of the Comets. LV-POY, c/n 6430, first flew at Hatfield on 15th February 1960 and was delivered to the airline on 8th March. It was re-registered LV-AHR and named Alborada and later Arco Iris. LV-PPA, c/n 6434, was built at Chester and first flew on 20th July 1960, with the aircraft being delivered on 26th July, re-registered LV-AHU and named Centaurus. The ceremony was conducted by Mrs Betty Thomas, the wife of a Comet pilot, and Mrs Margaret Seligma, the widow of a Comet pilot who had recently been killed in a car crash. The Bishop of Omas de Zamora gave a blessing and the occasion was attended by officials from the airline and the Government. The airline had also taken delivery of a sixth aircraft, LV-POZ, c/n 6432, which first flew on 18th February 1960 and was delivered on 19th March, being the first of three that were built at Chester, and was re-registered LV-AHS and named Las Tres Marias and later changed to Alborada.

Aerolineas Argentinas acquired a seventh Comet on 27th April 1962. It was c/n 6460, a Comet 4C, which was built at Chester for MEA and first flown on 21st August 1961. It was first registered G-AROV and then LV-PTS. On delivery it was re-registered LV-A1B and named President Kennedy. The aircraft had been flown in MEA colours at Farnborough in September 1961, but MEA did not take delivery of it.

The third Comet that the airline was to lose, LV-AHR, crashed at Campinas Airport, Sao Paulo, Brazil, on 23rd November 1961. The aircraft took off for Trinidad at 05.38 hours and reached an altitude of about 100 metres before crash-landing in a eucalyptus forest. The aircraft was destroyed and the twelve crew and 40 passengers died in the accident.

The flight had originated at Buenos Aires and the aircraft had flown a total of 5,242 hours, 2,242 of which had been flown since the last overhaul and about six hours since the last 90-hour inspection. Unfortunately it was not possible to check the maintenance reports regarding the 30 days prior to the accident. The crew on board the aircraft at the time of the accident consisted of a Pilot, a Co-Pilot and ten other crew members. The Pilot was sitting in the right-hand seat, presumably acting as instructor at the time of the accident. He had flown a total of 12,550 hours of which 11,246 were as pilot-in-command or instructor and held a valid IFR rating with 5,791 hours by night. On the Comet, he had 1,612 hours of which 584 had been as Pilot-in-Command or Instructor.

Delivered in April 1962, LV-AIB (previously LV- PTS), was destined to be the sole Comet 4C used by the Argentinian airline. Here we see the aircraft at Heathrow on a murky June day in 1964 preparing for the return flight to Buenos Aires.

The Co-Pilot had flown a total of 13,427 hours of which 1,074 had been on the Comet. He had flown 2,833 hours at night, and also held a valid IFR rating. The crew had only served about three hours during the preceding twenty-four so it was not thought that the accident had been caused by fatigue.

Neither was it believed that the weather contributed to the accident although it was a dark night due to stratocumulus at 400 metres and altostratus at 2,100 metres. At the time of take-off, the aircraft's weight was 1,087kg below the MTOW and the centre of gravity was within the prescribed limits. According to the ATC, the take-off run was approximately 2,000 metres, some 240 metres shorter than estimated before departure.

Tests were carried out with LV-AHU and it was concluded that the take-off run took about 40 seconds. The ATC concluded that the aircraft's climbing angle was around 4.5° and that the aircraft reached an estimated altitude of 100 metres. Taking into account the minimum climbing angle of 4.5°, the aircraft should have reached an altitude of 120 metres.

It was concluded that LV-AHR should have reached the IAS of 170 knots. At that moment LV-AHR was midway between the take-off point and the first impact point. It was estimated that the aircraft flew a total distance of 3,170 metres, and the point where the aircraft started losing altitude was estimated as the middle distance between the point where the aircraft became airborne and the first impact point.

At an IAS of 170 knots, the pilot was required to alter the elevator change gear from the 'coarse' setting to the 'fine' setting, an action which tended to cause the aircraft's nose to drop. This had to be counteracted by using the manual trim tab and it was believed that the unit was being adjusted when the accident occurred. As it was deduced that the aircraft hit the first eucalyptus tree in a nearly horizontal attitude, it was concluded that the pilot had been trying to regain climbing attitude but, due to the elevator being in the 'fine' position, the aircraft took longer to respond. At 120 metres after the first impact point, the aircraft adopted a climbing angle of approximately 25° with this conclusion being reached because the eucalyptus trees at that spot were burned from the top down, probably by turbine exhaust gas. At that point, the elevator counter balance collided with a eucalyptus tree which tore it off. About 145 metres after the first impact point, the aircraft collided with a larger eucalyptus tree resulting in a fire in the left wing pod tank, and moments later a further impact occurred with another tree in the No. 1 engine area and the aircraft collided with the ground about 303 metres from the first impact point and exploded.

It was surmised that the instructor, who was Pilot-in Command, may have failed to brief or supervise the Co-Pilot

LV-AIB is serviced at Heathrow in preparation for the return flight to Argentina, via Paris, Madrid, Dakar, Recife and Rio de Janeiro.

properly. Consequently, the Argentinian Government determined that the cause of the accident was "Failure to operate under IFR (Instrument Flight Rules) during a take-off by night in weather conditions requiring IFR operation, and failure to follow the climb procedure for this type of aircraft. A contributory cause was the lack of vigilance by both pilots during the operations." [21]

Having lost three Comets in service, the airline decided in September 1965 to begin to replace the aircraft with the Boeing 707-320B. The first of four purchased arrived in November 1965. Over a period of seven years, LV-AHS, LV-AHU, LV-AIB, and LV-PLM were gradualy retired and sold to Dan-Air.

Following his retirement from the airline, a former flight instructor, Captain Ronnie Daintree, gave an interview to the airline's in-house publication in which he stated: "We pilots break airplanes. Airplanes don't break by themselves. In propeller times we had accidents and then came the big change with the Comet 4 and still we had three major accidents. So then the president of the airline called me to his office and said 'Would you like to take over flight instruction because we've lost three Comets?' and I said 'Yes, why not?' After that, we had no other major crash. Whether that was thanks to me or not, I don't know. We didn't lose any more Comets, and then we did the Boeing

707 course at Boeing, which was a good course, better than the one the English gave us for the Comet, which I attended here, not in England. Some of the pilots didn't qualify though, it was just too much for them. From the Boeing 707 on, we never had a major accident in international service. If you're looking for a reason why we improved so much in terms of flight safety, I'd say it was because of Boeing. The training was simply better."

IN SERVICE WITH MEXICANA

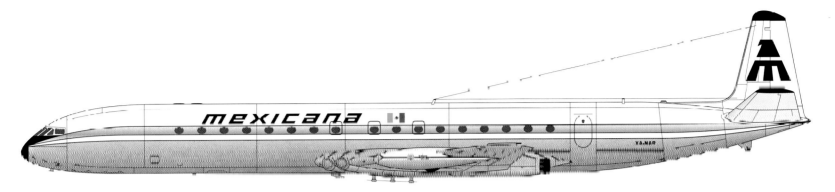

The first order for the Comet 4C was from Mexicana Airlines. On 30th October 1959, the airline announced its intention to purchase three aircraft at a total cost of $14 million including spares. Its first aircraft, XA-NAR, flew at Hatfield on the following day, carrying the temporary British registration G-AOVU, for its Certificate of Airworthiness and development flying. The FAA certified the Comet 4C in March 1961 and the tests carried out by them involved the first Mexican aircraft. The tests resulted in only a few, mainly minor, modifications to suit American operating procedures.

The second aircraft for Mexicana, XA-NAS, carried the temporary registration G-AOVV when it made its first flight at Hatfield on 3rd December 1959. It was the first to be delivered to Mexico City when it departed from Hatfield on 14th January 1960, and was joined by XA-NAR on 8th June. De Havilland were in a position to make prompt deliveries of the first two aircraft following a decision made a few months earlier to complete two Comet 4Bs, originally assigned as the fourth and fifth aircraft for BEA, as Comet 4Cs. This was done by fitting Comet 4 type outer wing sections and pinion tanks to the already partly completed aircraft. Prior to being temporarily

The first customer for the Comet 4C was Mexicana who used three 4Cs bought new and two secondhand 4s purchased from BOAC. Here we see XA-NAS, the first aircraft delivered to the airline, during the first flight on 3rd December 1959.

The second Comet 4C delivered to Mexicana XA-NAR 'Golden Aztec', flares for landing at Mexico City in May 1965. This aircraft is preserved at the Seattle Museum of Flight in BOAC livery, with plans for a repaint in the near future into Mexicana colours.

registered as G-AOVU and G-AOVV, the aircraft had been registered G-APMD and G-APME in anticipation of their completion and delivery to BEA.

The third aircraft ordered by Mexicana flew at Hatfield on 7th October 1960 with the temporary registration G-ARBB. It left Hatfield as XA-NAT on 29th November for delivery to

Prior to flight at Mexico City Airport, the crew of 'Golden Aztec' discuss the forthcoming itinerary.

Mexico City, flying via Gander and Chicago. The aircraft took off from Hatfield at eight in the morning and reached Mexico City at 8.19 pm local time, the whole journey of 5,880 miles taking just under 15 hours, with Captain Roberto Pini of Mexicana Airlines, the first Mexican to qualify as a civil jet pilot, at the controls.

Mexicana operated what it called the 'Golden Aztec' international routes, linking the USA and the Caribbean with Mexico City. Destinations on the international network included Chicago, Los Angeles and San Antonio, Texas. The airline chose the Comet 4C in preference to other jet airliners because of the ease with which it could operate the required stages with a full payload from Mexico City Airport, an airport which combined an altitude of 7,350ft with high ambient temperatures. The aircraft was adaptable for Mexicana's volume of traffic and the accommodation layout was for twenty-two First Class and 64 Tourist passengers.

The airline had an option on two further Comet 4Cs, c/ns 6457 and 6463, which were under construction at Hatfield and due to be registered XA-NAD and XA-NAE. However, owing to the airline's financial problems, these options were not taken up and after being stored on the production line at Hatfield for a short while, the aircraft were sold to Sudan Airways.

In addition to its Comet 4Cs, the airline purchased two Comet 4s. In 1965 BOAC sold G-APDR to Mexicana, which was initially registered XA-NAZ, then again reregistered XA-NAP, serving the airline until the summer of 1971 when it was sold to Channel Airways who used it for spares until it was later acquired by the Stansted fire school. The second BOAC Comet 4 was G-APDT which was bought by Mexicana in 1966 and initially registered XA-POW. This aircraft was later registered XA-NAB, but the airline disposed of it late 1969 to BOAC who used it as a cabin trainer before it was handed over to the BAA for fire rescue training.

Mexicana withdrew its three Comet 4Cs from service in December 1970 and in July 1973, XA-NAR was acquired by Westernair of Albuquerque, New Mexico who reregistered it as N888WA. It remained at Mexico City for a period of two years undergoing a full refurbishment both to the interior and the exterior. After a number of potential parties were involved in negotiations to purchase the aircraft, it was finally sold in November 1979 to Redmond Air, a subscription club airline based at Redmond, Washington. The aircraft was ferried to Salt Lake City for work to be done to upgrade the electronics, then flown to Paine Field, Everett, where it remains to this day under the care of the Seattle Museum of Flight. In June 1974, XA-NAS was also bought by Westernair and reregistered N999WA. After sale to Redmond Air, this aircraft eventually ended up in Chicago,

A view of the interior of a Mexicana Comet 4C, looking toward the rear.

where it was subsequently scrapped in 1979. The final aircraft involved in the sale to Westernair XA-NAT, was reregistered N777WA. It consequently languished at Mexico Airport until the 1980s, when it was moved to the middle of a children's playground adjacent to the airport, where it now sits in derelict condition, painted overall blue with a brown cheatline and tail.

The scene at Mexico City in November 1966 after the crash landing of XA-NAT 'Golden Knight'.

XA-NAS approaching the gate at LAX, Los Angeles International Airport in November 1967, demonstrates the simple uncluttered lines of the Comet.

XA-NAT taxies out for the return flight to Mexico in August 1970, (three months before the infamous crash at Mexico City Airport) displaying the revised Mexicana colours.

IN SERVICE WITH BRITISH EUROPEAN AIRWAYS

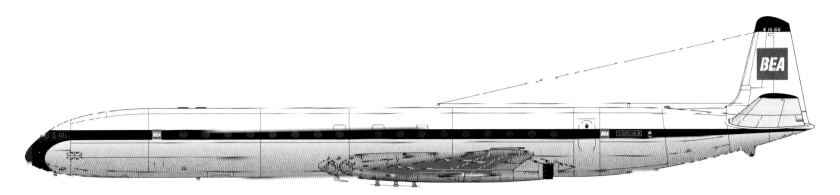

In the 1950s, it was widely believed that the jet airliner could not compete economically with the turbo-prop airliner on relatively short stages such as those operated by BEA. Nevertheless BEA were not slow to realise that formidable jet competition was looming over the horizon and, in August 1957, the airline decided to order six Comet 4Bs for their short-haul operation, with deliveries scheduled to commence late in 1959 and to be completed by the Spring of 1960.

G-ANLO, which was initially used as a prototype for the Comet 4, was modified by removing the pod tanks and redesignated the Comet 3B in order to test the proposed Comet 4B wings, although the aircraft retained the shorter length fuselage of the mark 4. It made its first flight in this form on 21st August 1958 then made its first public appearance, in the old BEA livery, two weeks later at the SBAC display at Farnborough.

On 20th July 1959, it was announced that BEA and Olympic Airways had entered into a consortium and that the Greek national airline had ordered two Comet 4Bs. This order was subsequently increased in two stages to four, so that the consortium eventually had a fleet of eighteen Comets operating on the European and Middle East network. It thus came about that BEA, with Olympic Airways, were able to meet jet competition everywhere in Europe and thus avert what might well have been a catastrophic loss of traffic had they not been in a position to do so.

Comet 4B G-APMB 'Walter Gale' in BEA 'red square' delivery colours, stands awaiting passengers at Nice in the South of France in July 1961.

A classic portrait of BEA's G-APMG 'John Grigg' taken during the first flight on 25th July 1960.

On 12th August 1959, Mr Anthony Milward, Chief Executive of BEA, announced that the order for six Comet 4B aircraft had been increased to seven, with deliveries commencing in October two months ahead of schedule. BEA's first Comet, G-APMA, took to the air for the first time at Hatfield on 27th June 1959. On 11th July it made a day return trip to Athens, taking about 3 hours and 30 minutes each way, giving travellers from England 5 hours and 30 minutes in the Greek capital, yet bringing them back in time to dine in London in the evening. Later the Comet flew from Northolt to Le Bourgét in 28 minutes and 30 seconds on 19th July 1959, winning a special prize of £1,000 in the Daily Mail London to Paris race while carrying the BEA Airline Syndicate entry. By 13th August, the aircraft had completed 100 hours of development flying. The second aircraft, G-APMB, made its public debut at Farnborough in September. The first two Comets delivered to BEA were G-APMB and G-APMC. They were handed over at Hatfield on 16th November 1959 to

prepare for route familiarisation flights throughout Europe in preparation for full Comet schedules to commence on 1st April 1960, when five aircraft entered service. The delivery dates beat the contract dates by six and ten weeks respectively.

Captain Geoffrey T Greenhalgh, MBE, the Comet Flight Manager of BEA, calculated that the airline needed about 90 pilots to operate the seven Comets. The nucleus of Training Captains took over the first aircraft in November and the programme of base training for about 80 other pilots followed the route-proving flights early in December. All these pilots had been on Viscounts and so had a basic understanding of the turbine, of fairly high speed, and of the Smith's Flight System. After a five week ground course on airframe and engine, they spent two weeks on the Comet 4B simulator which BEA had built by the Air Trainers Link Division of General Precision Systems and which was installed at Heston. Each pilot first did some 40 hours on the simulator, divided between the left and right hand seats and the systems panel. This period was followed by about eight hours of base flying, then two or three 'route flights' on the simulator followed by anything from ten to twenty sectors of line training with a Training Captain. In all, each pilot had some 70 to 90 hours of simulator and flight training. The plan worked well and there was the same enthusiasm among flight crew as there was among cabin crew and ground staff for the introduction of what Captain Greenhaigh called 'the gentle jet'.

For their Comets, BEA adopted the policy of a three pilot crew with the third pilot keeping an eye on the systems panel, a radio operator being carried only on the long distance routes. A method of 'monitored' landings, in which the duties were shared between the Captain and the First Officer, was standard practice for manual approaches in bad weather. Under this system, the First Officer made the approach to break-off height while the Captain watched for the first glimpse of the approach lights. As soon as contact was positively established, the Captain took over the controls and completed the landing. This method avoided the problem of transition from instruments to visual flying.

Following their delivery in November 1959, an industrial problem delayed the introduction of the Comets into revenue earning service. During the intervening period, one of the few passengers carried on a BEA Comet was Sir Winston Churchill. Captain A J Angus and his crew flew Sir Winston, Lady Churchill, a lady-in-waiting and a detective to Nice, where the party were to holiday. During the flight, Captain Angus went back to the passenger cabin to check that all was well and Sir Winston, then in his twilight years, asked "Haven't you got anything else but fish?" Captain Angus replied that it was a Friday to which Sir Winston exclaimed "Ugh!" with a twinkle in his eye [22].

Three BEA Comets took to the air on 1st April to inaugurate the Comet services. The first regular scheduled service of a Comet 4B was flown by G-APMB, which departed from Tel Aviv at 8.00 GMT commanded by Captain John Affleck. On the same day G-APMD took-off from London Airport for Istanbul and G-APMF, flown by Captain W Baillie, departed at 23.00 for Moscow. Out of a total BEA fleet of 93 aircraft, the six Comets operating in the Summer of 1960 produced no less than 15% of the airline's total of seat-miles. The airline's seventh Comet was delivered at the end of July, ahead of schedule.

At the BEA maintenance hanger at London's Heathrow Airport, G-APMC 'Andrew Crommelin' undergoes an airframe check. Note the unique BEA red wings livery, worn by all aircraft in the fleet until the amalgamation with British Airways in the early 1970s.

For the 1960s, the interior design of the BEA Comet 4B was a stylish combination of navy blue and pink. Above is a view of the economy section with seats arranged five abreast.
Below we see the first class section fitted with a larger more comfortable seat arranged in a four abreast layout.

The speed of the Comet naturally brought about a considerable time saving on BEA's routes and also made it possible to introduce non-stop flights to more distant destinations such as Athens and Moscow. Another factor which enhanced the standard of service on the BEA Comets was the sound design of the galleys, which greatly simplified the task of the cabin crews. With a galley at each end of the cabin, an improved meal service could be provided for both First Class and Tourist Class passengers. The Comet 4B was adapted from the long range Comet 4. From BEA's point of view, with the need to cater for high load factors on short-haul routes, two passenger doors and a larger baggage hold with loading doors would have been desirable. These requirements were brought to the attention of de Havilland and taken into consideration in the design of the Trident, then under development specifically for BEA.

BEA found that at London a Comet could be away in 50 to 55 minutes after its arrival on the departure stand. During this time the aircraft was replenished with fuel and with water for the 'domestic services', catering supplies were loaded to the two galleys, fore and aft, and the mail was put on board. Passengers' luggage arrived in two loads at the aircraft at between 20 and 30 minutes before departure, followed shortly by the passengers in three coaches, the last load of passengers arriving some 10 minutes before the aircraft moved away. At intermediate stops, the standard turnaround time was 45 minutes and this was normally accomplished without difficulty.

During the first three months the BEA Comets flew some 2,350 hours, carried 48,000 passengers and logged more than 42,000,000 passenger miles. It was not uncommon for a Comet to arrive at London Airport from Moscow at 9.30, to leave again for a return flight to Copenhagen, arriving back at London in the early afternoon in time to do a return journey to Nice and ending the day back at London Airport at about 23.00, having covered about 4,200 miles in the day.

Following the success of the Comet in service, BEA placed a further order for three aircraft in May 1960 followed, on 28th November, by another order for four more, all for delivery by September 1961. This was the fourth repeat order for Comets by BEA and increased the airline's total order from ten to fourteen.

In October 1960, the nose wheel axle of a BEA Comet fractured while the aircraft was taxiing at London Airport and the next day a similar taxiing incident occurred to another Comet at Zurich. Emergency action was taken by de Havilland and BEA. All axles were changed and a strengthening bolt was introduced and all of the airline's seven Comets were passed as serviceable within 24 hours. With the exception of Malaysian Airlines, BEA were the only operator to experience this particular problem, although Comets operating with other

Comet 4B G-ARJL at Heathrow Airport in late 1969, carrying a hybrid Olympic/BEA livery used at various times during the aircraft's lease to Olympic from BEA from February 1964, until return in February 1970.

airlines had by then accumulated some three times as many flying hours as those of BEA. On the other hand, while BEA's Comets made, on average, one landing every one and a half hours in contrast to the long-haul operators who landed about once every four and a half hours, the airline experienced a much lower incidence of brake wear and replacement than other airlines and consistently obtained more than three times as many landings per tyre than other Comet operators. On the other hand the different 'landing' procedures adopted by BEA led to the necessity for local strengthening in the flaps. On

average, the airline experienced only 8.8 technical delays of over five minutes for each 100 departures.

"Nobody has a bad word for the Comet. It is a pilot's aeroplane if ever there was one." This was a commonly held view among BEA's pilots and the handling qualities of the Comet came in for high praise. It was "beautifully controllable and has a nice amount of float" was how one pilot put it. This was borne out by the relative ease with which BEA pilots, the majority with no previous jet experience, had converted to the

This view of the ladies dressing room gives a good idea of the spacious surroundings enjoyed in 1960-70s Comet travel.

An alternative view of the Comet 4B passenger interior in the first class section.

EUROPE'S FOREMOST AIRLINE BEA

BEA Comet 4B

The Comet 4B, the big jet for Europe, brings European and Middle Eastern destinations closer than was ever dreamed possible. Powered by 4 Rolls-Royce Avon jet engines and with a cruising speed of over 500 m.p.h., the Comet 4B is a convincing reminder that BEA is Europe's Foremost Airline.

Comet. In some cases, five hours of Comet flying had been sufficient for certain pilots to qualify for passenger carrying although in fact they put in some further route proving time before the passenger services officially started.

The start of the Comet operations represented a major factor in BEA's forward planning. It had a great impact on the airline's main booking centre at Dorland House in Regent Street, London, where a new section was opened to meet the demand of the Mediterranean area bookings alone. BEA's telephone exchange received 1,500 calls per hour and more than 10,000 calls per day. A special feature of the exchange was the recently introduced queue calling system, which employed telltale indicator lights on the switchboard and enabled waiting calls to be stacked and distributed in correct sequence. BEA was soon in the market for a computer to handle the volume of business that the airline was attracting.

BEA's Comets brought the European community closer together. From London Airport, Nice was one and a half hours away, Rome two hours, Malta two hours and Moscow less than three and a half hours of flying time. Such Comet schedules were the harbinger of increased demand for travel in a community already striving for increased business and

social contact. At that time BEA carried more than two million passengers a year, a greater number than any other airline outside the US and, by 1967, it was estimated that the airline would be carrying more than seven million passengers per year. BEA's network was composed entirely of short-haul routes with a high proportion of the traffic due to holiday travel, and more than two thirds of the annual passenger total was carried during the six summer months. On a peak day in August the traffic was three times as much as on a typical winters day.

A mixed-class arrangement accommodated 89 passengers — 22 First Class and 67 Tourist Class — while an all tourist plan accommodated 102 passengers, 47 in one cabin and 55 in the other. The initial fleet of seven 89-seaters carried about one fifth of all BEA passenger traffic and for the next few years the Comet was the prime express airliner of BEA. The airline was by then the principal European operator.

The consortium between BEA and Olympic Airways greatly strengthened the Comet position throughout Europe and the Eastern Mediterranean. In the early period, the two Comet 4Bs of Olympic Airways worked with the seven BEA Comets, introducing a greatly improved service not only on the stage from London to Athens but also between several other European cities. BEA developed their own aircraft maintenance organisation and undertook Olympic Comet maintenance as well, with the de Havilland and Rolls-Royce spare parts stores at London Airport at their service.

With the introduction of the Comet, BEA instituted a system of balanced maintenance which was a method of dividing a period of maintenance work into a convenient number of equal parts, each of which required the same number of hours. Balanced maintenance was not necessarily the cheapest method from the maintenance aspect but if the number of equal divisions was correctly chosen, in relation to the size of the fleet and the airline's programme of operations, it could be the means of producing more aircraft flying hours and of producing them at periods when they were most needed. When first introduced, the system called for Check 1s at periods of 145 hours carried out at night, and eight balanced Check 2s at periods of 500 hours. Approval was soon obtained from the ARB for the number of Check 2s in a full cycle to be reduced to six at intervals of 750 hours.

For their Comets, BEA chose 145 flying hours between Check 1s, a figure which tallied with the rest of the BEA fleet compared with the de Havilland recommended figure of 125 hours. BOAC had already obtained approval to fly 175 hours between Check 1s based on their long-haul Comet operating experience, at that time of some 72,000 hours.

A Check 1 on the Comet could be completed during a night shift which meant that aircraft were never off service for minor maintenance. Similarly a balanced check was accomplished in four days and took on average just under 1,000 hours. The annual direct labour requirement for all maintenance checks was only about 10,000 hours per aircraft.

An increase of some 30% in revenue was expected on the BEA Comet routes in the first year or so of service. An 86-seater Comet 4B did the work of three Viscount 701 aircraft and the seven Comets offered as many seat-miles as 25 Viscounts. Due to fuel requirements and other limitations imposed by operating conditions on the Copenhagen–Moscow leg, a maximum of 25 passengers was carried by the Viscount but the Comet flew from London to Moscow with its full complement of 86 passengers. On the Moscow service, the 1,600 mile journey time was cut from the 6 hours and 50 minutes taken by the Viscount — with a stop at Copenhagen — to 3 hours and 30 minutes and the Comets flew from London to Vnukovo Airport, Moscow, twice per week.

The last of the fourteen Comet 4Bs was delivered on 4th August 1961, however two of BEA's Comets were later lost in crashes. The first one was on 21st December 1961 when G-ARJM crashed shortly after take-off from Esenboga Airport, Ankara. It was concluded that the aircraft had stalled due to an instrument fault which allowed the pilot to execute a climb that was too steep. The aircraft hit the ground near the

The aircraft that flew the last BEA Comet service on 31st October 1971, G-APMA 'Sir Edmund Halley', stands in reserve for use in the event of a Trident failure, at the BEA maintenance base on 13th June 1971.

On a sunny morning at Gatwick in April 1972, G-ARCP, in the colours of the charter arm of BEA, passes a line of Dan-Air Comets while taxiing to the stand carrying another load of holidaymakers returning from Spain.

airport boundary, killing the seven crew and twenty passengers, with six passengers seriously injured.

G-ARJM had been on a scheduled flight from London to Rome, Athens, Istanbul, Ankara, Nicosia and Tel Aviv. From Istanbul the flight was operated by BEA on behalf of Cyprus Airways and the operating crew, employed by BEA, consisted of a captain and two first officers. Also aboard were four cabin staff employed by Cyprus Airways along with 27 passengers.

Snow had fallen during the 46-minute stopover at Ankara and on take-off the aircraft had a light covering of snow on the upper surface of its wings, however this had no bearing on the accident. The take-off run, rotation and unstick were normal but a second or two after unstick, the aircraft rapidly assumed an excessively steep climbing angle. One witness put the angle achieved as about twice the normal, another estimated it as 45° to 50°. Witnesses also spoke of a wing drop and of variations in the engine noise during this climb. The Comet stalled, with the left wing down, at a height of about 450ft and then sank to the ground in a relatively flat attitude, being almost completely destroyed by the impact and the ensuing fire. The accident site was 1,600 metres from Esenboga's ATC tower and

occurred at 21.43 GMT. The Captain had flown a total of 13,240 hours including 785 on Comet aircraft. The aircraft was in good order and there was no record of any defect or repair during the recent operation of the aircraft which could be considered to have any bearing on the accident.

The Captain's director horizon was examined by the RAE at Farnborough when it was found that the pitch pointer 'spider' was obstructed by the upper left dial mask screw, which had unscrewed sufficiently for its head to be in the plane of movement of the 'spider'. To attain this position, the screw had to be three and a half turns from the fully tightened condition. Examination of the screw head, the washer and the surface around the screw hole in the dial mask flange showed that the screw had not been tightened down fully during the assembly of the instrument. Local disturbance of the paint of the flange suggested that the assembly was tightened to within about half a turn from the fully tightened state.

The position of the impact point in relation to the unstick point, the fact that the aircraft did not begin to assume an abnormally nose-up attitude until a second or two after unstick, and the fact that the landing gear was not selected up, together gave a strong indication that something unusual

This shot of three aircraft taken in August 1972, gives a good idea of the extensive use made of Gatwick by the BEA Airtours Comet fleet from its foundation in 1970.

occurred immediately after unstick. From unstick the aircraft assumed an increasingly steep angle which reached about 45°, about twice the normal, before it stalled. The pitch pointer in the Captain's director horizon was the only fault in the aircraft and its equipment that could account for the abnormally steep climb. It was calculated that the time interval between unstick and the stall was approximately eight to ten seconds.

The outer engines may have begun to fail due to fuel starvation after the angle became excessive. However, as this occurred very close to the stall when recovery was impossible, it was not considered a contributory cause of the accident. Only the lap straps of the crew's safety harnesses were fastened and it was thought probable that the three pilots would have survived had they used the shoulder straps also.

The second crash was caused by a bomb. On 12th October 1967, G-ARCO was reported missing off the coast of Turkey. The aircraft had crashed in deep water, killing all the occupants and leaving only a few seat cushions and other debris floating amongst the bodies. It was one of the seat cushions that provided the vital clue which proved that a bomb had been placed under one of the passenger seats, blowing a hole in the cabin and severing the controls. The obvious target was a senior Turkish military figure, General Grivas, who had switched to another flight at the last minute. Those responsible for the bombing were never caught [23].

BEA's Comet 4Bs were withdrawn from service in March 1969. Along with the Olympic Airways' Comets, they were stored in the open at Cambridge but a number were temporarily returned to service during peak periods in 1970 and 1971. The last of this group, G-APMA, was retired on 31st October 1971 and subsequently scrapped at the Engineering Base at Heathrow. Of the remainder, ten were delivered to Gatwick in January 1970 to form the core fleet of the newly formed BEA Airtours. The subsidiary had been formed to operate on the Inclusive Tour routes, thus giving BEA a share of the lucrative holiday charter market and in so doing, the Comets were given a new lease of life.

The first BEA Airtours charter was from Gatwick to Palma on 6th March 1970, after which the aircraft served with distinction, building on the rapid success of the company to a point at which an urgent replacement was required. In 1973, BEA decided to replace the Comets with ex-BOAC Boeing 707s and the Comets were gradualy acquired by Dan-Air. The last BEA Airtours Comet service was flown by G-ARJL on 31st October 1973. As the Comet fleet was retired, the aircraft were ferried to Lasham for storage and repainting for service with their new owner, with the exception of one aircraft which was taken out of storage at Cambridge and sold to Channel Airways.

IN SERVICE WITH EAST AFRICAN AIRWAYS

East African Airways came into being in 1945 and the first scheduled service took place on 1st January 1946. From its inception, the airline had to rebuild the civil air communications of the East African Territories of Kenya, Uganda and Tanzania which had lapsed during the war years. At the outset EAA had six DH 89A Dominies to cover a territory some 680,000 square miles in extent, stretching from the Rhodesias in the South to the Sudan in the North, the Belgian Congo in the West and to the Indian Ocean in the East.

For many years EAA watched the steady growth of air traffic between East Africa and the rest of the world, while their role as a purely internal airline became more and more

difficult to carry out without incurring heavy losses. The airline therefore decided to enter the international field, with the twofold object of earning revenue to assist in the operation of the internal services and keeping a proportion of the money spent on air fares within the East African Territories.

The first of EAA's international services to Europe, Pakistan and India were operated by Canadair C4s, acquired from BOAC. The first service was on 14th April 1957 then, in 1958, a Britannia 312 was chartered to cope with the rising traffic. It soon became evident that the airline's Canadairs would not be competitive with the Britannias and Boeing 707s scheduled for introduction on routes to Africa in 1959 and

Originally registered as VP-KPK on delivery to East African Airways in September 1960, 5H-AAF on re-registration in March 1964 became the only Comet to appear on the Tanzanian register. Here the aircraft stands ready for service at Heathrow in April 1964.

Passengers pose for the camera before the inaugural EAA Comet service at Heathrow on Saturday 17th September 1960.

1960, and EAA therefore made plans to replace the Canadair fleet with an aircraft which would be suitable to operate high frequency, high density routes at a speed attractive to the public and which would give a good utilisation. Although a study was undertaken of the existing jet aircraft, the choice of the Comet 4 was almost inevitable. It alone combined the necessary range capabilities with a carrying capacity matching the market potential. Even more important perhaps was the fact that the Comet's airfield performance made it particularly suitable for the difficult altitude and high temperature conditions to be found at many of the airports served by EAA.

The order for two Comet 4s was placed in August 1958 with the aircraft due for delivery in June and July 1960. EAA

A view of the EAA symbol on the tail of the second Comet 4 delivered to the airline.

planned to use the Comet 4s on routes from South and Central Africa to East Africa and onwards to the United Kingdom, as well as to Karachi and Bombay. The difference in flying times on these routes would be vast and by the early 1960s EAA was operating to 35 airfields in East Africa. Within Africa the airline operated to Lumbo, Beira and Lourenço Marques in Portuguese East Africa, to Blantyre, Ndola and Salisbury in the Central African Federation and to Durban and Johannesburg in the Union of South Africa. Further afield the airline operated to Khartoum, Benghazi and Rome on the route to London and to Aden, Karachi and Bombay to the East.

Following the orders, preparations were undertaken for the Comet 4 airframe maintenance to be carried out in the EAA maintenance hangar and workshops at Nairobi's Embakasi Airport. Engine overhauls and engine changes were to be undertaken on EAA's behalf by BOAC at London Airport and an agreement was reached whereby EAA purchased engine hours for the Comets from BOAC. In the event, engines were changed as and when necessary by BOAC during the fourteen hour layover which occurred at London Airport each Friday.

EAA were fortunate in that the timely move to the new Nairobi Airport at Embakasi provided an opportunity for the erection of a compact and modern engineering base, with the equipment carefully selected so that as far as possible it had a universal use, resulting in good utilisation. Before this the airline's activities had been split between Nairobi West airfield for internal services, and Eastleigh Airport for the international routes. The engineering workshops, stores and administration headquarters were located on a convenient site at Embakasi and it was there that the maintenance work was carried out on the airline's Comets, Canadair C4s and nine Dakotas. The skilled working staff consisted of 130 Europeans, 200 Africans and about 200 Asians. According to some observers, one of the main reasons for EAA's fine maintenance record lay in the fact that there was a notable absence of dogmatic trade segregation and no one minded helping out, within his capabilities, on another part of the job.

EAA also established a programme to train its flight crews for the Comets. The first flight crews arrived in England in January 1960 and underwent courses at de Havilland, Rolls-Royce and with BOAC, where they received instruction on the Smith's Automatic Flight system and the Comet simulator. During the training, the EAA crews flew as supernumeraries with BOAC on the Comet routes to Africa which enabled them to gain invaluable practical experience of both the aircraft and the routes over which they were to operate.

One of the two Comet 4s landed at Nairobi Airport on a technical flight in preparation for the inaugural service, prior to the delivery of the first two aircraft, registered VP-KPJ and VP-KPK, which took place on 25th July and 12th

On 14th July 1960, the first East African Airway's Comet 4 to fly was VP-KPJ.

August 1960, a little behind schedule. The acquisition of these two Comets had the effect of trebling the airline's fixed assets at a stroke and with the delivery of the first aircraft, a short but intensive flight training programme with BOAC instructors was undertaken. To avoid the traffic congestion of London Airport and over the South of England, the aircraft were based at Shannon. The flying training programme was concluded with two proving flights from London to Nairobi during August and when the aircraft arrived in Nairobi, another training programme was started by EAA at Embakasi to bring the total strength up to ten crews.

EAA, operating in conjunction with BOAC, opened their southbound service on Saturday, 17th September 1960 when VP-KPJ took off from London Airport at 18.40, bound for Rome, Khartoum, Entebbe and Nairobi. It reached Nairobi at 11.00 the following morning with an elapsed time — including three halts of forty-five minutes — of twelve hours. The northbound service was inaugurated in the early hours of 19th September when the same aircraft set out on its return journey on the same route. From then on the service was thrice weekly, with one service omitting Entebbe and extending to Dar-es-Salaam.

From the start, all three East African capitals were served by the Comet then, in October, one of the three services was extended to Johannesburg. On 2nd January 1961, a Comet service across the Indian Ocean was inaugurated and the route from Nairobi to Karachi and Bombay was flown twice per week in both directions, once with a Comet and once with a Canadair.

The Comet covered the 3,271 statute miles to Karachi and Bombay in an elapsed time of nine hours against the seventeen-and a half hours of the Canadair, which made an additional traffic stop at Aden. The following month EAA placed an order for another Comet 4, for delivery in the spring of 1962.

On the routes between East Africa and London the traffic was to some extent seasonal, with a northbound trend in the english Spring and Summer as expatriates went home for leave, and a southbound trend during the early Winter. In later years these peaks showed a tendency to level off, but another 'seasonal' rush occurred at the time of the english school holidays and there were occasions when the flights to and from London were almost wholly occupied with schoolchildren. Such flights, known as 'lollipop specials', were a challenge for the cabin crews who sometimes had to cope with experienced teenage travellers who demanded champagne.

A turnaround time of 45 minutes was easily achieved in practice in spite of having only one passenger loading door and some inevitable congestion near the forward services door when catering supplies were being taken aboard. The luggage loading hatches came in for some criticism, a detail which de Havilland were to correct in the Trident.

EAA's results with the Comet were encouraging. From the time the services started in 1960 up to the end of May 1961, the Comets flew 2,929 hours and carried 17,500 passengers, representing some 5,641 million seat-miles at an average passenger load factor of 67.5%. In the ten

In-flight over Africa, 5H-AAF displays the colourful revised East African livery adopted to coincide with the delivery of the Vickers Super VC10s into the fleet.

months to the 31st May 1961, the two Comets earned £1,675,000. During the same period, the passenger load factor on the Nairobi to London services averaged 70% with peaks exceeding 80%. Matters were somewhat helped by the need to evacuate around 1,500 people from Bukabo and Stanleyville, in the Congo.

With a full complement of passengers, a payload of 1,150kg was generally available for mail and freight, of which some 800 to 850kg was freight. Among the many urgent consignments carried in the Comet were tea and coffee samples, vaccines and serums, and football pools coupons which were dispatched by agents in bulk packages. There was also considerable traffic in fruit and vegetables including mangoes, capsicums, avocado pears and strawberries. Vegetables such as peas and French beans were also carried, the latter fetching as much as seven shillings a pound in Covent Garden market at the beginning of the season. Other items of freight included raw cured crocodile skins and teaplant seeds to India, each one the size of a marble which had to be planted within three days of being picked. Southwards there was a consignment of milk from Nairobi to Dar-es-Salaam five days of the week.

EAA pilots liked the Comet and they particularly appreciated the aircraft's reserve of power which made light work of the high-altitude airports and the high ambient temperatures with which they had to contend. At Nairobi Airport the runway was 10,000ft long, situated at 5,327ft above sea level with temperatures ranging up to 80°F. The Comet 4 was able to take-off at all times without restrictions of range or payload. Of all the airfields used by EAA's Comets, only at Benghazi was there a potential restriction. Yet even there, the 6,600ft runway met EAA's maximum load requirements in zero wind conditions at temperatures of up to 93°F. The longest non-stop stage was from Nairobi to Karachi, a distance of 2,726 statute miles and even on this sector the residue of fuel was of the order of 8,000kg, enough for a good two hours flying.

On one occasion, when Benghazi was unexpectedly closed, the northbound Comet from Entebbe over-flew to Rome where it arrived with more than an hour of fuel in reserve. The pilots of EAA constantly strived to get the best out of their aircraft and many of them evolved their own operating technique, thereby achieving results which showed a considerable improvement in speed, range and fuel economy as compared with 'the book'. Over the years, expatriate pilots in EAA acquired the sobriquet 'Bush Pilots', a tag that may have emanated from the manner in which many had first learnt to fly, using private aircraft on private airstrips before graduating to formal pilot license training [24]. It was perhaps in this spirit that one aspect of the Comet's handling was regularly demonstrated to new flight crew; while cruising at quite a high airspeed, the high pressure fuel cock was turned off, causing a small change in heading, and once it was opened again the engine spooled up without hitch [25].

The Comet routes however presented some navigational problems. On the routes between Nairobi and Karachi and between Entebbe and Benghazi, navigation aids were few and far between and on both of these routes, the aircraft were navigated solely by celestial means for periods of up to three hours or more. Communications also left something to be desired. Over much of the Sudanese and Libyan deserts, only HF/RT was available and this was often badly affected by static. The Comets were not equipped with either Doppler or Dectra and while such systems would have been effective they would have required the presence of a navigator to operate them. The advantage gained would have been small and the expense and weight penalty hard to justify.

EAA's fleet was based at Embakasi Airport, some ten miles from Nairobi which, from a pilot's point of view was one of the finest to be found anywhere in the world. Situated on a plateau, the surrounding country was absolutely flat with virtually no obstructions higher than a tree and very few of them for miles around. The highest object anywhere nearby was the radar aerial on the airport water tower which was a surveillance radar. The airport also had an ILS and while the 10,000ft long runway was quite adequate, plans were in hand for an extension to 13,500ft.

EAA's initial Comet network covered some 12,500 statute miles and involved about 90 hours flying each week. While it was unusual for an airline to undertake such an operation with only two aircraft, EAA made it a success which was, in a very large measure, due to the excellent maintenance which the aircraft received from the engineering staff. The airline decided that the most practical method was to fly one aircraft continuously for fourteen days whilst the other underwent maintenance and was held in reserve. During this period the aircraft in the hangar also provided a full kit of spares, a factor which greatly eased maintenance during the introductory period.

By this method, one aircraft flew all the Comet schedule services for two weeks with only transit maintenance averaging between twelve and thirteen hours flying per day. It was as ambitious a schedule as any yet attempted with a Comet or any other type of aircraft. Only once was there a cancellation and on only four other occasions was the reserve aircraft substituted, and in each of these four cases the delay caused was not serious.

By the end of 1960 the airline had decided to order a third Comet 4 for delivery in 1962. In July 1961, the Comets joined EAA's Canadairs in assisting the Britannias, Beverleys and Hastings of the RAF Transport Command in an airlift of troops to Aden and Bahrain as a result of the Kuwait crisis. The third Comet, VP-KRL, was delivered on 10th April 1962 and following its delivery, the airline sold its two surviving Canadairs. The Comets operated seven flights a week to

Seen at Nairobi Kenya, on 14th December 1971. East African leased G-APDD from Dan-Air as 5Y-AMT from 28th December 1970 until 22nd February 1971, due to the lack of capacity caused by the retirement of two Comets due to corrosion.

Taken in early 1968, a view over the wing on take-off of the last Comet service from Entebbe, Uganda.

London via Rome, two flights a week to Karachi and Bombay and two flights a week to Johannesburg.

In December 1963, both Kenya and Zanzibar became independent and the national flags of Kenya, Tanganyika, Uganda and Zanzibar were then emblazoned on the fins of EAA's aircraft. Following the revolution in Zanzibar in January 1964, Zanzibar joined Tanganyika in the newly formed nation of Tanzania and thus only three flags were shown on the aircrafts' fins. During the colonial era, all of EAA's aircraft had been registered in Kenya with the prefix VP-K but, in January 1965, a committee was appointed to review the constitutional position of the airline following the independence of the three constituent nations. It was decided that ownership of the aircraft should be divided as equally as possible between the three nations. VP-KPJ was re-registered in Uganda as 5X-AAO, VP-KPK was re-registered in Tanzania as 5H-AAF and VP-KRL was re-registered in Kenya as 5Y-AAA. In October 1965, EAA unveiled a new livery for its fleet which featured the main colours of the three countries' flags: red, yellow, green, blue, white and black. The national flags were reproduced on the tail arranged in a triangle — with the flag of the nation of registration at the apex — within a twelve-pointed yellow star. At the same time, the word Airlines was dropped from the title on the fuselage. In the same month EAA leased a Comet 4 from BOAC, G-APDL, which went into service in October 1965, using the registration 5Y-ADD until its return to BOAC in March 1967.

Early in 1965 a committee was set up to look into the options available to the airline for a Comet replacement. An initial list of nine possible types was reduced to three, namely the DC8, the Boeing 707-320 and the Super VC10. The latter was chosen and, by the end of 1966, the airline's two newly acquired VC10s had taken over from the Comets

on the route to London. In the same year, the Comets achieved a utilisation of eleven hours per day.

In November 1968, the Comets were taken off the route to India and Pakistan but continued to be used on the medium-haul routes within Africa and on an inter-city service linking the capitals of Nairobi, Dar-es-Salaam and Kampala. Long haul flights at the time were usually charter operations to London via Entebbe and Benina airport, Bhengazi, with an elapsed time of around 10 hours and 45 minutes. In order to extend their service life, all three Comets had to be returned to de Havilland for modification and one was returned in November 1967 and the other two followed in 1968. In 1960 EAA had set up a subsidiary, named Seychelles-Kilimanjaro Air Transport and in 1968, EAA's Comets were transferred to SKAT and the subsidiary started to operate long-haul charter flights. On the regional routes the Comets were replaced by Fokker F27 Friendships.

On one epic occasion in June 1969, 5Y-AAA abandoned its take-off at the start of a flight to London with a faulty airspeed indicator. After a replacement was fitted, the Comet took off for Benina and on approach to land there a high oil temperature was indicated on the No. 2 engine. No fault could be found during the stop-over and the flight left for London two hours behind schedule. On approach to Heathrow an overheat warning was indicated and the No. 1 engine had to be shut down then, a short time later, a leading edge bay fire was indicated. Both of the latter faults were traced to faulty sensors in the system [26].

5X-AAO and 5H-AAF were withdrawn from service in November 1969 due to corrosion and both were sold to Dan-Air for use as spares. 5X-AAO was delivered to Dan-Air on 16th November 1970 followed by 5H-AAF in January 1971. 5Y-AAA was also sold to Dan-Air and was delivered on 8th February 1971.

Following the cancellation of an arrangement to lease a DC9, EAA leased a Comet 4, G-APDK, from Dan-Air to operate alongside 5Y-AAA. The aircraft was operated by EAA with the registration 5Y-ALD from 9th January 1970 until 23rd March, when it was returned to its owner. Due to the brevity of the lease it retained most of its Dan-Air livery, and it was returned once a more permanent arrangement could be made which involved the leasing of Dan-Air's Comet 4, G-APDE, which was operated by EAA with the registration 5Y-ALF. This later aircraft was delivered to EAA on 22nd February 1970 and then returned to Dan-Air in the December however, because of a further delay with the planned introduction of the DC9, EAA leased another Comet 4 from Dan-Air, G-APDD, which was reregistered 5Y-AMT during its service with EAA and was delivered on 28th December 1970 and returned on 22nd February 1971.

IN SERVICE WITH OLYMPIC AIRWAYS

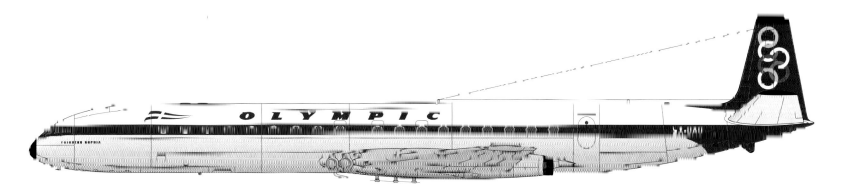

Olympic Airways, the official Greek airline, was formed in April 1956 when Aristotle Onassis assumed the ownership of the existing national Greek airline, TAE. Onassis pursued a policy of reorganisation and modernisation and took the decision to introduce jet travel on the airline's international network. On 20th July 1959, Olympic Airways announced its intention to adopt the Comet 4B for its main operations and on the same occasion, Onassis for Olympic Airways, and Lord Douglas of Kirtleside for BEA, stated that a consortium agreement had been signed between the airlines, providing for joint operational and commercial exploitation of routes between Britain and Greece and the Eastern Mediterranean and the Middle East.

BEA's first Comet 4B, G-APMA, flew to Athens on 11th July and two passenger flights around southern Greece were made during the day, with Mr Garofalides, President of Olympic Airways, and Mr C Konialidis, the Managing Director, both on board. The flights were of technical interest because the runway in use, 'Zero Three', was only 5,705ft long compared to London's longest runway which was 9,500ft. The Athens airfield was also obstructed by hills up to about 3,000ft within three to four miles, with one hillock of 75ft in line with the runway and within 1,500ft of its end. Pilots knew that the minimum approach height was no less than 7,000ft. but this posed no problems for the Comet. Using the reverse thrust fitted to two of its engines, the Comet made all its Athens landings without even applying wheel-brakes.

One of the Comet's take-offs from Athens was a spectacular demonstration of the aircraft's capabilities. With many technical people from Olympic Airways aboard, one engine was cut back at 95 knots during the take-off run. Nobody on board appeared to notice and the other three

Olympic Airways' Comet 4B, G-APZM, taxies to the runway at Paris Orly Airport on 25th July 1965, on route to Athens.

Taken during the first flight on 7th April 1960 before delivery to Olympic Airways,
G-APYC displays the short 4B wingspan, devoid of pinion tanks.

engines were throttled back from take-off power to normal climb power, in the usual way, just after leaving the ground.

In preparation for the opening of the Comet services, some 50 engineers of Olympic Airways attended technical courses at Hatfield and with BEA. The courses started in November 1959 and covered the maintenance of Comet airframes, engines, instruments and electrical apparatus. Flight crews also underwent short ground familiarisation courses at Hatfield as part of their training. As Olympic Airways operated with Flight Engineers, they had to have a de Havilland employee overseeing their training, and BEA were able to satisfy this legal requirement by having a supervisory First Officer on board [27].

The first Comet 4B, SX-DAK, named Queen Frederica, arrived in Athens on 30th April 1960 after flying from London in the record time of 3 hours 14 minutes. Prior to its delivery the aircraft was registered G-APYC. The second aircraft, SX-DAL, named Queen Olga, was delivered on 14th May and prior to its delivery, was registered G-APYD. The first service was flown on 18th May and Olympic Airways adopted a mixed layout for the passenger accommodation, with twenty-two First Class seats and sixty-four Economy Class seats.

Although the Comets did not go into operation until May 1960, they contributed considerably to the airline's increased annual traffic. During 1960 the airline carried 16.2% more passengers, 260.5% more cargo and baggage and 35% more

mail than in the previous year. The third and fourth Comets to fly with Olympic Airways had British registrations as they were owned by BEA. G-APZM, named Queen Sophia, was delivered on 14th July 1960 and G-ARDI, named Princess Sophia, was delivered on 25th March 1961. With the introduction of the fourth Comet, Olympic Airlines were able to operate a Summer Schedule which included 48 flights per week between London and Athens with the average daily flying time during the summer of 1960 being six and a half hours per Comet.

Four of Olympic Airways' Comet 4Bs, along with one BEA aircraft, were purchased by Channel Airways from storage at Cambridge, for use in the Inclusive Tour Market.

SX-DAK is serviced on the apron at Paris Orly, previous to the return flight to Athens.

IN SERVICE WITH MISRAIR — UNITED ARAB AIRLINES

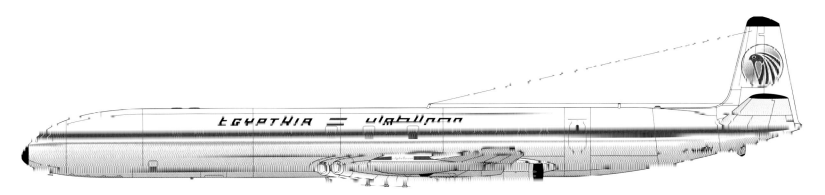

The Comet became pre-eminent on routes throughout the Middle East. As well as BOAC, BEA and Olympic Airways who operated Comet services to the region, the aircraft was also bought by Misrair, Middle East Airlines and Kuwait Airways. Misr Air was founded by the Egyptian bank Misr and the airline soon became known as Misrair. A close association between Misrair and de Havilland was formed in 1932 when, in conjunction with Airwork Ltd of London, a flying school was set up at Almaza Aerodrome, near Cairo, with Gipsy Moths and the company soon established a leading position in the Middle East.

In 1949 the airline became completely Egyptian-owned and changed its name to Misrair-SAE. An all-out effort was made by both the Americans and the Russians to sell jet aircraft to the airline which required an aircraft that would be capable of showing profits not only on main trunk routes such as the European services, but also on the branch lines where the average number of passengers could be smaller. The Comet 4C was chosen for its great flexibility and avoided the airline having to operate a variety of aircraft types. The airline's network comprised both express services between western Europe and Cairo and shorter stages linking Cairo with Khartoum, Jeddah and Beirut. The Comet 4C could fly the London to Cairo stage of 2,200 statute miles non-stop in under five hours and could carry its capacity payload of 19,630lb for a stage length of 2,820 miles, with the usual diversion fuel reserves.

The first Comet 4C for Misrair, SU-ALC, under construction at Chester in February 1960.

Misrair Comet SU-ALC, formates with the company Dove during its first flight on 21st May 1960.

SU-ANI arrives at Tokyo in April 1968. This aircraft was destroyed in a crash at Addis Ababa, Ethiopia on 14th January 1970.

Comet 4C SU-ALL taxies away from the stand at Fiumicino Airport, Rome, in March 1967.

On 30th December 1959 following more than two years of study and investigation, Misrair SAE signed a contract for the purchase of three Comet 4Cs. It was the second order for the Comet 4C and, with equipment and spare parts, the sum involved was about £4 million. The aircraft were due to be delivered in the Summer of 1960 and the purchase represented one of the most important events following the re-opening of diplomatic relations between Britain and the United Arab Republic in the wake of the Suez crisis. It was stated at the time that the difficult political atmosphere had not influenced what were described as 'amicable discussions' between the airline and de Havilland. The delay in satisfactorily concluding the contract was attributed to monetary exchange difficulties between the two countries.

The first Misrair Comet 4C, SU-ALC, made its first flight from Chester to Hatfield on 21st May 1960 and was handed over to Misrair on 9th June, within 23 weeks of the order being placed. The following day it was flown to Cairo, piloted by Captain Helmi Shams, Misrair's Chief Pilot and Operations Manager taking 4 hours and 17 minutes. The second aircraft, SU-ALD, was built at Chester and flew for the first time on 15th June and was delivered to Misrair on 29th June. Training and other preparations were undertaken and the Comets were put into service on 16th July 1960.

Five return services were operated each week between Cairo and London and, for traffic reasons, each flight called at Rome and one other city, either Geneva, Zurich or Frankfurt. By the end of the month two services were operated each week from Cairo to Jeddah and Khartoum. At the same time, Misrair and Syrian Airways merged to become United Arab Airlines and the airline experienced an immediate increase in traffic following the introduction of the Comets as the aircraft proved extremely popular from the start, and traffic was heaviest between Cairo and Rome and Cairo and Jeddah. During the first five and a half months of operation, no Comet service was missed on any of the routes, however one service westbound from Rome was cancelled due to exceptionally bad weather. The utilisation rate was just over seven hours per day per aircraft which was quite an achievement given that the airline only had two Comets, one of which was almost always on standby. Between them, the two Comets logged about 90 hours per week on scheduled flights and 10 hours per week on charters and training. The introduction had gone smoothly in every respect.

In September 1960, President Nasser used one of the national airline's Comets for a visit to the United Nations' Headquarters in New York. Altogether three return flights were made on that occasion and, on one of the outward

Above: John Cunningham at the handover
of the first Misrair Comet.

Below: President Nasser of Egypt, on arrival at Idlewild
Airport, New York in September 1960, to attend
the United Nations General Assembly.

journeys, against strong prevailing westerly winds, the aircraft was airborne for eight and a half hours from Shannon to New York. On the final return journey the aircraft flew from New York to Cairo, a distance of some 6,000 miles, with one stop at the Azores. President Nasser also paid a state visit to Sudan in the November, again flying on one of the airline's Comets.

At London, Frankfurt, Zurich, Geneva and Rome, BOAC were on hand to provide spares and technical assistance when required by UAA, but the airline relied entirely on its own flight engineers for normal maintenance and turnaround checks. Not having previously employed flight engineers, Mr Shehabeldin, Chief Engineer of UAA, decided to train ground engineers for these duties. These men took the de Havilland course at Hatfield and then had simulator training with BOAC and by 30th November 1960, ten ground engineers had qualified. The Cairo shops of UAA had been well experienced on the Viscount, and on the Comet, Check 1s were carried out after 125 flying hours which initially took three days. A Check 2 was carried out every 250 hours taking seven days but times were soon reduced to one and a half and four days respectively.

Routine engine changes were undertaken by BOAC at London Airport, usually taking place on a Wednesday during an overnight halt in London. Spare parts were all held at Cairo, along with one spare Avon which was for emergency use only. A spares pooling agreement was made between BOAC, BEA, Olympic Airways, Middle East Airlines and UAA, whereby the spares of each company, at allotted stations, were available to all. UAA were allotted Cairo, Frankfurt, Khartoum and Jeddah. BOAC had London and Rome, BEA had Zurich, and MEA had both Geneva and Beirut. Field Aircraft Services repaired the UAA's Comets, American radio equipment and held their radio spares.

Captain Shams decided to train sixteen Captains first, so that they would have experience of the right hand seat as well as the left hand seat, and it proved to be a successful system. De Havilland pilots, headed by John Cunningham and Peter Bruggé, participated in the early base and route training and from November 1960, the second phase of training fifteen Co-Pilots commenced.

The third aircraft flew to Cairo from Hatfield on 23rd December, covering the 1,918 statute miles in 4 hours 15 minutes. This aircraft, SU-ALE, operated the regular Cairo-London service the next day and averaged fourteen and a half hours daily in its first week. With the introduction of the third Comet in service, the network expanded to include services linking Cairo with Benghazi, Tripoli, Kano, Lagos and Accra.

The scene at Munich on 9th February 1970, where Comet 4C SU-ALE lies on its belly
after crashing on take-off. The aircraft was subsequently written-off and scrapped.

On 15th January 1961, an order for two more Comets was announced and the fourth Comet 4C, SU-ALL, was delivered on 12th June followed by the fifth aircraft, SU-ALM, on 15th July.

The Cairo to London service increased from five to seven round trips per week in June and a service from Cairo to Moscow began in July. The airline witnessed a fall-off in traffic each October followed by a rise starting in November for the North European winter tourist season when Egypt, with its archeological wonders and holiday resorts, became a popular destination.

A further two aircraft, SU-AMV and SU-AMW, were ordered and were delivered on 6th and 16th April respectively. The last aircraft was lost, however, on 19th July 1962 when it crashed in thick jungle in Thailand being replaced by SU-ANC, which was delivered to Cairo on 22nd December 1962.

SU-ALD was lost in the sea en route from Bangkok to Bombay on 28th July 1963 and replaced by SU-ANI, the last civil Comet built, which was delivered to Cairo on 26th February 1964. SU-ALE abandoned a take-off at Munich on 9th February 1970 and overshot the runway. Although there were no fatalities, the aircraft was damaged beyond economic repair.

A view of the comfortable First Class cabin
in the United Arab Airlines Comet 4C.

On the change of name from United Arab Airlines to Egyptair, a number of Comets carried this hybrid livery for a short period.

This rare shot of SU-ALL in the attractive full livery of Egyptair, was taken at Cairo in 1974 when in use as a reserve.
In October 1976 the aircraft was bought by Dan-Air for spares recovery and then scrapped.

IN SERVICE WITH MIDDLE EAST AIRLINES

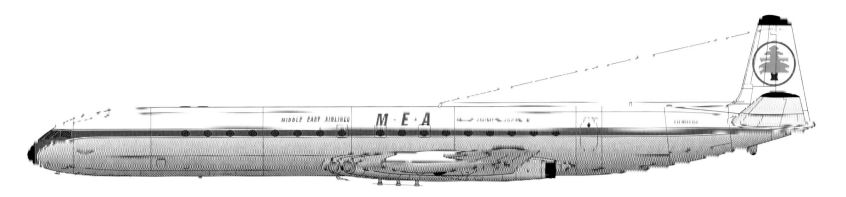

Middle East Airlines started a local network in November 1945 with three de Havilland Dragon Rapides and later acquired a number of DC3s. A partnership with Pan American Airways was entered into in 1949 and later in March 1955, MEA became an associate of BOAC. While the link with Pan Am was retained, 51% of the airline's shares were held by Lebanese interests and 49% by BOAC. A fleet of Viscounts was bought in 1955 and three Avro York freighters were put into service in June 1957.

The rapid economic and industrial development in the Middle East area since the war, coupled with the almost complete absence of satisfactory surface transport, afforded reason enough for the growth of air traffic at a rate considerably greater than the world average, and in January 1960 MEA placed an order worth £5.5 million for four Comet 4Cs which they planned to have in operation by April 1961.

The decision to order Comet 4Cs was taken after an extensive technical evaluation of every available jet and propeller-turbine aircraft. The airline's technical team concluded that a medium sized jet was the most suitable aircraft for the future. MEA spent two years examining their options and de Havilland won the order against intense competition from a number of other manufacturers. The airline placed emphasis on the need for frequency in the region, where urgent business travel was in demand, and on low passenger fares for the tourist traffic which was on the increase. The Comet 4C was ordered as it was versatile and able to work profitably in the varied conditions demanded by MEA's route patterns, and it could carry full loads safely in and out of existing airports of moderate runway length.

MEA leased G-APDM from BOAC as OD-AEV, in full Middle East Airlines/Air Liban colours, for a three month period in 1967. Here we see the aircraft at Heathrow on the 26th June 1967 after the completion of the lease.

The only Comet to survive the Israeli attack on Beirut in December 1968 in which three sister ships were destroyed, OD-ADT served into the early 1970s, until the aircraft was sold to Dan-Air for spares and broken up at Lasham airfield.

In November 1960, MEA chartered a BOAC Comet 4 for five months. G-APDG provided MEA with handling and traffic information, so the introduction of its new aircraft into service would go smoothly. The aircraft operated two return services to London each week, one via Rome, Beirut, Doha and Bahrain and the other via Geneva, Beirut and Bahrain. MEA captains and first officers flew as observers and two MEA stewardesses shared passenger duties with three BOAC cabin crew. The passenger appeal of the Comet was immediately realised.

By November 1960, two MEA pilot training courses had been completed in England. They included coverage of what were referred to as the Hatfield and Derby syllabuses and instruction on the BOAC simulator. About 40 MEA ground engineers completed their courses at the same time as did half of the flight engineers. Rolls-Royce and de Havilland engineers were stationed at the MEA Engineering Department in Beirut, where they found excellent facilities and organisation in two fine hangars which had been completed in 1959.

The first Comet for MEA, OD-ADK, made its first flight on 3rd December 1960 and was handed over at Hatfield on 15th December to Sheikh Najib Alamuddin, about four months ahead of schedule. The aircraft was delivered to Beirut on 19th December and re-registered OD-ADR. As soon as the first Comet arrived in Beirut, a programme of pilot conversion started, with base training by de Havilland pilots headed by John Cunningham and Peter Bruggé. The first few crews were trained and then the aircraft was put on service four days per week, continuing base training on the other three days. MEA

MEA leased aircraft from BOAC when short of capacity. On this occasion G-APDK is prepared for flight in March 1960.

had originally planned to introduce the Comets with the 1961 Summer schedules on 1st April, however, with careful planning and early training, the airline was able to start operating the first aircraft on 5th January in preparation for large scale Comet operation by April.

The second Comet, OD-ADQ, was delivered on 15th February, followed by the third and fourth OD-ADS and OD-ADT, on 14th and 18th March respectively. MEA's Comet 4Cs were known as Cedar Jets and operated services to London, Geneva, Rome, Beirut, Frankfurt, Vienna, Istanbul, Dhahran, Bahrain, Karachi, Bombay, Jeddah, Aden, Doha, Baghdad, Teheran and Cairo. In addition to scheduled services during 1961 the Comets were engaged in carrying 1,500 United Nations' troops in each direction between Beirut and Scandinavia, on a charter basis, in connection with troop rotation. The standard accommodation layout on the aircraft was for twenty First Class and fifty-nine Tourist passengers and it was the first time that MEA provided both First Class and Tourist Class seating, although a high density, 98-seat layout was often used for charter work.

From the Comet's introduction into full operation in May until the end of September, the airline's passenger traffic increased by 45% over that for the same period in the previous year and on the London to Bombay route, MEA's traffic rose 250%. New offices were opened in Glasgow, Manchester and Birmingham and sales staff were tripled in a reorganisation of the airline's London branch. For the Comet crews, the airline selected pilots who had a minimum of 2,000 hours in command of Viscounts and the average command experience was 8,000 hours. In association with de Havilland,

MEA produced a method of flight planning which cut flight plan preparation down to five minutes and the load sheets were designed to make loading and trim adjustments as straightforward as possible. While it was rare for the Comet to suffer any payload penalty, many of the stages flown were short enough to require the take-off weight to be limited in order to keep within the weight limits for landing at the destination. The most difficult runway for the Comet on MEA's network was at Doha in Qatar where the runway was only 6,000ft long, temperatures were high and there were no approach lights. However, operations could be safely undertaken provided very strict operating procedures were adhered to. The Comets were unable to fly to Kuwait until the city's new airport was opened in late 1961.

The fifth Comet on which MEA had an option, G-AROV, made its first flight from Chester on 21st August 1961. Although the aircraft flew in MEA colours and took part in the SBAC Show at Farnborough in the September, it was not purchased by MEA and was delivered to Aerolineas Argentinas on 27th April 1962.

MEA's first three Comets, OD-ADK, OD-ADQ and OD-ADS, were destroyed at Beirut Airport on 28th December 1968 when Israeli Forces made an attack on the airfield. The action was carried out in retaliation for an attack made by two Palestinians on an El Al airliner at Athens on 26th December. This left MEA with only OD-ADT, so they leased two Comet 4Cs and one Comet 4 from Kuwait Airways — 9K-ACA, 9K-ACE and 9K-ACI — in order to continue operating an international service.

Out of service because of thick fog at London Airport on 21st September 1965, Comet 4C OD-ADT enjoys a rare quiet moment.

Alternative views of Sudan Airways' Comet 4C ST-AAW.
Top: A superb study taken during the maiden flight of the aircraft from Hatfield on 5th November 1962.
Bottom: On a sunny day at London's Heathrow Airport on 23rd September 1965, the aircraft awaits departure.

IN SERVICE WITH SUDAN AIRWAYS

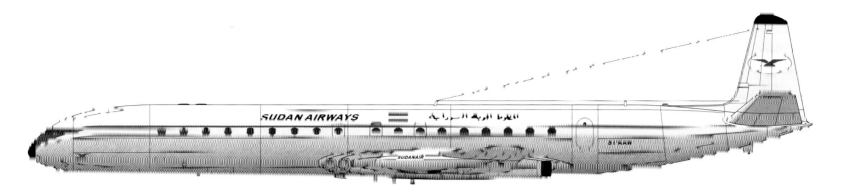

Sudan Airways was founded in 1947 and was established as a government-owned subsidiary of the Sudan Railway System. In 1954 the airline started international services and bought two Comet 4Cs which were originally allocated to Mexicana. The first one was completed as ST-AAW and made its first flight on 5th November 1962 from Hatfield. Shortly after this, it was registered G-ASDZ enabling de Havilland pilots to fly it to Sudan on 14th November for the Independence celebrations at Khartoum two days later. The aircraft returned to Hatfield via Rome on 18th November for crew training and was finally delivered to Sudan Airways on 8th December. The second aircraft, ST-AAX, which was the last Comet built at Hatfield, first flew on 8th December and was delivered to Khartoum on the 21st.

Crew training for Sudan Airways' continued with the delivery of ST-AAW to Khartoum. Apart from base training in Sudan, en route training for the Flight Engineers was carried out on the four flights each week to London which began in December 1962. The departures to London were always at around 22.00 hrs local time, and the flights often carried a vast assortment of freight, including livestock, which was

Wearing the revised livery of Sudan Airways, ST-AAW approaches Heathrow Airport on 30th October 1971.

The last Comet built at Hatfield, ST-AAX, taxies out to begin the journey home to Khartoum from London in January 1972.

stowed away in the freight bay. This bay was part of the temperature controlled area within the fuselage, separated by its own grilled door and rear passenger cabin curtains. On one crew training flight, Hatfield-based Flight Engineer M V Parker left the flight deck to investigate a furore, only to be engulfed by a snowstorm of feathers and multi-coloured missiles. Thirty wild finches had escaped from their cage and were flying around the cabin, causing mayhem and panic. Parker reasoned that if they could contain the panic amongst the passengers while the lights were turned off, the finches would settle down and it would be easier to catch them. A stewardess explained what was about to happen and when the lights were put out the birds did indeed settle down and with the aid of a torch all the escapees were returned to their cage. [28]

The return flight from London was via Rome, Athens and Cairo, where passengers and fuel were taken on board. The Comet was usually on the approach to Cairo at around midnight, twelve hours after its departure from London. On one flight the aircraft was committed to a landing when it became clear to the two pilots that they were on approach to a main road, well to the right and at about 2° divergence from the runway centre line. The aircraft overshot and made a second, more accurate approach, much to the relief of the flight deck crew but not without a rebuke from Cairo ATC, who threatened to withdraw landing rights. [29]

On another flight, the Senior Stewardess came to the flight deck as the Comet taxied out prior to take-off for Beirut early one morning. "One of the pod tanks, he is peeing" she reported and Flight Engineer M V Parker walked down the cabin and looked out to see a fair jet of fuel squirting out from the underside of the port tank pod. The Comet taxied back to the ramp where the faulty booster pump seal was isolated. [30]

One of the minor problems with the Comet was that the hot end of the engines passed through the rear spar requiring the Flight Engineer to keep an eye on the spar temperatures. During one training flight involving circuits and bumps at Khartoum, the temperatures came close to their limits and so the Captain decided to go out of the circuit for an hour or so and fly low south of Khartoum, following the White Nile down to Juba. Below them the crew could see villagers and wildlife running for cover as it was no doubt the first time they had ever seen or heard a jet aircraft. [31]

Both of Sudan Airways' Comets continued in service until the mid-1970s when Dan-Air acquired them. ST-AAW was withdrawn from service in October 1973, reregistered G-ASDZ and ferried to Lasham where it was broken up and used for spares. ST-AAX was reregistered G-BDIF and ferried to Lasham on 21st August 1975.

IN SERVICE WITH KING IBN SAUD

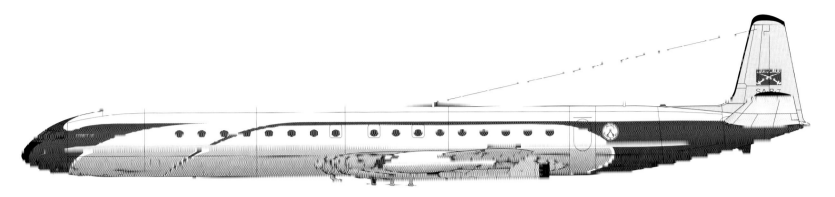

The Comet 4C built for the personal use of King Ibn Saud of Saudi Arabia was the most interesting of the series. The aircraft was ordered at the Farnborough Show in September 1961 and SA-R-7 was built at Hatfield and became the most luxuriously appointed and expensive VIP jet of its day. It was painted externally in green, black, white and gold and the accommodation included a night suite in the forward cabin and seats for 50 people in the aft cabin. It was operated on the King's behalf by Saudi Arabian Airlines and the aircraft made its first flight at Hatfield on 29th March 1962. Its first overseas flight was to Pisa and Rome on 15th June and in August the aircraft made a visit to Jeddah before commencing crew training at Hatfield during September and much of October.

The aircraft visited Saudi Arabia on 25th October and continued with the crew training and occasional trips for the King, and then on 19th March 1963, the aircraft flew from Hatfield to Geneva and then flew the King from Geneva to Nice. However on a flight on 30th March, it crashed in the Alps near Cuneo while en route from Geneva to Nice in the early hours of the morning, killing all on board, including some of the King's entourage. The American Saudi Arabian Airlines crew were being checked out by two de Havilland

The unique Saudi Arabian Royal Comet 4C SA-R-7, taxies to the runway at Hatfied on 29th March 1962 for its first flight.

personnel, Test Pilot John Hanslip and Flight Engineer Ken Rowse who were resting at the time of the accident following a long period of duty.

During his time with the Comet in Saudi Arabia, Rowse had, out of necessity, devised a method of calculating the Comets c of g by measuring the nose oleo extension with a six inch steel rule. It was a practical response to the difficulty he had faced of calculating the weight of the items being loaded on a Royal flight, given that it was often not clear how many passengers might arrive and how much luggage they might bring with them. [32]

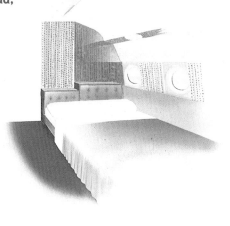

Settee daytime
configuration

Sideboard unit combining
secretarial position

Artists impressions created for the approval of King Saud, before the fitting-out of the Comet interior.

Lounge and dining room

Settee convertible to bed
for nightime configuration

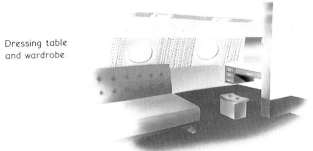

Dressing table
and wardrobe

De Havilland Comet 4C
Special Interior

for

His Majesty King Sa'ud ibn 'Abd al-'Aziz
ibn 'Abd al-Rahman Al Faisal Al Sa'ud
King of Saudi Arabia
Riyadh

IN SERVICE WITH KUWAIT AIRWAYS

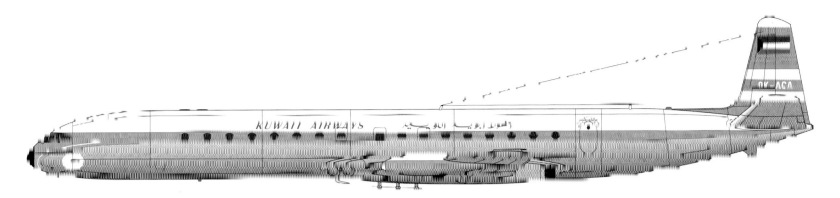

Kuwait National Airways was founded in 1953 and the airline's initial fleet of DC3s was operated and maintained by BOAC. In July 1956 the airline leased two Handley Page Hermes 4s which were soon replaced by DC4s. The airline was re-named Kuwait Airways in 1958 and by the following year it was operating three Viscounts.

Kuwait Airways was the last airline to order the Comet 4C. 9K-ACA first flew on 14th December 1962 and was delivered to the airline on 18th January 1963. In order to realise capital and expand its fleet still further, Kuwait Airways was nationalised in 1962. The airline ordered one more Comet 4C,

9K-ACE, which was delivered to Kuwait on 2nd February 1964, covering the distance of 3,169 miles in a record time of 6 hours and 2 minutes. Following its delivery, the airline inaugurated a service to London with stopovers at Geneva, Frankfurt or Paris.

On 9th December 1966, Kuwait Airways bought Comet 4 G-APDG which was then reregistered 9K-ACI and operated with the airline for nearly three years during which time it was briefly leased to Middle East Airlines, before being sold to Dan-Air in September 1970. In April 1971 9K-ACA and 9K-ACE were also sold to Dan-Air, becoming G-AYWS and G-AYVS.

Kuwait Airways Comet 4C 9K-ACE makes a spirited take-off from Heathrow in September 1966.

Top: Kuwait Airways Comet 4C 9K-ACE, soars above Hatfield on 17th December 1963 during its first flight.

Bottom: On 7th November 1965 at Heathrow Airport, G-APDN of BOAC wears Kuwait Airways stickers during a three month lease period.

IN SERVICE WITH MALAYSIA SINGAPORE AIRLINES

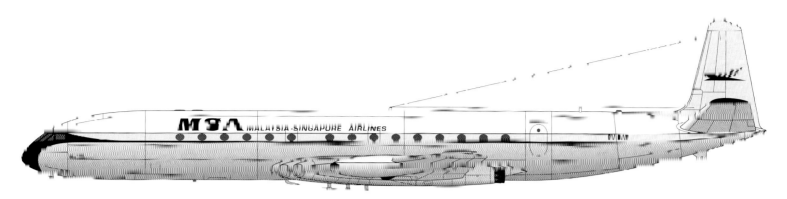

The first air services to the Malayan Peninsula were started in 1930 by KNILM and KLM. In October 1935, plans were in hand to establish a new airline to operate between Singapore, Kuala Lumpur, Ipoh and Penang, and Imperial Airways and a local shipping company, Straits Shipping Company Ltd, were involved in the venture. The airline, Malayan Airways Ltd, was not in fact registered until October 1937 and, due to a number of factors, did not start operations until April 1947 using three Airspeed Consuls. The airline later operated five DC3s, two DH89

Dragon Rapides, a DC4 and two Viscounts. Prior to the Comet, the final acquisition for the airline was a fleet of five Fokker F27 Friendships.

In December 1962 the airline leased BOAC Comet 4, G-APDH. The Comet service was known as the 'Silver Kris Jet' linking Singapore with Hong Kong, Kuala Lumpur, Jakarta and Bangkok, and in its first four months of service, the Comet was operated at a projected annual rate of 3,231 hours.

Less than two months after entering service with Malaysian, Comet 4 9M-AOE is prepared for service at Hong Kong on 1st December 1965.

Surrounded by a fascinating array of ground equipment, 9V-BAS of renamed Malaysia-Singapore Airlines is prepared for flight in April 1967, at Hong Kong.

On 16th September 1963, the eleven states of the Malayan Federation joined with Singapore, Sarawak and Sabah to form the Federation of Malaysia. The change in the political arena led to a change in the name of the airline to Malaysian Airways Ltd.

On 22nd March 1964, G-APDH was damaged by fire following a landing at Singapore in which the aircraft's starboard undercarriage collapsed. There were no fatalities but five of the 70 passengers suffered serious burns. A replacement Comet was leased from BOAC and, at the end of August, it was announced that MAL were to buy five BOAC Comet 4s for delivery the following year. In June 1965 the first Comet was painted by BOAC in the MAL livery and delivered to the airline in September. Prior to that, Singapore seceded from the Federation of Malaysia and a new national prefix, 9V, was used from January 1966 onwards. The airline was known as Malaysia-Singapore Airlines from 1st January 1967 and it was shortly after this change that the airline ordered Boeing 707s and 737s.

In July 1966, a Comet service to Manila was introduced and by April 1967, the Comets also served Taipei and Perth. 1968 was the airline's twenty-first anniversary and in that year a Comet service to Phnom Penh was added to the network. In the same year the airline took delivery of its first two Boeing 707s and on 21st August 1969 MSA became the first airline in Asia to operate the Boeing 737, heralding the end of Comet operations. The Boeing 737s replaced the Comets on the routes from Singapore to Kuala Lumpur, Penang, Bangkok, and Kota Kinabula and by the end of the year they had been retired and sold to Dan-Air.

G-APDA was sold to Malaysian Airlines on 9th December 1965 and registered 9M-AOA. It was later registered 9V-BAS with MSA and was sold to Dan-Air in November 1969 and used for spares. G-APDB was sold to Malaysian Airlines on 11th September 1965 and registered 9M-AOB. It was also sold to Dan-Air in October 1969 and flown by the airline until April 1973. G-APDC was sold to Malaysian Airlines in October 1965 and registered 9M-AOC. It was registered 9V-BAT with MSA then sold to Dan-Air in September 1969 and used for spares. G-APDD was sold to Malaysian Airlines on 8th November 1965 and registered 9M-AOD until it was sold in October 1969 to Dan-Air who operated it until it was withdrawn from use in August 1972. G-APDE was sold to Malaysian Airlines on 5th October 1965 and registered 9M-AOE. It was later registered 9V-BAU until it was also sold to Dan-Air in November 1969. G-APDH was leased to Malaysian Airlines but was written off at Singapore on 21st March 1964 when the undercarriage failed.

Top: MSA Comet 9M-AOD approaches Singapore on the completion of another flight in early April 1967.

Bottom: 9M-AOD is serviced on the apron at Paya Lebar, Singapore, while the competition, in the form of a Convair 880 of Cathay Pacific, taxies by to the terminal.

In the maintenance hanger at Paya Lebar Singapore, a MSA Comet undergoes work on the wing pinion tanks.

G-APDM was leased to MSA on 20th January 1968 and served the airline until August that year when it was acquired by Dan Air. During its year with MSA it was registered 9V-BBJ. G-APDP was leased to MSA from 30th November 1967 and registered 9V-BBH. It was operated by MSA until 23rd January 1968 and was acquired by Dan-Air on 13th February 1969. In all, Dan-Air acquired five Comet 4s from MSA in 1969, all of which were ex-BOAC aircraft. Both 9V-BBH and 9V-BBJ were leased by MSA as two of their Comets had cracked front spar fittings which required the attention of a de Havilland repair team. When the two MSA aircraft had been repaired, 9V-BBH and 9V-BBJ were returned to BOAC.

After lease to Middle East Airlines as OD-AEV, BOAC Comet 4 G-APDM is seen in the process of being repainted into the full MSA livery in the company hanger at Paya Lebar Singapore, in January 1968.

Top: Comet 4 G-APDL overflies London on the start of another holiday flight from Gatwick in July 1969.

Bottom: Delta Lima taxies to a halt at Manchester's Ringway Airport in June 1969, at the completion of another sector.

IN SERVICE WITH DAN-AIR

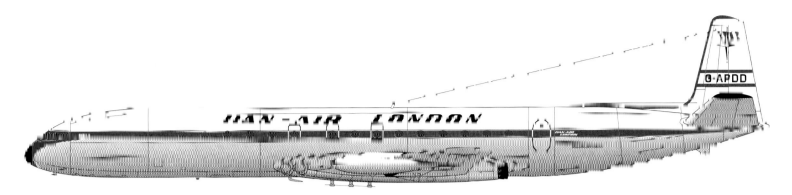

In 1922 two gentlemen, Davies and Newman, established a business as shipbrokers specialising in the oil tanker trade. In the early 1950s, the business expanded into the aircraft broking market and over the next ten years the company operated DC3s, ex-RAF Yorks, Bristol Freighters, Airspeed Ambassadors and Doves. In 1966 the airline bought two Comet 4s from BOAC and with the acquisition, Dan-Air became the second independent airline in Britain to operate jet aircraft. BUA were the first, with their recently acquired VC10s.

The Comets began service in the Winter of 1966, under contract to one of Britain's largest IT companies, Clarkson and Horizon Holidays when the aircraft were operated on short stages with high passenger loads. As the ratio of landings to flight hours was high, coupled with the fact that the aircraft were carrying more passengers and less fuel, Dan-Air sought the assistance of Hawker Siddeley Aviation at Hatfield to modify the aircraft. Tourist passenger accommodation was increased to 99 seats and the cabin floor and some of the wing structure was strengthened to meet the unique requirements of the airline. Following the Comet 1 losses, a close watch had been kept on the fatigue life of all Comets and the actual loadings endured by aircraft in different configurations had been monitored. The Comet 4s had been expected to be good for about 12,000 flights in the type of long-haul work on which BOAC had been using them. Dan-Air was thus required to modify the wing front spar top and

Dan-Air Comet 4 G-APDL was written-off during a wheels-up landing on a training flight, at Newcastle-upon-Tyne on 7th October 1970.

In June 1975 Comet 4B G-APZM of Dan-Air sits at Gatwick wearing the early version of the company livery.

bottom booms, the rear spar top boom and the bottom skin panel in the area of the wheel well cut out, before operating them fully. BOAC had already modified the front and rear spar top booms to allow a further 2,000 to 4,000 flights, before selling the aircraft to Dan-Air.

During 1967, the airline's first full year of operation, 45,643 passengers were carried. In order to train its flight crews, the airline opened a ground school at Horsham, near Gatwick and a ten-year-old Comet simulator was purchased from BOAC and installed by BOAC's simulator engineer in an operation that took twelve weeks. The machine could simulate ten different scenarios, ranging from normal flight to a full emergency. When pilots joined the airline they spent eleven weeks at the centre, during which they flew a total of 28 hours on the simulator. Comet 4, G-APDE, was used as a training aircraft and was based at Teesside.

In May 1967, Dan-Air acquired a third Comet 4 from BOAC and, during the same month, G-APDK landed at Glasgow in front of a crowd of 30,000 football fans who had come to welcome the aircraft's passengers, the Glasgow Celtic football team who were returning from Lisbon where they had just won the European Cup. Teesside Airport was the venue for another Comet event of note when the Newcastle Evening Chronicle and a tour operator staged an event one January evening which attracted a crowd of 15,000 who were willing to queue in the rain for the chance to look inside a Comet and a BAC 1-11.

Foreign exchange restrictions in 1968 prompted a slowdown in the airline's growth but even so, in May the airline acquired a fourth Comet. It also purchased £1m worth of Comet spares from BOAC, enabling it to place ground engineers at Luton, Manchester, Glasgow and Berlin with a supply of essentials spares. In the same year the airline also started to operate IT flights from West Berlin's Tegel Airport to Malaga for a German tour operator, Neckerman und Reisen, with the first flight taking place on 31st March. One Comet was permanently based in West Berlin while the others were based at Gatwick. Dan-Air operated 300 Comet flights to Malaga in the Summer of 1968 then in November, the independent airline British Eagle went into liquidation, leaving two holiday companies, Lunn-Poly and Everyman, without service provision. Dan-Air was awarded the contract and in January 1969 acquired three more Comets. The Comet fleet continued to grow that year with the acquisition of four more aircraft from MSA and as these were all ex-BOAC aircraft, the modifications required were a matter of routine for Dan-Air. In October that year the airline operated its first trans-atlantic flight, flying tourists to Port-of-Spain, Trinidad.

During 1970 and 1971, the airline acquired another Comet 4 from MSA, three Comet 4s from EAA, two Comet 4Cs and a Comet 4 from Kuwait Airways, and three Comet 4s and a 4C from Aerolineas Argentinas. All these aircraft were ferried to Lasham and thoroughly overhauled, and modifications were carried out which took on average 1,500 hours spent on each aircraft. Seating was initially

Caught on approach to Gatwick in June 1978 Comet 4B, G-APZM, displays the ample flap area of the aircraft.

standardised at 99 but, in due course, this was increased to 106 in the Comet 4s and 119 in the Comet 4Cs and Comet 4Bs. While it proved difficult to establish a standard cockpit layout, the basic navigation and communication equipment and the autopilot and flight systems were standard. Dan-Air operated its Comets with two pilots and an engineer and four cabin staff, and interestingly three of the first officers were women. During 1971 the number of crews increased from 28 to 43 and a total of 22 Captains and 28 First Officers undertook the training course, putting in a total of just under 4,000 hours. By the following year, the airline had more than 100 Comet flight crews.

At the beginning of July 1970, Dan-Air announced that it had signed a £2.5m contract with IT company, Global and the airline was engaged to operate flights on behalf of the holiday firm from Birmingham. Just two days later, however on 3rd July, Dan-Air's Comet 4 G-APDN crashed while on the final stage of a flight from Manchester to Barcelona. The 105 passengers and seven crew were all killed. The aircraft had taken off from Manchester for Barcelona eight minutes late at 16.04 on a regular charter flight. At 18.05 Barcelona ATC requested the Comet's altitude and G-APDN reported passing 4,000ft. At 18.07 the ATC called the aircraft for confirmation that it was still on course and G-APDN did not reply to the transmission, nor to other calls which were subsequently made. The site of the accident was Latitude 41°47'45" North and Longitude 02°27'34" East and the altitude of the site was

about 3,900ft up in the Sierra del Montseny mountains, some 65 kilometres to the north-east of Barcelona Airport.

G-APDN was originally acquired by BOAC in April 1959, then bought by Dan-Air in 1969 and the aircraft had flown 25,786 hours. A British commission was appointed to collaborate with the Spanish authorities in investigating the cause of the accident. The inquiry deduced that, due to a combination of erroneous information, the Comet had not followed airway UB31 which was the route to Barcelona that it had been allocated, but had in fact been flying approximately 30 kilometres to the east. [33]

Dan-Air had to retire G-APDL, a Comet 4, when it was damaged beyond repair at Newcastle Airport on 7th October 1970 in a wheels-up landing during training. The early 1970s saw Dan-Air operating at their peak with twelve Comet 4s then, in early 1972 when BEA Airtours began to dispose of its fleet of Comet 4Bs, Dan-Air acquired two from BEA and also five of the type from Channel Airways. One was based at Southend and used for spares while the other four entered service. The following year, the airline acquired eight more Comet 4Bs and one Comet 4C from MEA and by the end of 1973, Dan-Air had acquired no fewer than 38 Comet 4s, 4Bs and 4Cs out of the total of 74 built. However, due to the on-going retirement of the older aircraft, the number of Comets in service with Dan-Air at any one time was in the range of fifteen to twenty and many

Wearing the second version of the Dan-Air livery, Ex Sudan Airways Comet 4C, G-BDIF, approaches Newcastle in August 1978.

of the latter acquisitions were used for spares only. During 1973, the airline reached the decision that the Comet was beginning to look old fashioned when compared to the newer jet aircraft then coming into service in the burgeoning IT market, and therefore decided to begin phasing out the type.

Nonetheless, Dan-Air continued to purchase second-hand Comets as and when they came onto the world market and during the 1970s they acquired eleven more. Two were bought from Sudan-Airways, with one entering service and the other used for spares. Five were bought from 216 Squadron and these were especially valuable as they had relatively low hours and fewer landings. Finally, in October 1976, four Comets were bought from Egyptair and of these one was stripped of useful components and abandoned in Egypt, and the other three were stored at Lasham and used for spares. During 1975 the Comet fleet operated a total of 17,217 hours and by the Autumn of 1976 they had a combined utilisation for the year of 23,123 hours. During 1976 Dan-Air flew eighteen Comets in commercial service; nine Comet 4Bs and nine Comet 4Cs.

One pilot who flew both the Comet 4B and the 4C later explained his preference for the latter. "I much preferred the 4C as it allowed some really smooth landings because of its 'slower' wing, and 80 degrees of inboard flap — which trapped a nice cushion of air that let you down very gently." [34]

Most of the work at that time was what was known as 'there and backs', taking holiday makers to sun spots all over Europe, and occasionally there were 'specials' taking football supporters to see their team play abroad. ATC delays in the mid-1970s were legendary, six hours was common and twelve hours was not unusual. Captain Wayt recalled a flight on 28th August 1976 which involved six hours on the ground at Ibiza and as the Comet had no APU for air-conditioning, the only way to get a through breeze was to remove the over-wing emergency exits. During the 1970s Dan Air acquired a reputation for delays and other incidents which undoubtedly led to the nickname Dan-Dare. [35]

During the Winter of 1976, half the Comet fleet was withdrawn from service and stored temporarily at Lasham. However, it was found that restoring them to service for the Summer peak proved more expensive than maintaining all aircraft in flight status at a lower monthly utilisation. Three Comets were retired in 1976 and the remaining fifteen were maintained through the Winter and operated throughout 1977. The average annual utilisation across the Comet fleet worked out at about 1,500 hours per aircraft. The seasonal nature of IT operations meant that during the Summer peak the aircraft were flying up to 360 hours per month.

The last commercial Comet flight took place on Sunday, 9th November 1980. Dan-Air's Comet 4C, G-BDIW, was chartered

Ex Royal Air Force Comet 4C G-BDIW, sits in a quiet corner of Ringway Airport Manchester, sporting the latest company livery in June 1980, a matter of five months from retirement. This aircraft is now preserved at Hermeskiel Germany.

by Ian Allan Travel for a 1 hour and 10 minute return trip for enthusiasts from Gatwick. The aircraft was under the command of Captain John Kelly, with Co-Pilot Captain Simon Searle and Flight Engineer Gordon Moores. The two Captains had flown 31 and 34 different Comets respectively.

G-BIDW took off at 14.08 and flew at 2,000ft towards Heathrow, passing over Reigate, Woking and Windsor. After seventeen minutes in the air, the Comet turned to the starboard and made an approach to Heathrow's runway 10R. The aircraft descended to 400ft, initiated an overshoot and climb-out sharply to starboard, then headed northwest to complete another dramatic overshoot at 300ft at Brize Norton before flying southwest to its former base at RAF Lyneham for a fly-past. During the flight, passengers queued in the aisles in order to get a glance in the cockpit and ask the crew for their autographs. From Lyneham, the Comet flew south at 2,000ft to Bournemouth and turned to port to cross the Solent and proceeded towards Portsmouth. The aircraft then headed northeast on a course for Gatwick where it landed at 15.20 hours. It was G-BDIW's 10,933rd landing.

One of the notable Comet retirements from Dan-Air was G-APDP, which was converted at Dan-Air's Lasham engineering base to serve as a trials aircraft for the Nimrod development programme. The choice of Lasham was a tribute to the airline's engineering expertise.

Among the Dan-Air Comets that were not scavenged for spares or otherwise broken up were G-APDB, G-APDK and G-APYD. G-APDB, the second production Comet 4, was flown by BOAC before it was bought by Dan-Air. It flew the first passenger carrying flight across the Atlantic on 4th October 1958 and on retirement, Dan-Air donated it to the then East Anglian Aviation Society, which later became the Duxford Aviation Society, for their collection at Duxford, near Cambridge.

G-APDK remained at Lasham and was used as a clubhouse for the Air Scouts before finally being scrapped. G-APYD flew the last Dan-Air holiday flight when it returned from Crete to Gatwick on 23rd October 1979.

On 1st November Comet 4B G-APYD was flown by Captain Joe Wright to Wroughton, near Swindon, where it was preserved with the Science Museum's Civil Airliner Collection. En route the aircraft performed a low fly past at Lasham and the landing at Wroughton was the Comet's 18,586th and it had flown around fifteen million miles in 32,738 hours. During their service with Dan-Air, the Comet fleet flew around 95.5 million miles in some 238,000 flying hours. One ex Dan-Air pilot managed to acquire the 'name plates' of G-BDIW, G-BDIF, G-BBUV and G-APME and he presented that of G-BDIW on a plaque to the Comet Fleet Manager, Captain 'Don' Warburton DFC, when he retired.

A collection of images taken on the occasion of the last commemorative Comet passenger flight by Dan-Air from Gatwick carrying a full load of enthusiasts on Sunday, 9th November 1980 under the command of Captain John Kelly with Captain Simon Searle and Flt Engineer Gordon Moores and four stewardesses.

IN SERVICE WITH CHARTER OPERATORS

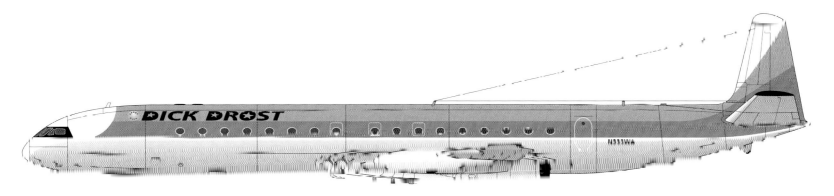

A number of airlines operated Comets on a charter basis, and the first to do so was South African Airways which leased Comet 1s from BOAC and operated them on the route from Johannesburg to London. The service was known as the Springbok service and it operated twice per week, alongside SAA's Constellations. The service commenced from the newly opened Jan Smuts Airport in October 1953, following initial trials from Palmietfontein. The aircraft retained the BOAC livery and carried the Flying Springbok symbol on the nose and fin.

Among the Comet 1s leased from BOAC were G-ANAV, G-ALYS, G-ALYU, G-ALYW, G-ALYX and G-ALYY. However, on 8th April 1954, G-ALYY was lost off Stromboli, near Naples, while on charter to SAA, and the leasing arrangement was terminated soon after with the withdrawal of the Comet 1s from service around the world.

A BOAC Comet 4 was chartered by Qantas Empire Airways for the sector from London to Singapore on the joint BOAC Qantas Kangaroo service between London and Sydney. Agreements whereby Comet 4s were chartered bearing stickers, over the BOAC logo, were entered into with Air Ceylon, Air India, Tasman Empire Airways, Malaysian Airways, Central African Airways and Nigerian Airways. Cyprus Airways and Transportes Aereos Portugueses chartered a BEA Comet 4B under a similar agreement, a Mexicana Comet 4C was chartered by Guest Aerovias and a number of MEA Comet 4Cs were chartered by Kuwait Airways.

Channel Airways, an independent airline which was formed in January 1946, operated a fleet of Comet 4Bs from 1969. The decision to acquire the Comets was taken after Lyons Tours Travel Agency signed a contract in April 1969 to

Comet 4B G-APZM was one of five aircraft used that remained in the colours of its previous owner Olympic Airways, and never carried the full livery of Channel Airways.

An Unusual Opportunity

WE/TERNAIR *of Albuquerque now offers*

A Complete Jet Airline
for less than $2,000,000

A Complete transportation Package

Three 100 passenger DE HAVILLAND *comet 4c*

RR *Power*

U.S.A. - FAA Type certificate
7A10 Jet Transport category

A Redifon 4C flight simulator
A total parts inventory
A complete array of ground support equipment

TOTAL PRICE: $1,975,000

(Consider individual sales but would prefer a package deal.)

WE/TERNAIR *of Albuquerque, Inc.*
We are owners - not brokers - consider trades and offers - can deliver.
RICHARD F. DURAND, JR. ——●—— RICHARD DURAND III
P.O. Box 9127 AMF Albuquerque, New Mexico 87119
Telephones: (505) 247-1528 and (905) 571-2034

A US company Westernair of Albuquerque, purchased the Mexicana Comet fleet on retirement, refurbished the aircraft and then marketed the three Comets and associated equipment for a total of $1,975,000. Sadly the offer received little interest for the then first generation jet Comet 4C. After passing through a succession of owners (none who flew the aircraft) each in turn was scrapped, culminating in the last aircraft to survive XA-NAT which still exists in derelict condition in a children's playground in Mexico City, painted in a gaudy red and green colour scheme.

A selection of shots that illustrate well the gaudy colours carried by the ex-Mexicana 4Cs. The top two were taken at Mexico City in April 1974 and the bottom at Chicago, Illinois, USA, in October 1977.

operate IT tours from 1970 to 1972 and Channel Airways was chosen to operate the flights. The airline bought five Comet 4Bs from BEA and Olympic and the deal, worth just under £2 million, was signed on 27th August 1969. The first of five Comets to be delivered, G-APYC, arrived at Stansted on 26th January 1970 fitted out with 109 seats, an arrangement adopted by the rest of the fleet, G-APMB, G-APYD, G-APZM and G-ARDI. The Comets flew services from

Birmingham, Bristol, Glasgow, Manchester, Newcastle and Stansted to Alicante, Basle, Gerona, Milan, Palma, Rimini, Tangier and Trieste. Further IT tours were flown from Bournemouth, East Midlands and Teesside on behalf of other tour operators, including Mediterranean Holidays and Trident Holidays, both subsidiary companies of Channel Airways. G-APYC flew the airline's first Comet IT service from East Midlands on 17th May 1970 when it carried a party of

Air Ceylon leased Comet 4 G-APDP from BOAC, for their once-weekly service to London from April 1962.
Here we see the aircraft parked out of service at Heathrow on 7th November 1965.

holidaymakers from Castle Donington to Palma. Most of the airline's Comet services for Lyons Tours also started in May 1970. In June 1971 Channel Airways bought an ex-Mexicana Comet 4, G-APDR, for use as a source of spares and its remains were transferred to the Stansted Fire School the following June. G-APMB, G-APYC, G-APYD and G-APZM were

sold to Dan-Air in April 1972 and G-ARDI was used for spares and dismantled the same month.

On 20th May 1976, a Dan-Air Comet was wet leased for a service from Manchester to Malta and back on behalf of Air Malta who provided the cabin crew.

Area of Ecuador used a sole ex-BOAC Comet 4 HC-ALT, on its route network from Quito from March 1966
for a period of two years, after which the aircraft was stored at Miami until broken up in February 1978.

IN SERVICE WITH THE ROYAL CANADIAN AIR FORCE

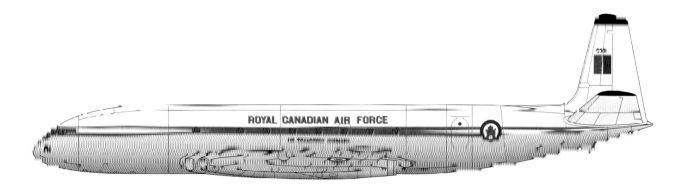

The Canadian Government placed an order for two Comet 1As for the Royal Canadian Air Force, making the RCAF the first Air Force to order and operate Comets and also the first to operate the aircraft across the Atlantic. The RCAF and the RAF pioneered military jet transport services and together they accrued some 20,000 flying hours with their Comets flying to almost every country in the world.

The RCAF flew the first Comet to the North American Continent on 29th May 1953, when the RCAF's Comet 1A, registration 5301, landed at Uplands Airfield, Ottawa, after completing the flight from England via Keflavik and Goose Bay. The total flying time for the journey was 10 hours and 20 minutes and the elapsed time was 14 hours and 34 minutes. On 16th June the second RCAF Comet, 5302, flew over the same route from London to Ottawa, cutting by nearly one hour the time taken by the first aircraft. The two Comet 1As were operated by 412 Squadron RCAF and were used primarily for high speed communications. They were also employed as targets for high altitude interception practice with the fighter squadrons of the RCAF.

For some months prior to the delivery of the two Comets to the RCAF, the Canadian crews were engaged on a jet conversion course at Hatfield. Pilots, Navigators, Radio Officers and Flight Engineers were chosen from Air Transport Command's most experienced line aircrews and the first eight pilots chosen had almost 50,000 flying hours between them. When the aircraft were delivered, they took an intensive flying training course under the supervision of BOAC during which they covered over 60,000 miles on the routes to South Africa, India and Singapore. On 9th May, one of the Comets established an unofficial record by flying non-stop from London to Beirut, a distance of 2,250 miles in 5 hours and 10 minutes then, on 5th June, the other aircraft flew non-stop in the reverse direction in 5 hours and 20 minutes.

The RCAF operated its Comets alongside two Canadair C5 North Stars, DC3s, Expeditors and Mitchells. The Air Force removed the first of the Ghost 50s for overhaul after more than 830 hours, a figure which represented an extension of 80 hours on the manufacturer's overhaul life of 750 hours and 30 hours on the RCAF's recently approved overhaul life of 800 hours.

A superb study of the Royal Canadian Air Force Comet 1A, 5301, on the occasion of its first flight on 21st February 1953.

Comet 1A, 5301, in-flight on 25th July 1958 displays subtle changes to the RCAF livery.

In the wake of the Comet 1 crashes, the RCAF's Comet 1As were withdrawn from service and returned to Chester to be modified. The aircraft were later returned to the RCAF in September 1957 and re-designated Comet 1XBs. The Comets had previously flown approximately 1,000 hours and were given new C of As, then the two Comets, in silver livery, were engaged on crew training from Hatfield which included a number of overseas flights, one of which took both aircraft to Johannesburg on 26th September. The two Comets left Hatfield together for Uplands, via the Azores and Chatham, New Brunswick, and the overall time for the journey was 14 hours and 40 minutes.

RCAF personnel examine the Comet 1A flightdeck interior on 25th August 1958.

By mid November, training had been completed and the Comets started a wide range of scheduled and unscheduled flights. The aircraft also maintained overseas commitments, one of which was a scheduled flight from Ottawa via Montreal and Gander across the Atlantic to Marville in northeast France. These flights were made every first, second and fourth week of each month and their purpose was to transfer service personnel to and from the RCAF Fighter Wing based at Marville, supporting the Canadian Sabres and CF 100 Squadrons serving with Canada's No. 1 Air Division. One of the fastest Atlantic crossings took little more than three and a half hours from Gander to overhead Shannon, and the 2,100 mile flight between Ottawa and Vancouver was one of the many unscheduled domestic flights made by the Comets.

At the outset it was the RCAF's practice to take spares on the flights to Marville but this practise was soon dropped and the spares were pre-positioned. The basic crew compliment on such flights was two Pilots, a Navigator, a Radio Officer, one Flight Engineer, a Movement Control Assistant and a Cabin Steward. As the only trained Comet technicians within the RCAF were based at Uplands, the usual procedure on overseas flights was to take along two Flight Engineers and an Airframe Fitter.

Another important function of the Comets was the carriage of military VIPs, particularly those concerned with Air Defence Command functions. 5301 and 5302 were withdrawn from service during 1963 when plans were in hand to sell one of the aircraft to Aeronaves del Peru SA of Lima, Peru, and it was

In June 1961, 5301 displays the final livery carried by the two Comets prior to retirement.

fitted out with an appealing passenger interior using surplus Viscount seats acquired from Air Canada. However, a warning from Hawker Siddeley concerning the anticipated fatigue life of the Comet 1s led to the cancellation of the sale. Hawker Siddeley predicted a safe life of 7,000 hours without extensive and expensive refurbishing and at the time of the proposed sale, both Comets had total times of about 5,500 hours. Both aircraft were flown for storage to Mountain View, near Trenton, Ontario, the headquarters of what was then the RCAF's Air Transport Command. 5301 was broken up and various components were used in 5302. The entire forward fuselage of 5301 is still intact and is in storage at the Rockcliffe Air Museum. According to a rumour circulating at the time, 5301

was accidentally damaged by a ground vehicle and the decision was then taken to scrap the aircraft.

Mr Eldon Armstrong of Islington, Ontario, bought 5302 and the aircraft was registered CF-SVR. Approval was obtained to fly it for five hours and an RCAF crew ferried it to Hamilton's Mount Hope airport, where it was parked for some time until Armstrong relinquished his ownership and the aircraft was advertised for sale. In 1967 CF-SVR was sold to Dallas Airmotive Inc then, in early 1968, the American firm re-sold it to a Mr Buddy Reid of Miami, where it was reregistered N3735. The aircraft remained there for some time until it was eventualy scrapped.

Comet 1A 5302 was bought by Mr Eldon Armstrong from the RCAF in early 1965 and registered as CF-SVR. Unfortunately due to a restriction notice issued regarding the use of the aircraft by the manufacturer, the aircraft remained unused until resale in late 1965.

Above: Ex Air France Comet 1A F-BGNZ was converted to 1XB standard by de Havilland in 1957 for the Ministry of Supply as G-APAS, and transferred to de Havilland Propellers as XM823 in whose service this shot was taken in October 1963.

Below: A nostalgic scene at Singapore in 1958 involving Royal Air Force Transport Command Comet C2 XK671 'Aquila', newly arrived from the UK.

IN SERVICE WITH THE ROYAL AIR FORCE
216 SQUADRON

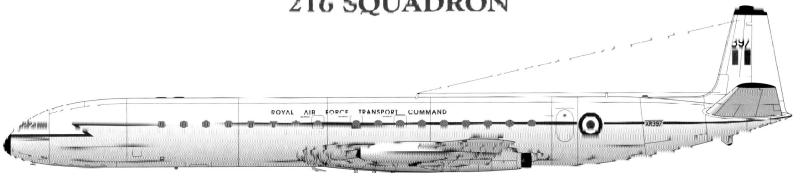

216 Squadron was formed at Manston, Kent, in 1917 with the amalgamation of 2 and 16 Squadrons of the Royal Naval Air Service. During its history the Squadron has operated Handley Page bombers, DH10s, Vickers Vimys, Victorias, Valentias, Bristol Bombays and Hastings. In 1955 a decision was taken to operate the Comet C2 and the first Comet T2 to arrive at RAF Lyneham was XK670, formerly registered as G-AMXF with BOAC. It was flown from de Havilland's factory on 7th June 1956 and the following day it was joined by the other Comet T2, XK669, formerly G-AMXB with BOAC. XK669 was transferred to the RAF Handling Squadron at Boscombe Down for preparation of the Pilot's notes and both the first and second Comets were used for crew training and route-proving trials. They were later converted to become Comet C2s and were the first military aircraft to enter service with a full civil passenger carrying C of A. This allowed the aircraft to be operated at its maximum differential pressure of 8lb per square inch.

With the exception of these two aircraft, the RAF Comets had a modified internal layout to allow them to serve as troop carriers, VIP carriers or casualty evacuation carriers. The floor of the front compartment was strengthened to carry freight or baggage as an alternative to seats, and special racks could be fitted for the casualty evacuation role.

All ground instruction on the aircraft was done at the manufacturers and all pilots attended a four-week course at de Havilland and a one-week Avon engine course at Rolls-Royce. Navigators and signallers attended a two week course at de Havilland and a one-week course at Marconi, while the engineers attended an eleven-week course at de Havilland and a one week course at Rolls-Royce. Flying experience was backed by training on the Redifon Comet simulator at RAF Lyneham.

All Captains and Co-Pilots were given a Meteor jet conversion course at RAF Manby followed by a short course at the Canberra Operational Conversion Unit for the navigator's benefit. All Captains completed the Manby course but, for administrative reasons, only six completed the Canberra course. A Comet conversion course of 55 hours a 'day' and 20 hours 'night' flying was arranged in order to bring the pilots up to passenger carrying standards. This programme was broken down into eighteen hours dual flying, seventeen hours solo flying and 40 hours screened route flying. Before being granted a Transport Command Passenger Carrying C category, all Captains had completed 75 hours dual and solo flying.

All the crews had to be familiar with both civil and military procedures and they had no undue difficulty in converting to jet transport operations. Much of the conversion training was done at El Adem, Libya, where the kinder weather made it possible during the work up to take on an increasing load of operational commitments. In the course of training a goodwill mission to Ghana was carried out, the Ship's Company of HMS Newcastle was ferried to Bahrain where the vessel was recommissioned, supplies were carried to Aden, troop movements to and from Cyprus were undertaken and many official inspections and visits were carried out. This varied programme allowed ground crews on and off the trunk routes to familiarise themselves with the Comet. The RAF received no complaints of excessive noise and the civil authorities at Le Bourgét on occasion permitted RAF Comets to pick up passengers immediately outside the main terminal buildings.

With regard to take-off and landings, the main requirement of the Comet was for a hardstanding surface that was able to take the weight of the aircraft. In practice even Pierced Steel Plate proved acceptable as a temporary measure, provided sharp turns when taxiing were avoided. The combination of rain and runways with poor drainage sometimes made operations difficult, and when pools of water were present the low set flaps were liable to damage from water thrown up by the main wheels. The approved technique

Delivered to 216 Squadron on 8th June 1956, XK669 had the distinction of being the first Comet for RAF Transport Command.

in such circumstances was to land with only half flap selected, retracting them immediately on touchdown. Pools of water were also a problem occasionally on take-off as, at around 50 knots, the nose wheels threw up water across the front of the inboard engines causing them to surge and flame out, and the resultant damage to swirl vanes necessitated a double engine change. An intermittent but persistent problem was the occasional freezing of the pitot and static lines to the pressure flight instruments and the loss of these instruments at altitude was rather disconcerting.

The first operational flight in Squadron service was of historic interest. On 23rd June 1956, XK670 landed at Moscow Airport carrying the Secretary of State for Air and senior RAF Officers who had been invited to attend the Soviet Union Air Display at Tushino Airport. The Comet flew an obligatory non-stop, indirect route via Berlin and Warsaw, a distance of about 1,700 statute miles and it was the first British jet-engined aircraft ever to visit Russia's capital.

For the first month the Squadron had the assistance of DH Technical Representatives stationed down the route and a limited number of spares were prepositioned. Thereafter, once the Comets were away from base, technical support was the responsibility of servicing personnel at overseas staging posts, whose experience on the Comet was naturally limited in the early stages.

Scheduled Comet flights to Singapore were introduced in June 1956 and the trip took 24 hours. The schedule was soon extended to Adelaide and Brisbane and marked the start of full scale Comet C2 operations. Over time the route to Singapore varied considerably, due mainly to events in the Middle East, and Comets bound for Hong Kong flew there from Singapore and returned on the same day. Hong Kong's Kai Tak airport required specialised local knowledge and the Comet landing there for the first time picked up a Captain of the Far East Air Force Hastings aircraft, for return to England.

In August, two flights were made to Bahrain in support of operations in the Muscat area, and two flights to the Middle East in support of RAF Bomber Command aircraft. With only four aircraft in service, 216 Squadron was involved with operations at Suez in early November, flying troops and equipment to Malta and Cyprus. The tenth built and last aircraft to arrive was XK716, which was delivered on 7th May 1957 and which was the first and only Comet C2 to be built at Chester. The final four aircraft were the only ones to make their first flights in military markings.

During September 1957, two Comets flew to Pinecastle AFB, Florida, via Aldergrove and Gander, in support of RAF V Bombers taking part in a USAF Bombing Competition. These were the first non-stop westbound crossings of the North Atlantic by any jet transport aircraft, the Aldergrove to Gander leg taking just over five hours. In September 1957, a Comet set off westbound with a small staff to survey a new route which was to provide a high speed courier service across the Atlantic and North America and then on across the Pacific to Christmas Island. The survey flight was successful and RAF staging posts were established at Goose Bay, Offut AFB, Travis AFB and Hickam AFB.

The 19,000 mile round flight took 3 days and 18 hours and the flying time was approximately 45 hours. Slip crews were positioned at Goose Bay, Travis and Hickam to eliminate crew rest problems and to make full advantage of the Comet's high work capacity. A weekly service was operated with passengers leaving Britain on a Tuesday morning and arriving at Christmas Island after little more than 24 hours in the air.

During the first year of operations, the RAF's Comets made promotional or inspection visits to Turkey, Cyprus and Kenya. In Turkey, XK670 was demonstrated to senior officers of the Turkish Air Force and was the centre of attraction during stops at Istanbul, Ankara and Eskeshir.

In their VIP role, 216 Squadron's Comets carried out a variety of tasks. On 4th June 1957, the Queen and Prince Philip flew in a BOAC Comet from Marham in Norfolk to Leuchars in Scotland, and then back to London Airport on the same day. On 20th April 1959, the Queen Mother and Princess Margaret left London on board XK698 for an informal visit to Rome and, on 28th August 1959, President Eisenhower and the British Prime Minister Harold Macmillan boarded a Comet at RAF Benson and flew to Scotland and back. This was

believed to have been the first time that a President of the United States had flown in a foreign aircraft.

The leatherbound visitors' books of 216 Squadron continued to record the names of kings and queens, princes and presidents, heads of state and leaders of the Armed Forces who were carried by the Squadron. The last entry in one of the books was that of Miss Leila Khaled, a failed air hijacker, who was returned to Egypt by the RAF on 30th September 1970 after an uninvited stay in Britain. She gave her address as Haifa, Palestine, and in the same book was the signature of King Hussein of Jordan and other Arab leaders whose entries bore the bleak addendum 'since assassinated'.

216 Squadron's Adjutant ensured that the books remained under lock and key at RAF Lyneham, apart from their flying trips. One visitor offered five thousand dollars for just one page on which were the signatures of Queen Elizabeth, the Queen Mother, Queen Frederika of Greece, Princess Sophie of Greece and Princess Margaret. Also at the headquarters was a cupboard with 33 national flags for use on overseas visits, including the Royal Standard and the personal colours of Prince Philip and the Chief of the Defence Staff.

On one VIP trip, a Comet was found to be unserviceable at Muharraq, in Bahrain, with a damaged engine. A replacement engine was quickly flown out from Britain and two engineers worked in over 100°F to replace the damaged engine in less than eight hours. The Comet was able to catch up with its VIP passenger who had continued his journey in another aircraft.

The only RAF Comet C2 to escape the breaker's torch, XK699 'Sagittarius' is preserved on the gate at RAF Lyneham. Here seen in more active days at London Airport in the company of a BOAC Comet 4.

At Moscow, on 29th June 1956, Comet C2 XK670 'Corvus' stands awaiting the Minister of Transport and Civil Aviation, Mr Nigel Birch, for his return trip to the UK.

During their first year of operation with 216 Squadron, the Comets flew many 'Specials', conveying military and civilian VIPs to destinations abroad. Many of these were arranged at very short notice and, together with the scheduled services, they represented a volume of operating experience that far exceeded that indicated by the 8,500 hours flown up to the 6th January 1958. The Comets had by then visited some 30 countries and flown more than 50 million passenger miles, with many of the destinations being far away from the spares backing and servicing facilities found on the trunk routes.

In the casualty evacuation role, the Comet C2 proved to be an ideal aircraft. It flew at sufficient altitude to be above the weather, it had a high performance over a satisfactory range and its pressurised cabin eliminated the need for general oxygen. The cabin heating was fully controllable over a wide range, a humidifying unit was incorporated and the near complete absence of vibration meant much to seriously ill passengers. The introduction of the Comet in this role revolutionised the whole concept of casualty evacuation flights and the effect on the morale of patients was considerable. Prior to the Comet, flights from Singapore had taken seven days and the journey from Cyprus had taken two days.

The normal medical team on the Comet was four, consisting of two Flight Sisters from RAF hospitals in England, and two male nursing staff, one fully trained and one under training, known as Air Ambulance Attendants. A Medical Officer was not normally carried as the average stage time was only four to five hours and patients were seen by a Medical Officer at every stop. Up to 36 patients could be transported by Comet. There were six stretchers in three pairs in the forward cabin of the aircraft for the seriously ill, and in the rear cabin there were reclining seats for the most needy of the ambulatory patients. The remainder travelled in trooping seats together with the medical staff and other passengers. Due to the lightness of the forward load represented by six stretcher cases, baggage and freight were also put in the front compartment.

The RAF was responsible for all patients and stretcher-cases were emplaned in the forward cabin of the aircraft direct from the ambulance. The loading was carried out through the crew entry door and the change in the level of vehicles was accommodated by means of a portable covered ramp which was manoeuvred into position. The stretchers were secured to the floor of the aircraft and the patient made comfortable. New equipment was soon introduced, using tubular racks which accommodated patients in pairs, one above the other. The shorter flight times achieved by the Comets could easily represent the difference between life and death and the rapid flight meant that many passengers previously considered fit to return only on stretchers were allowed to travel as sitting patients.

One problem the RAF encountered with its Comet C2 operations was that of liaising effectively with ATCs around the world. On the route from Britain to Singapore and Australia, the RAF experienced no difficulty in obtaining clearance for a cruise-climb and a slow landing from about 100 nautical miles. However, clearance to cruise-climb was rarely obtained on the route across Canada and North America. For this route, level cruises had to be used and the 4,000ft step between each successive height meant that the aircraft was sometimes 3,000ft from its optimum cruise-climb height. The North American Air Traffic Control were seemingly unaware of the serious fuel penalties caused by holding jet aircraft on the ground or in the air at low level, but initial ATC problems en route were steadily overcome with the cooperation of the US civil and military authorities.

Contrary to airline practice, in the RAF it was the Navigator's responsibility to compile the flight plan for each succeeding leg which took the form of a combined navigation and fuel plan. A special form was designed for use with the Comet and this included a 'Howgozit' which pitted fuel against distance. Both the critical point and the point of no return were plotted graphically on it. Initially, the flight plan was prepared using the graphs but matters were soon simplified by the use of a specially designed slide-rule and the introduction of tabular presentation.

The Comets possessed both the ten channel TR1998 VHF for the military frequencies and the 140-channel STR 12D which covered the whole civil band. They were also equipped with radio and radar aids, twin ADFs, ILS, Gee, Loran, Eureka Mk 7 and a cloud warning radar with the facility for viewing coast lines. While the navigation equipment was generally found to be satisfactory on the route to the east, there was a need for an independent fixing aid on long stages over the sea in daylight, or at night when an Astro-fix was not possible. On the route to the west, the Loran performance was initially disappointing but it gradually improved.

The speed of the aircraft made it necessary to ensure that passengers were suitably clothed to cope with the rapid changes from temperate to tropical climates and the reverse. It was held that it was better medically for passengers to be too hot than too cold, thus in the British winter season, service passengers left the United Kingdom in blue and in summer they wore khaki drill. Baggage was stowed so that, in the event of a night stop, a change of clothing could easily be made without the necessity of unloading the whole aircraft.

While the average day of flying for the crew of a conventional four piston engined transport was seven to eight hours, that of the Comet crew was longer. Generally it consisted of two four hour legs divided by a flag stop of one-and-a-half to two hours, during which no relaxation was possible. The reduced noise levels, lack of vibration and better comfort and in-flight amenities on the Comet reduced the importance of the fatigue factor.

Over time 216 Squadron's Comet C2s were dispatched to 51 Squadron and the number serving the Squadron was steadily reduced. By early 1966 there were eight. XK715 was allocated the maintenance serial number 7905M on

Currently preserved at Scotland's East Fortune Aviation Collection in Dan-Air colours, Comet C4 is seen here in earlier days on a visit to the USA in June 1972.

Comet C4 XR397 one of five ordered for use by 216 Squadron RAF, was delivered on 15th February 1962.

22nd March 1966 and ferried to Cosford on 5th April. Three weeks later, XK669 was ferried to Brize Norton where it served as a trainer for Air Quartermasters until it was burnt in September 1969. Towards the end of 1966, XK696 was taken to Watton by road for use as a static test-bed where it remained until it was eventually scrapped in November 1969. XK670 was retired to RAF Lyneham as 7926M where it arrived on 29th November 1966 to be used for fire-rescue training until it was burnt out in 1968.

The remaining aircraft were officially withdrawn in April 1967. XK697 transferred to 51 Squadron, while XK716 was flown to Halton on 4th May and serialised 7958M. It was used for fire training and reduced to scrap by 1976. XK698 flew its last sortie with 216 Squadron on 1st April 1967 and was then withdrawn to the 27 MU at Shawbury on 8th June where it was given the instructional serial 8031M on 13th September. The aircraft was transferred to St Athan on 11th December and scrapped in April 1973. XK699 was the last to leave 216 Squadron. It was ferried to Henlow on 14th June 1967 and serialised 7971M before being transferred to RAF Lyneham as the Gate Guard, where it remains to this day.

On 5th September 1960, it was announced that a contract had been negotiated for the purchase of five Comet

C4Cs for 216 Squadron, for delivery during 1961 and 1962. The Comet C4Cs were serialised XR395 to XR399 and were all constructed at Chester. XR395 took to the air for the first time on 16th November 1961, and was delivered on 6th January 1962 but did not enter service with the Squadron until the 4th June. XR399 was the last to leave Hatfield when it flew to RAF Lyneham on 26th April. The Comet C4s carried 94 passengers compared to the 44 carried by the Comet C2s and, for a brief period, the two types operated together.

In normal service the Comet C4s carried 80 passengers but, for high density troop movement, this was increased to 96. Two of the Comets were capable of rapid conversion for VIP duties and the forward cabin was equipped with a dining table, armchairs and divans. In their casualty evacuation role they could be arranged to carry twelve stretchers with attendants and 47 sitting cases or passengers. The Comet C4s were intended to bridge the gap between the earlier Comet C2s and the VC10s which were due to enter Royal Air Force service in the mid 1960s.

216 Squadron was disbanded on 30th June 1975 and the five remaining Comet C4Cs were ferried to the 60 MU at Leconfield Beverley, Yorkshire and by September all five had been sold to Dan-Air.

IN SERVICE WITH THE ROYAL AIR FORCE
192 & 51 SQUADRONS

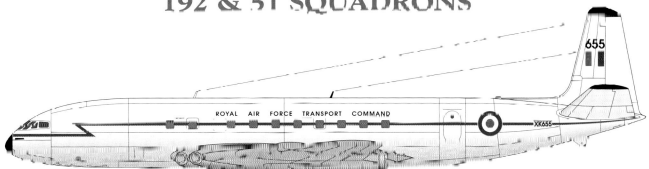

When it came into operation, the Comet presented itself as an ideal aircraft for Elint gathering missions. Its ability to fly at high altitudes, together with its spacious interiors, made it an ideal choice for conversion which was partly undertaken by Marshalls of Cambridge. These Comets were among the last to be delivered to the RAF, and were designated the title Comet 2R replacing the Boeing RB29A Washingtons flown by 192 Squadron at Watton Thetford, Norfolk. It is understood that the first to be delivered was XK663, which was allocated to 192 Squadron on 18th April 1957 and left Hatfield on the following day, via Wyton where installations were added. XK659 was also allocated to 192 Squadron on 12th July 1957 but did not arrive at Watton until 14th March 1958. The final aircraft, XK655, was delivered directly to Watton on 24th March.

192 Squadron was renumbered 51 Squadron and the Comets were transferred on 21st August 1958 where they remained with 51 Squadron until replaced by the Nimrod R1 in 1974. It is understood that the Comet 2Rs were equipped for monitoring the Warsaw Pact signals traffic and the analysis of radar transmissions and the aircraft were believed to have operated along the western and southern margins of the Eastern Bloc, with some of the aircraft detached to Cyprus from time to time.

51 Squadron moved to Wyton Huntingdon in March 1963, and official records give the date of the transfer of the aircraft to 51 Squadron as March 1963, some five years after 192 Squadron disbanded. In the interim, another aircraft had joined the Squadron but one was destroyed in a fire. XK715 joined the Squadron on 1st May 1962, but was returned to 216 Squadron at RAF Lyneham on 17th September and the following day it was replaced in 51 Squadron by XK671. It is understood that XK663 was destroyed in a fire in a hangar at Wyton on either the 13th September 1957 or the 3rd June 1959. No official explanation was published but it is believed that electrical equipment was left running and overheated whilst the aircraft was being prepared for delivery to Watton.

XK695 joined 51 Squadron on 8th March 1963 after undergoing modifications by Marshalls which took nineteen months to complete. By then, XK671 had run out of flying hours and was finally withdrawn on 14th November 1966. The aircraft was flown to Topcliffe where it was registered 7927M and its airframe was used for training. Part of its hulk remains at the airfield. The last aircraft to join 51 Squadron was XK697 which arrived on 1st March 1967 and it is understood this aircraft was used as a trials installation aircraft until it was withdrawn on 20th December 1972. The aircraft remained at Wyton as a static aircraft for use by the local Air Scouts.

51 Squadron's three remaining Comets were eventually replaced by three Nimrod R1s; XW664, XW665 and XW666. The Nimrod was formally commissioned on 10th May 1974 and the Comets were withdrawn in the same year. XK659 was withdrawn on 8th April and ferried to Ringway on 13th May. It was then dismantled and transported to the Pamona Dock, Manchester, where it was installed as an annex to the

On 20th April 1970 Comet C2R, XK655, sits on the ramp at Honington.

XK655 ended its days at the Strathallan Aircraft Collection in Perthshire, Scotland, where it was broken-up in the late 1990s. The nose section was transported to the rooftop aviation park at Gatwick Airport, where it was restored and put on display.

North Westward Ho Bar in Hulme Hall Road. XK655 was the next to leave when it was flown to Strathallan Aircraft Collection Perthshire, Scotland, on 22nd August to join the Roberts collection. The aircraft suffered a hard landing in which the starboard undercarriage leg hit an earth bank just short of the runway. The undercarriage came off in the incident and the aircraft slid to a halt, however the damage was repaired and the aircraft was placed on static exhibition until being scrapped in 1990. The final Comet, XK695, was ferried to Duxford on 10th January 1975 to join the Imperial War Museum's collection, until being scrapped in 1992 due to extensive corrosion in the main undercarriage.

One of two Comet 2E aircraft used for trials by BOAC before the introduction of the Comet 4, XN453 was used for most of its life by the RAE as a flying laboratory. Here seen far from home on the ramp at Bermuda on 5th April 1967.

THE COMETS IN GOVERNMENT SERVICE

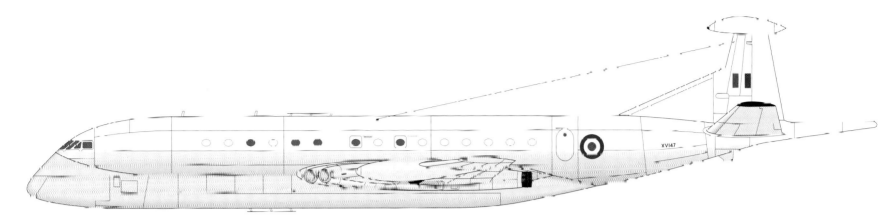

A number of Comets were used in a variety of experimental roles in military markings and in 1954 the MoS obtained two ex-Air France Comet 1As. F-BGNY was converted to Mk 1XB standard with strengthened skins and swept out exhausts. It was serialised XM829 and used at the A&AEE Boscombe Down for Decca/Dectra navigational equipment trials until it was acquired by the MOA Fire School and ferried to Stansted on 20th February 1964. F-BGNZ was also converted to a Comet 1XB and was registered G-5-23, later G-APAS, and issued with serial XM823. It was used by de Havilland Propellers/Hawker Siddeley Dynamics for testing missile equipment until retirement to 27 MU at RAF Shawbury, Shrewsbury, in April 1968 and allocated serial number 8351M. Later it was moved by road to the Cosford Aerospace Museum on 17th September 1973 where it is displayed in BOAC markings as G-APAS.

G-ALYT, the Comet C2 prototype, spent most of its life test flying for the MoS. Its final flight on 28th May 1959, piloted by John Cunningham, was to RAF Halton near Aylesbury which was equipped with a 3,800ft grass runway. It became an instructional airframe with the School of Technical Training and was given maintenance serial 7610M until September 1967 when it was scrapped.

BOAC's Comet C2, G-AMXD, was registered XN453 and transferred to the RAE, Farnborough, where it was used for long-range radio development trials. The aircraft was withdrawn in September 1975 and, by late 1976, it had been moved to the dump. In early 1977 its wings were removed and it was transported to Woodford where the remainder of the aircraft was left in the company of several Comet 1s which had been used for fatigue tests.

G-ANLO, which started life as the Comet 3 and later became the Comet 3B, was delivered to the Blind Landing Experimental Unit on 21st June 1961 and was registered XP915. For more than ten years it was used at Bedford and the RAE at Farnborough for a variety of trials and at one time it was modified

to carry a nose probe. It was also used for retarded landings, being run into a carpet of plastic foam on the runway, as well as research into the Autoland technique. On 21st and 22nd August 1973, it was transported by road to Woodford where it was used as a systems mock-up for the Nimrod AEW3. Its place at Bedford was taken by XS235 which was delivered on 2nd December 1973 and transferred to A&AEE Boscombe Down in 1975.

Another BOAC Comet C2, G-AMXK, was delivered to Bedford for the RAE as XV144 on 18th November 1966. The aircraft also spent some time at the College of Aeronautics at Cranfield before it was transferred to Farnborough on 21st January 1970. The aircraft was withdrawn in 1974 and cut-up in August 1975 for disposal at a scrap yard in Halifax.

The MoD acquired some ex-BOAC Comet 4s for research and trials. Comet 4, G-APDF, became XV814 and was operated by the DRA at Farnborough for radio communications, navigation and avionics trials work. A pannier was fitted under the fuselage and, to ensure stability, a dorsal modification was added to the fin. During 1986, XV814 was further modified and acquired a Nimrod fin with a radome at the top. The aircraft's last trip was completed on 18th December 1992 when it returned from a flight around the world finally being retired from service that month, making its last flight to Boscombe Down as a spares source for XS235 on 28th January 1993. Over time it was gradually stripped of its parts and kept in open storage until it was broken up for scrap on 12th August 1997 in an exercise that lasted just six hours.

Similarly, G-APDS was serialised XW626 and fitted with a Nimrod type fin and converted to carry a Nimrod AEW3 radar in a new bulbous nose. It flew for the first time in this mode on 28th June 1977. G-APDP was serialised XX944 and delivered to Farnborough on 19th July 1973 where it was used in the Nimrod development programme for early trials. The aircraft was withdrawn early in 1977 for instructional use by RAE technical apprentices. Three other civilian Comets,

G-APAS taxies out to the runway at Chester for the first flight after the completion of the conversion to Comet 1XB standard in March 1957.

G-APYC, G-APZM and G-BBUV, were bought in 1978 for spares to maintain the RAE and A&AEE aircraft. G-APYC acquired RAF finflashes when seen with 5 MU at Kemble later that year.

The two final military Comets were c/ns 6476 and 6477, being unsold civil Comet 4Cs. 6476 was first flown as G-5-1 at Chester in October 1965, using the registration originally given to the Comet prototype. The aircraft was powered by

Rolls-Royce Avons and flown to Woodford for conversion to the Nimrod prototype. 6477 remained at Chester for similar modifications and was powered by Rolls-Royce Spey engines. The aircraft underwent service trials at A&AEE from 23rd December 1975 then, in 1979, was transferred to the RAE at Bedford and later to Woodford to undergo fatigue tests. The two aircraft later became XV147 and XV148 and they formed the opening chapter of the Nimrod story.

Two Comet 4Cs were completed but unsold. Both were converted to Nimrod prototypes; one XK147 with Avon power, and this aircraft the second prototype XV148, was flown to Chester to be converted to the Nimrod specification with Spey power.

To mark the retirement of the only Comet 3B still flying, a unique formation was flown in April 1972, comprising XP915 (Comet 3) XN453 (Comet 2E) and XV814 (Comet 4).

Comet 2E XV144 was operated by the Blind Landing Experimental Unit, first at RAE Bedford from November 1966 until being transferred to Farnborough in May 1971, then until 1974 when finally withdrawn from use. The aircraft was broken up at Farnborough in August 1975.

A dramatic view of XW626, the former BOAC Comet 4 G-APDS used in the aborted Nimrod AEW radar trials.

Originally delivered to BOAC as G-APDF on 31st December 1958, XV814 was acquired by the Ministry of Technology in February 1967, when the aircraft was used for radio radar and avionics trials. Retired in January 1993, it was eventually broken up on 12th August 1997 donating many parts to the Museum of Flight in Seattle for the restoration of their Comet 4C XA-NAR.

IN SERVICE WITH CANOPUS XS235

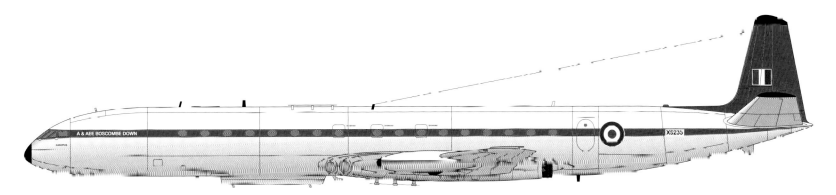

The world's last airworthy Comet was allocated the serial XS235. It was constructed at Chester and first flew on 26th September 1963 and, after shakedown and acceptance flights, was delivered to Boscombe Down on 2nd December. The Comet was named Canopus after the second brightest star in the sky, while Sirius, the brightest, was the name given to another Comet operating from A&AEE when XS235 arrived. It used the call-sign 'Gauntlet'.

XS235 was built specially for the Ministry of Aviation as a flying laboratory, in which a variety of airborne navigation equipment could be tested, and was held to be superior to any comparable aircraft in the West. The aircraft was a standard Comet 4C which was extensively modified during manufacture. Extensive trunking was fitted down both sides of the fuselage interior so that cable for trials equipment could be channelled tidily. A second sextant was mounted in the top of the fuselage in addition to the one in the flightdeck, an astrotracker was located in the top of the fuselage and moveable datum posts were fitted in the fuselage at two points. The datum points were used to establish an extremely accurate fore and aft aircraft datum, in order to harmonise all on-board equipment to an accurate common datum during its initial installation. A number of extra aerials of various shapes and sizes were mounted on the outside of the fuselage, including a large boat shaped fairing for testing Doppler Aerials, fitted below the fuselage and forward of the wing.

In March 1967, XS235 was flown to northern Greenland and Canada to test equipment in extreme cold conditions. The Comet was flown on the 8,000 mile route to experience the coldest attainable temperatures during ground-stops and two items of equipment, the Decca ADL21 Loran C/A and Decca Doppler 67M, were tested in the cold environment. The response of the Doppler 67M over the ice cap and the performance of a new type of Loran C aerial were also evaluated. The route took the Comet from Boscombe Down to Keflavik, on to Thule in Greenland, then on to Toronto and back to Prestwick.

There were 27 personnel on the trip. The flight crew consisted of three pilots, an engineer, a navigator, a radio officer and an air quartermaster, while the trials crew of eight included staff from A & AEE and a number of RAF navigators. The servicing crew included one man for each trade. Also on board was a photographer, two trials instrumentation engineers, two technical representatives from the Decca Co and a scientist from RAE Farnborough who measured ozone levels throughout the flight.

The flight deck of XS235 was modified to incorporate a high standard of navigation equipment, including twin Smith's Flight Systems, twin Marconi AD712 ADFs, twin VOR and Tacan equipment, Marconi 2300 Doppler and compass, Decca Navigator Mk 10 and a Kollsman periscopic sextant. All of the specialised navigation equipment was displayed in front of the navigator and radio officer who sat at a shallow table on the port side. The pilots also had displays of ADF, VOR Tacan and Doppler information, as well as the Smith's Flight System.

Immediately aft of the flight deck where toilets would normally be situated, were two store rooms and, on the port side, the space was turned into a photographic darkroom. The toilets themselves, and the only galley on the aircraft, were situated at the rear of the aircraft on the starboard side. The rear half of the fuselage was fitted out as two passenger compartments, the rearmost of which had ten standard RAF rearward facing seats. The forward compartment was configured in the manner of a conference area, with eight airline seats and two large tables on which charts and diagrams could be spread. The rest of the fuselage was taken up with trials equipment which amounted to just over half the total length of the Comet. The larger forward compartment housed four observation positions where the trials officers could control and watch the displays associated with the equipment on trial, as well as the displays of the datum reference equipment. Twenty-seven panniers of bulky cold weather clothing were also taken on the each trip.

A dramatic view of Comet 4C 'Canopus' taken on 29th July 1992, flying low over typical English countryside.

The aircraft lifted off from Boscombe Down's main runway at 09.59, exactly 34 seconds ahead of schedule. After flying a visual circuit at 1,500ft, the Comet made a practice ILS approach to Boscombe Down and overshot at 200ft. The aircraft then headed north on a 1 hour and 31 minute stage to Kinloss for a brief refuelling stop. Not long after getting airborne, the trials crew set up their equipment and started to take readings. The on-board crystal clock was synchronised to GMT, using a radio time signal which gave a visual digital reading every second and registered on the recording system each tenth of a second. Information from the test equipment was fed to the digital recorder for use in post-flight evaluations of the navigational aids under test.

The approach to Kinloss was delayed for ten minutes due to an emergency at nearby RNAS Lossiemouth where helicopters and aircraft were looking for a Buccaneer which had ditched off the coast. After 1 hour and 50 minutes on the ground, the Comet took off for Keflavik, at that time a US Navy base. The descent into Keflavik took the Comet into an area of developing low pressure which produced a 'whiteout', in which vertical reference and depth perception were difficult but the Comet landed on the snow covered runway from which snow-ploughing bulldozers had just vacated. The snow that greeted the Comet was in fact the first fall for two months which had caught the Icelanders unaware.

The accommodation allocated to the Comet's personnel was known as the BOQ, the Bachelor Officers' Quarters. The janitors employed by the USAF were Filipinos and Hawaiians who kept the temperature of the place at 90°F, well above that preferred by the phlegmatic British. The outside air temperature was low enough to enable some of the cold trials to be made and tests were carried out at 0°C, –10°C and –20°C. The aircraft was kept on the ground for four hours, due to the intensity of snow which had fallen and the drifting because of high winds. Prior to departure, the Comet endured three de-icing sessions in which antifreeze was sprayed all over the aircraft from high pressure hoses, and the slush was then brushed off by hand.

From the top of the descent into Thule, the cabin heating was turned off so that the aircraft would be as cold as possible, both inside and out, when on the ground. This saved 'cooling time' on the ground at Thule as the Comet had to depart within a specific time window in order to avoid exceeding crew fatigue limitations, and the delay in Keflavik had already put the crew closer towards their limit. During the descent the personnel on board donned their cold weather clothing in anticipation of temperatures of –20°C on the ground. The array of under-clothing included two string vests made of thick cotton cord knitted in a wide mesh, two pairs of long johns, a pair of normal service trousers, a loose-necked woollen shirt, a long sleeved ribbed woollen pullover and a neck square made of soft cotton. Over this a two piece cold weather flying overall was worn and an outer parka was provided for wearing over the flying overalls in extremely cold weather. On the hands, woollen wristlets and woollen inner gloves were worn, with a choice of leather working gloves or outer mitts made of soft leather on top. For the feet, three pairs of woollen socks were worn, each sized to fit over the other without creasing. Over them went a numnah sock made of blanketing, together with a thick felt insole, followed by a boot with a waterproof canvas upper extending over the calf and a rubber sole and galosh. The sole was ribbed for good traction on snow and the boot legs laced up.

On approach to Thule from the east, the three large hangars at Thule looked like isolated chicken huts when seen from 50 miles away. The first approach was a practice approach and from 300ft the aircraft climbed up the narrow valley in which Thule's one runway lay. The runway had a gradient so landings were always made from the seaward end and take-offs were towards the sea. After clearing the hills, the Comet made a twenty minute sortie over the ice-covered sea at 500ft to check the operation of the Doppler under those conditions at various angles of bank.

On the ground at Thule the temperature was −15°C and the Comet personnel found that it was possible to stand outside or sit in the aircraft without any discomfort whatsoever. It was only when they walked into wind that the searing cold was felt. The ink in their fountain pens and the paste in their toothpaste tubes solidified after an hour on the ground at Thule. In order to cool the aircraft quickly, the Comet's doors were left open and the emergency exits were taken out. Next, the equipment cases were unplugged from their racks and put out on the wings and while the ground crew kept watch, the trials crews took it in turns to supervise the trials equipment as it cooled. The rest of the personnel took refuge in the Officers' Club where steak and other imported delicacies were on offer, to the accompaniment of piped music.

The trials crew carried out the cold trials at −10°C and −20°C and after placing the equipment on the wings for as long as possible, a temperature of −21°C was achieved. The equipment warmed up normally when they were switched on and, after reaching operating temperatures, performed perfectly, thus proving their capability to operate after a cold soak and large internal temperature changes. It was dark when the rest of the personnel returned to the aircraft in an aircrew truck. There were no other aircraft in the open as they were all stored in heated hangars. The personnel assembled in the aircraft at the very last minute so that their body heat would not unduly warm up the equipment. Once all were aboard, the emergency windows were replaced and the engines were started up.

The aircraft had been scheduled to fly across Baffin Bay and Baffin Island to a point north of Igloolik and then run due south, but the area was declared off-limits and the aircraft had to make a considerable dogleg across Foxe Basin and around Hudson Bay, landing at Toronto after a twenty hour duty day from

Keflavik. On arrival at Toronto's large international civil airport, the British researchers had to wait for half an hour in the silent and darkened aircraft for a set of steps to arrive but, once out, they were taken quickly to a downtown Toronto hotel.

After a rest day the Comet took off from Toronto and flew direct to Scotland, helped on its way by a 187 knot tail wind which on occasion pushed the ground speed up to 585 knots. The stage from Toronto to Prestwick was used for Loran C work. The long stretch of open water also gave the researchers an opportunity to note the effect of sea surface movement on the accuracy of the Doppler measurements.

The scientist from RAE Farnborough was accommodated at a table in the rear passenger compartment. His task involved the measurement of ozone levels along the route to check whether theoretical calculations, which had been made for the purpose of Concorde flights, were correct. At that time little was known about the levels of ozone at very high latitudes and it is believed that XS235 was the first aircraft to be instrumented to check both the outside and inside levels of ozone simultaneously.

The Comet touched down at Prestwick for Customs clearance at 19.30 hours after six hours flying. The final landing at Boscombe Down was made difficult as the main runway had been blocked by an aircraft which had burst all its main tyres on landing and the Comet had to land on the short runway. XS235 returned to its normal Wiltshire environment and routine, flying on most working days throughout the year, both night and day, carrying the trials team and their equipment on more routine flights of up to six hours over Britain and the eastern Atlantic. On such flights, data collection was automatically controlled by a computer which was programmed before each flight according to the trial's requirements.

A significant proportion of XS235's work demanded that it be flown from overseas bases. In July 1968, it made the first flight with two inertial systems and the following month, flew around the world in an easterly direction. XS235 was first shown publicly at the Farnborough Air Show in September 1968 where it dominated the static park, and its livery remained the same as the day it was rolled out in 1963, apart from the red fin which was painted in early 1971. In May 1969 it flew around the world in a westerly direction and also made two flights across the geographic North Pole.

In November 1969, XS235 made history when it flew across Antarctica. It was the most ambitious overseas flight attempted to date, involving a 38,000 nautical mile route and nearly one month away from base. The flight across Antarctica took place during a trials exercise named 'Exercise Canopus', preparations for which got underway in June 1969. Amongst the equipment to be tested were two inertial systems, a new Loran C receiver, a Doppler/gyro navigation system with its own digital computer and Omega, a type of transmitter which, when linked with other Omega transmitters, would eventually give complete world fixing coverage. An array of technical, administrative and diplomatic issues had to be settled before the route could be conformed. In the end it took the aircraft from Boscombe Down to the Azores, Bermuda, Barbados, Lima, Santiago and Punta Arenas on the way south. On the return journey the route was Santiago, Guayaquil, Mexico City, San Francisco, Honolulu, Pago Pago, Fiji, Sydney, Port Moresby, Guam, Tokyo, Adak, Vancouver, Toronto, Argentina and Boscombe Down.

The decision to include an over-flight of Antarctica was of interest to the British Antarctic Survey and the Meteorological Office at Bracknell, England. The Comet departed from Boscombe Down on 20th November and, on 24th November, reached Punta Arenas which is the most southerly city in the world and also has the most southerly civil airport. On arrival the Comet shared the apron with a Boeing 707 freighter which was unloading a herd of dairy cows.

The unique sight of two generations of Comet flying together. Comet 4C XS235, in company with the only airworthy DH 88 Comet G-ACSS, on Wednesday 29th July 1992.

Take-off the following day was planned for 06.30 local time as this gave the optimum time over the photographic target areas. Due to the laboratory equipment on board, along with twenty personnel, the Comet would be 4,000lb over the normal take-off maximum with full tanks. As a full fuel load was essential for the trip, the aircraft had been cleared for this special take-off, at 166,000lb, before leaving Britain, and the special ODM sheets supplied by Hawker Siddeley showed that the take-off would present no difficulty.

The Comet took off at 10.28 GMT and once safely airborne, the flight crew found that it had to contend with very severe icing conditions and for twenty minutes it was necessary to use full engine and airframe anti-icing. At 33,000ft a northwesterly jet stream provided a tail-wind advantage. Early on in the sortie, the navigator reported a large mass 100 nautical miles away where none was shown on the charts and in time it became apparent that it was a large ice flow measuring approximately 30 nautical miles. As the Comet continued southwards over the Bruce Ice Plateau, the friendly voices of radio operators on Argentine Island and Adelaide Island seemed to relieve the desolation of the area. When breaks in the cloud occurred, the cameras made the best of the opportunity and as the Comet reached its most southerly point and turned for home, an excited Adelaide Island radio operator reported "I can see you at the end of your trail".

The 900 nautical miles back to Punta Arenas were a matter of routine. During the 5 hour and 40 minute flight, the Comet had spent some 36 minutes in the Arctic Circle. The inertial systems coped with the South Polar navigation problem without difficulty and although the photographic coverage obtained was limited, it turned out to be of a very high quality. It was the first small scale photography taken of the area and made a considerable contribution to the current mapping programme in the area. The Comet arrived back at Boscombe Down on 16th December after a 24 hour weather delay, having completed 98 hours flying in the 27 days it had been away from base.

On Wednesday, 29th July 1992, the 1934 DH88 Comet racer met up with XS235 when the distinctive twin engined red DH88 Comet, G-ACSS, was flown to Boscombe Down from Shuttleworth. On arrival at Boscombe Down it parked beside XS235 for a photocall and the two Comets then took to the air and headed for Hatfield via RAF Lyneham and RAF Brize Norton. From Brize Norton, the duo were accompanied by a Hercules cameraship and headed for Hatfield. For 2 hours and 10 minutes they formated at 200mph, a difficult exercise for a twin piston and a four jet aircraft to co-ordinate. XS235 returned to Hatfield where a welcoming party had gathered and presentations were made between British Aerospace, The Shuttleworth Collection and A&AEE.

Canopus flies at low level over the sea just prior to retirement in late 1996.

The final flight trials conducted by XS235 took place on 14th March 1997. It was the aircraft's last operational flight which was carried out to test and evaluate a modification of the GEC Marconi Avionics FIN 107.5 Inertial Navigation System for the RAF Harrier GR7. The tests involved some precision flying, over a designated track, with 45° bank and 2G turns.

The Comet took off at 11.00 hours under cloudy skies from Boscombe Down with John Cunningham as a guest, sitting in the radio operator's seat. The sortie took it overhead at Cardiff, RAF St Athan, Hawarden, Warton, RAF Wittering, RAF Brize Norton and RAF Lyneham before flying to Boscombe Down for a landing. Without shutting down systems, it then took off again for a short trial sortie before a second landing back at base, again without shutting down. Finally XS235 then departed for a last short trials flight, including an air-to-air photo shoot, before arriving at Boscombe Down for a final landing at 16.20 hours in glorious sunshine. The Comet was then taxied back to the Weighbridge hanger, where its engines were shutdown. The on-board dignitaries disembarked and a party was held in the RAF Officers' Mess. Somewhat synchronously, that evening the Comet Hale Bopp added its salute as it sped across the sky to the north west.

After nearly 34 years of service, XS235 ceased to be a trials aircraft, having flown only 8,280 hours. The aircraft was in excellent condition and after stripping it of its test equipment, the MoD planned to auction the aircraft on 8th May 1997. The MoD insisted that the Comet must be auctioned to the highest bidder and there were fears that this might mean that it would be sold overseas. While the aircraft had flown very few hours in its service life, it had never had a civil C of A and was unlikely to be granted one in view of the number of modifications it had endured. It was due for a major check and non-destructive testing of the structure in July 1998 and as this involved a complete paint strip, it would be both expensive and require considerable technical expertise. As that expertise was only available within the RAF, the work undertaken would not be acceptable to civil standards.

On 30th April 1997, Michael Portillo MP, announced that XS235 would not be sold at auction. It was one of the last acts of the Conservative Government which was defeated in the general election the following day after eighteen years in office. On 20th July 1997, the de Havilland Museum Trust was informed that its application to obtain the Comet had been successful. It had been planned to fly the aircraft to Hatfield but part of the forthcoming cinema film Private Ryan was being filmed at the airfield at the time so, on 30th October, the aircraft was delivered to Bruntingthorpe, Leicestershire, by Captain Mark Leonczek, with Co-Pilot Geoff Delmege, Flight Engineer Nick Newton and Navigator Cliff Ware. The Comet's GPS had been removed and the minimum

Nueva York a Cuatro Horas y Media de Caracas

LINEA AEROPOSTAL VENEZOLANA
HAS CHOSEN THE COMET
(Series 2 with Rolls-Royce Avon engines)
DE HAVILLAND

De Havilland advertised in the Aviation Press the successful sale of the Comet 2 to LAV of Venezuela, with the hope of more sales to come.

at the earliest opportunity and, in an effort to restore the Comet to flying condition, the National Air Pageant joined forces with the de Havilland Museum Society and researched the hurdles that had to be crossed. They plan to ferry the Comet to Lasham where the work necessary for a C of A will be carried out by ATC Ltd, whose engineers had worked on the Dan-Air Comets. ATC's Quality Manager, Steve Gerrish, headed a team which analysed the aircraft's military maintenance records, surveyed the aircraft, devised a work schedule to prepare it for a ferry flight and compiled a low utilisation maintenance schedule for submission to the CAA. [36]

At a meeting on 1st December chaired by BAe's former Vice-Chairman Syd Gillibrand, BAe decided that it could not offer the support required for an application for a C of A. The National Air Pageant were aware that the CAA would not entertain an application for a Permit to Fly, and thus it was decided that the option of transferring the Type Certificate to a third party would be looked into and Aviation Traders Ltd at Bournemouth expressed a strong interest. In February 1999 the National Air Pageant wrote to BAe and asked the company to relinquish the Type Certificate.

XS235 was powered by four Rolls-Royce Avon 524 three-stage turbine jet engines and, unlike other marks of the Avon which are still in service with Canberras and Hunters, the 524 was a rare type which was no longer supported by Rolls-Royce. In November 1998, Rolls-Royce at Filton expressed an interest in overhauling the engines as a way of contributing to the project. However, as the tooling required for the operation had been scrapped in 1987, a world-wide search had to be undertaken to obtain the required tooling, with Rolls-Wood of Aberdeen and Rolls-Royce in Canada and Brazil also joining in the search. Rolls-Royce Bristol were able to run a computer check to ascertain which of the tools were common to other Avon engines and found there were many similarities between the Avon 524 and the 527 which is still in use on some Caravelles.

of navigation instruments were in place on the flight deck at the time. Much of the flight was conducted with visual contact with the Foss Way, constructed during the Roman occupation of Britain. The crew made the most of what was then considered to be the Comet's last trip and the flight took one hour.

Newton inspected the Comet in September 1998 when it was parked outside as the only available hangar was being used to house a Vulcan undergoing restoration. He recommended that the Comet should be stored under cover

THE NIMROD AND THE DH111 BOMBER PROJECT

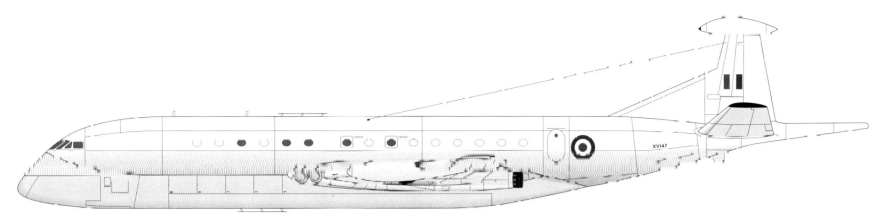

The Comet lives on to this day in the shape of the Nimrod. Two final Comet 4Cs, c/ns 6476 and 6477, were laid down at Chester but remained unsold until they were allocated to the Nimrod programme as prototypes. The first one, XV147, made its first flight on 25th October 1965, when it flew from Chester to Woodford as an unpainted 4C airframe and was subsequently shortened and converted to the Avon powered prototype, in which form it first flew on 31st July 1967. The second aircraft, XV148, remained at Chester where it was converted to Spey power and the fuselage was also shortened. This was in fact the first Nimrod to fly, on 23rd May 1967, when it was delivered to Woodford by John Cunningham and Jimmy Harrison. Both these aircraft retained all the original windows along the cabin, unlike the production aircraft, which have relatively few. The total final production consisted of the two prototypes, 46 Nimrod MR1s and three Nimrod R1 elint and sigint aircraft. From 1979 onwards, 35 of the Nimrods were converted to Nimrod MR2s by British Aerospace.

The Nimrod was designed to operate as an AWACS and an Elint platform. The first two variants were the Nimrod AEW3 and the Nimrod R1. The AEW3 performed as an AWACS platform while the R1 performed as an Elint platform. The Nimrod AEW3 was ordered as a replacement for the Shackleton AEW2. On 30th June 1969 an ex-BOAC Comet 4C, G-APDS, was acquired by the MoD and was serialised XW626 and used as a trials platform. The aircraft was fitted with a 'Nimrod type' fin, as well as a nose radar and radome, first flying in its modified form on 28th June 1977 at Woodford until its final flight on 28th August 1981 to Bedford, where it was stored until broken up in April 1994.

Eleven further development aircraft were produced from Nimrod MR1 airframes, with the first two beginning trials in 1980. The latter never entered service, and were scrapped after the programme was cancelled amid a political furore in favour of the Boeing 707 derived AWACS E3.

Another ex-BOAC Comet 4, G-APDP was serialised XX944 and delivered to Farnborough on 19th July 1973 and used for further trials on the Nimrod programme. The aircraft was withdrawn early in 1977 for instructional use by RAE technical apprentices.

By 1996 there were 28 Nimrod MR2s at Kinloss. In July that year, it was officially announced that twenty-one Nimrods would be modified to become Nimrod MRA4s, also known as the Nimrod 2000, for 2001 entry in sevice with the RAF. While based on the existing Nimrod airframes which were derived from the Comet, the future Nimrods will have new engines, wings, undercarriage, general systems, flight deck and detection systems.

A Comet variant that did not come to fruition was the DH111, referred to as the Comet Bomber Project. On 16th February 1945 de Havilland were given information concerning Operational Requirement 109, which called for a 500mph jet bomber capable of carrying a 6,000lb bomb load over a range of 1,600 miles, while operating at between 35,000 and 45,000ft. On 7th November 1946, copies of 'Top Secret' Specification B35/46 were sent to selected British manufacturers, including de Havilland, and the requirement concerned what was eventually to become the generation of V-bombers. The tenders submitted offered an innovative array of options.

At Hatfield, interest centred increasingly on the Comet and in 1948 de Havilland began to explore the military potential of the aircraft. De Havilland decided first to explore a high level photo reconnaissance adaptation of the Comet as at the time the Mosquito was still being used for elint gathering. A larger airframe was required and de Havilland submitted a proposal for what was known as the 'PR Comet', and the concept soon evolved into the design of the DH111 Comet Bomber. Details of such a possibility were submitted

by R N Bishop to Air Vice Marshal J N Boothman and Air Commodore T G Pike on 27th May 1948.

The proposed DH111 had a new 95ft fuselage, about 9ft deep and 6ft wide, making it narrower than that of the DH106. It was just able to accommodate the 'special bomb', namely the 10,000lb British nuclear weapon which at the time was thought likely to be 290in long and have a maximum girth of 60in, with some 80in aft of its nose. De Havilland argued that accommodating other weapons and equipment specified in B35/46 might lead to an unnecessarily large fuselage with all its weight and drag penalties. As it was, a bulbous front to the fuselage would be required to house the H2S MkIX radar scanner in the nose and additional fuel tanks carrying 2,400 gallons would be built into the fuselage.

A crew of four would be accommodated in an air conditioned cabin forward of the bomb bay and pressurised to 33° lb psi. That permitted prolonged operations at 45,000ft. De Havilland believed that a military crew would not require the same degree of comfort as middle aged passengers in a civil airliner and a pressurisation level with the equivalent of 25,000ft would be endured at 50,000ft. An emergency chute would enable the crew to leave through the bottom of the cabin and thermal de-icers would clear the engine intakes. The aircraft would be powered by four 5,700lb/st Ghost engines and be capable of flying an operational radius of 1,500 nautical miles when carrying an atomic bomb.

To ensure quick development and production, components would be the same as those on the Comet where possible. While the proposal did not fully meet the demands of B35/46,

de Havilland argued that their proposal involved a relatively straightforward design and this would mean that the RAF could be operating a long range jet bomber sooner rather than later.

Detailed examination of de Havilland's claims continued throughout the Summer of 1948. Officials believed that a range of 3,350 miles was attainable when cruising at 450 knots and the bomb could be dropped from 45,600ft. The aircraft's AUW was calculated as being 104,500lb, 500lb less than de Havilland reckoned. Its operating ceiling was thought likely to be 3,000ft higher.

The RAE studied the practicality of the DH111's layout, particularly its bomb installation. They were of the opinion that a number of equipment items would be heavier that de Havilland suggested and about 1,196lb would be added to the all up weight. It was also thought at the time that the first British atomic bomb might have a full cylindrical form instead of a streamlined shape. To accommodate any proposed large weapon, de Havilland had designed the rear spar to have an appropriate bend. Storage of a projected 21,000lb bomb was likely to cause immense problems. It remained possible that the aircraft would need a deeper fuselage and this raised doubts as to whether its eventual performance would be better than that of other proposed aircraft.

On 22nd October 1948 it was announced that the DH111 had no future as it was too small for its task. It was held that the aircraft would require essential additional equipment, such as missile jammers, which could raise the AUW by up to 2,000lb. That could only reduce the fuel load and thus compromise the vital range.

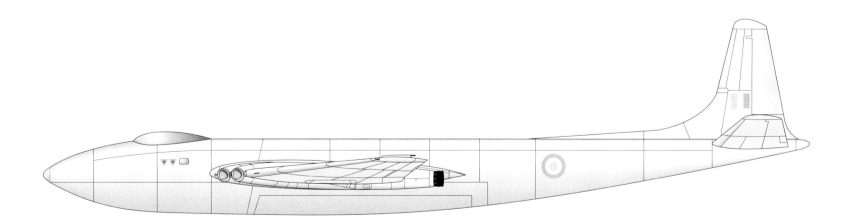

An impression of the DH111 Comet Bomber, carrying the 'anti-flash' nuclear white colours that would have been worn if it had gone into production.

CANCELLED SALES

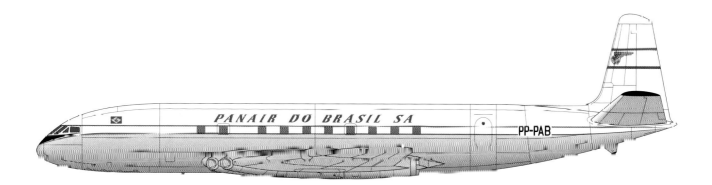

On 6th April 1951, it was announced that Panair do Brasil were contemplating the adoption of Comets to serve on their trunk routes to Europe and the Middle East. At the time the airline operated Constellations, Catalinas and DC3s, and the announcement was made in Rio de Janeiro at the conclusion of a visit made by de Havilland executives. It followed a long period of study by Panair, in the course of which Dr Paulo Sampaio, the President and General Manager of the airline, accompanied by several of his senior technical and operational team, had paid visits to the de Havilland factories. In February 1953 Panair do Brasil signed a contract for four Comet 2s for delivery the following year and an option for Comet 3s was also taken. However, the order was cancelled following the 1954 crashes.

On 20th October 1952, de Havilland Aircraft announced the purchase of three Comet 3s by Pan American World Airways, which was the first time in history that a British mainline transport aircraft had been chosen by a US airline operator. The aircraft were to be delivered in 1956 and Pan Am also took an option on seven additional Comets for delivery in 1957. The advanced delivery date was made possible because Sir Miles Thomas, Chairman of BOAC, had agreed to release three of the eleven Comets 3s which had been earmarked for BOAC.

It was a major breakthrough for both de Havilland and British aviation. Not for twenty years had US operators found it necessary to go beyond their own borders for aircraft and it was to have been the fruitful conclusion of a long association between de Havilland and US aviation. 95% of all the US production of aircraft for the 1914-18 War were built to de Havilland design and US built DH4s were used to carry US mail in the years between 1919 and 1927. Pan Am were to have been the first US operator to put jet airliners into service. Again, however, the Comet order was cancelled in the wake of the 1954 crashes.

Japan Air Lines was founded in 1951 and, on 18th November 1952, the airline concluded a purchase agreement with de Havilland for two Comet 2s. At the same time, JAL also ordered four Herons and four Doves but the Comet order was also withdrawn on 27th November 1955 in the wake of the 1954 crashes.

In June 1953, de Havilland announced that Air India International had decided to take up their option to buy two Comets 3s for delivery in 1957, but the purchase was subject to the conclusion of a contract which was then in the course of negotiation. Air India, who had a long association with de Havilland, planned to use the Comets initially on an express luxury service between India and the UK. The airline owed its existence to the energies of Mr J R D Tata, a pioneer of aviation in India who had owned a de Havilland Moth and who, in 1932, established Tata Air Lines which started operations with de Havilland Puss Moths and later operated Dragon Rapides. Tata Air Lines became Air India Ltd in 1946 and in 1948 Air India International, in which Air India and the Government were shareholders, was formed. Using Lockheed Constellations, the airline operated over the trunk routes between India and Europe and East Africa. However the order for Comets 3s was also cancelled following the 1954 crashes.

On 24th July 1956, de Havilland and Capital Airlines jointly announced that Capital Airlines had arranged to purchase fourteen Comets. Including spare parts and related equipment, the order was valued at £19 million with deliveries due to commence late in 1958 with four Comet 4s, to be followed in the second half of 1959 by ten Comet 4As.

Capital Airlines had pioneered the introduction of propeller-turbine aircraft on domestic services in 1955 with the Viscount. The airline operated one of the most important and elaborate networks of the US domestic airways system and, in 1955, the airline carried more than twenty-one million fare paying passengers and flew nearly 31 million miles. Based in

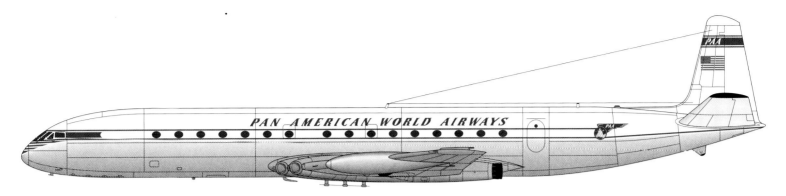

If Pan American had taken delivery of the three Comet 3 aircraft ordered, they would have appeared in the above livery.

Washington, DC, the airline connected the principal cities in the Eastern States, ranging westward from New York to the twin cities of Minneapolis and St Paul and from Buffalo southward to New Orleans. The network also included Chicago, Detroit, Milwaukee, Pittsburgh and many other major centres. The network embraced stages of varying length, for which the Comet's versatility as to stage length and economy was a significant factor.

In a document published at the time, Capital Airlines outlined the specification of the Comet 4A and its projected operating costs. It was estimated that its total cost per mile was $2.21 and this gave a cost per seat mile of $0.03. Among the specific requirements of the US airline were that the forward passenger cabin should be lengthened by 40 inches, with six passengers seated in a lounge. The canopy was to be modified to give a more satisfactory upward view and consideration was to be given to a means of taking advantage of the best downward view. US-manufactured instruments were to be fitted wherever practicable and

consideration was to be given to the introduction of individual cold air outlets for each passenger. Full provision for US radio equipment was to be made and consideration was also to be given to the substitution of British electrical equipment for US-manufactured equipment where the main generating system was not affected. In May 1957, the £19 million order was deferred due to financial difficulties and shortly after it was cancelled when Capital Airlines merged with United Airlines.

As late as 1962, de Havilland were still hopeful of receiving an RCAF order for several Comet 4Cs. As well as CPA, another Canadian airline had also taken an interest in the aircraft and, during the period from 1956 to 1958, Pacific Western Airlines applied to fly across Canada - in competition to Trans-Canada Airlines - and proposed to use three Comet 4s on its main routes. However, the airline withdrew its application after coming to an agreement with CPA by which PWA traded its interest in trans-continental flying for CPA's network of routes in northern Alberta and the North Western Territories.

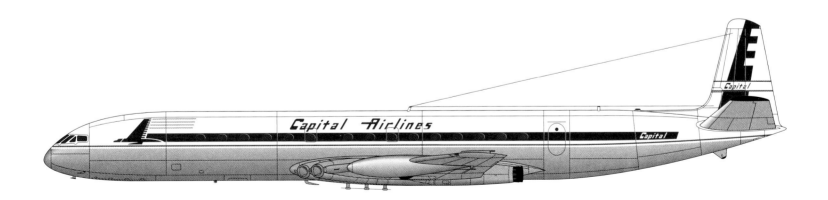

Capital Airlines, after operating Vickers Viscount aircraft with great success, decided also to purchase their jet transports from the UK when in April 1956 they ordered 14 Comet 4A aircraft, a mark designed especially for their US route network.

VARIATIONS ON A THEME

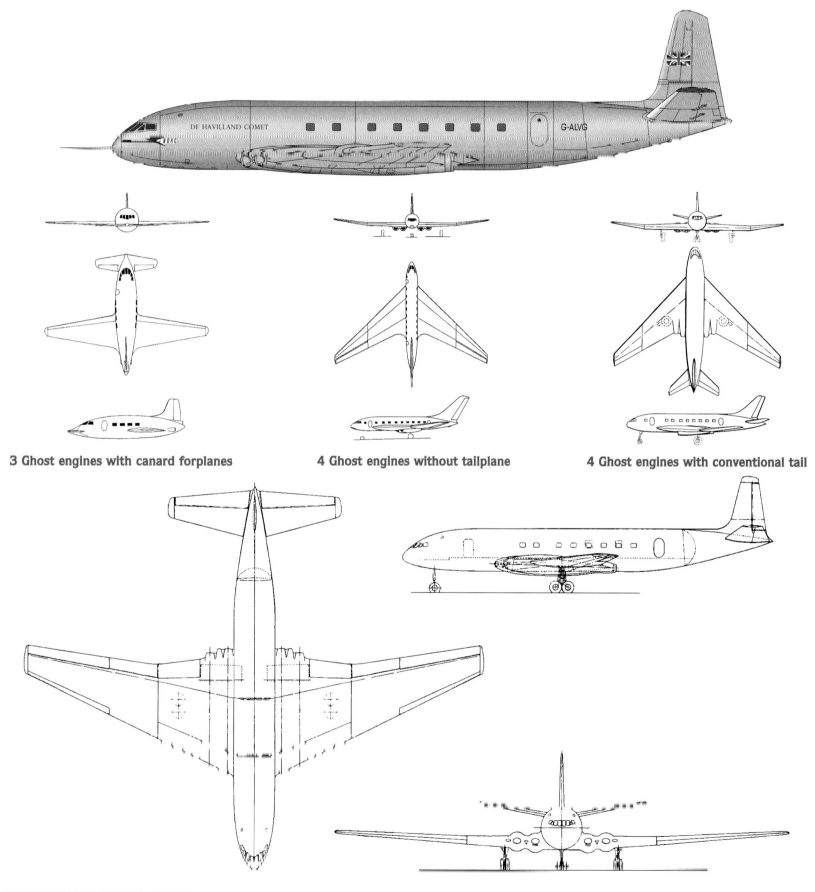

3 Ghost engines with canard forplanes

4 Ghost engines without tailplane

4 Ghost engines with conventional tail

DE HAVILLAND DH106 COMET 1

COMET 1 INTERIOR LAYOUT, 36-SEATER

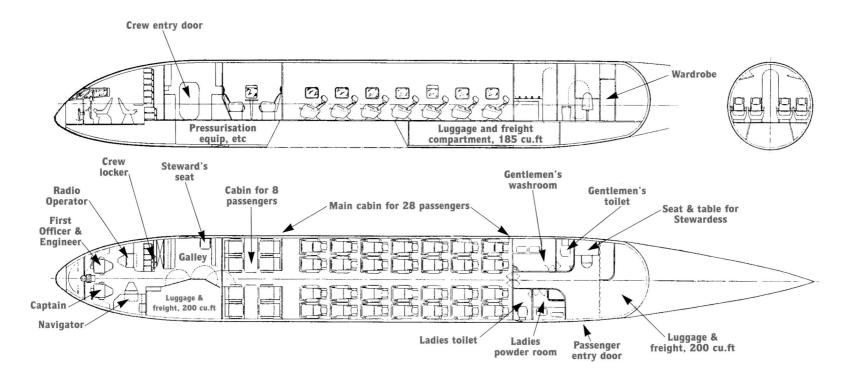

- Crew entry door
- Pressurisation equip, etc
- Luggage and freight compartment, 185 cu.ft
- Wardrobe

- Radio Operator
- First Officer & Engineer
- Captain
- Navigator
- Crew locker
- Steward's seat
- Galley
- Cabin for 8 passengers
- Luggage & freight, 200 cu.ft
- Main cabin for 28 passengers
- Gentlemen's washroom
- Gentlemen's toilet
- Seat & table for Stewardess
- Ladies toilet
- Ladies powder room
- Passenger entry door
- Luggage & freight, 200 cu.ft

COMET 1 INTERIOR LAYOUT, 48-SEATER

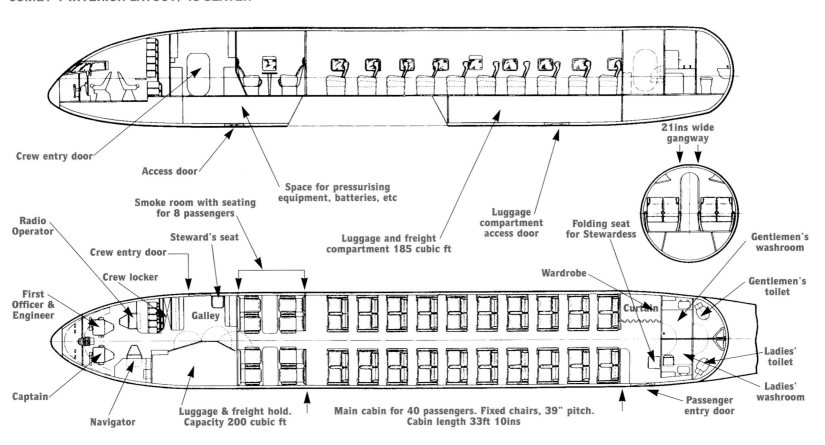

- Crew entry door
- Access door
- Space for pressurising equipment, batteries, etc
- Smoke room with seating for 8 passengers
- Luggage and freight compartment 185 cubic ft
- Luggage compartment access door
- 21ins wide gangway
- Folding seat for Stewardess
- Gentlemen's washroom
- Gentlemen's toilet

- Radio Operator
- Crew entry door
- Crew locker
- First Officer & Engineer
- Captain
- Navigator
- Steward's seat
- Galley
- Luggage & freight hold. Capacity 200 cubic ft
- Main cabin for 40 passengers. Fixed chairs, 39" pitch. Cabin length 33ft 10ins
- Wardrobe
- Curtain
- Passenger entry door
- Ladies' toilet
- Ladies' washroom

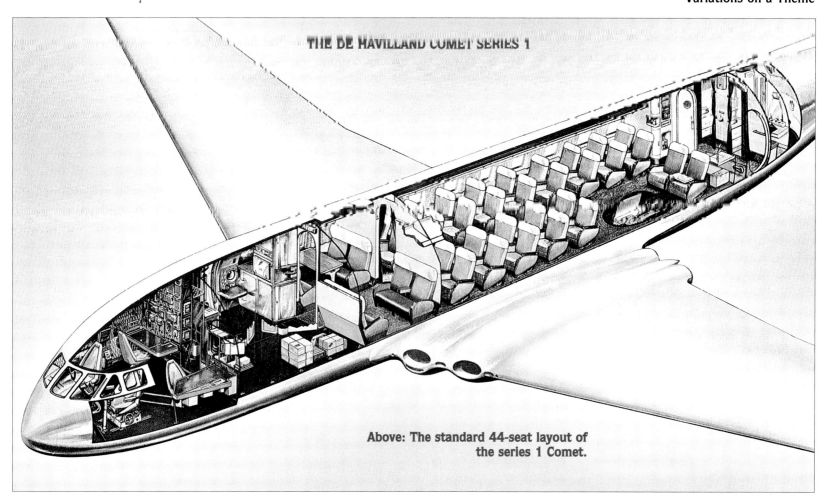

THE DE HAVILLAND COMET SERIES 1

Above: The standard 44-seat layout of
the series 1 Comet.

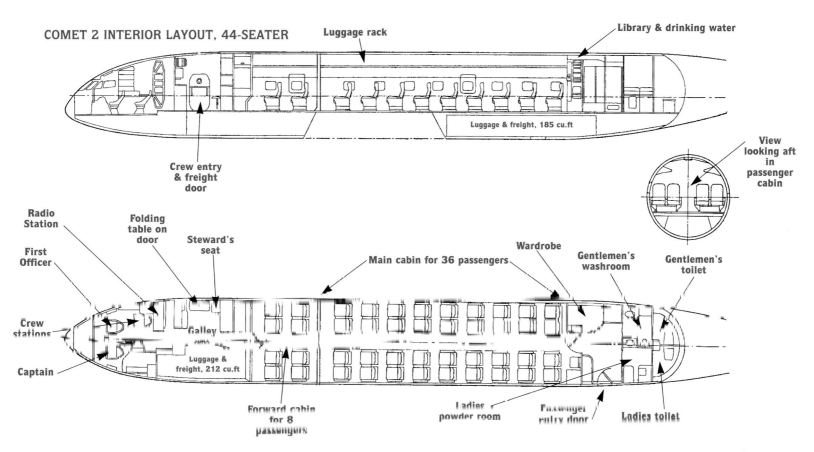

COMET 2 INTERIOR LAYOUT, 44-SEATER

Luggage rack

Library & drinking water

Luggage & freight, 185 cu.ft

Crew entry
& freight
door

View
looking aft
in
passenger
cabin

Radio
Station

Folding
table on
door

Steward's
seat

Wardrobe

Gentlemen's
washroom

Gentlemen's
toilet

First
Officer

Main cabin for 36 passengers

Crew
stations

Galley

Captain

Luggage &
freight, 212 cu.ft

Forward cabin
for 8
passengers

Ladies
powder room

Passenger
entry door

Ladies toilet

THE DE HAVILLAND COMET SERIES 2

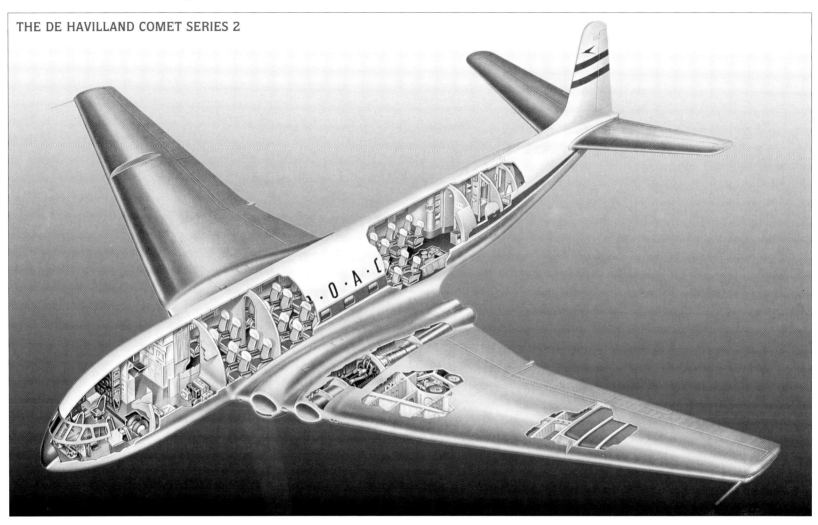

DE HAVILLAND DH106 COMET 2

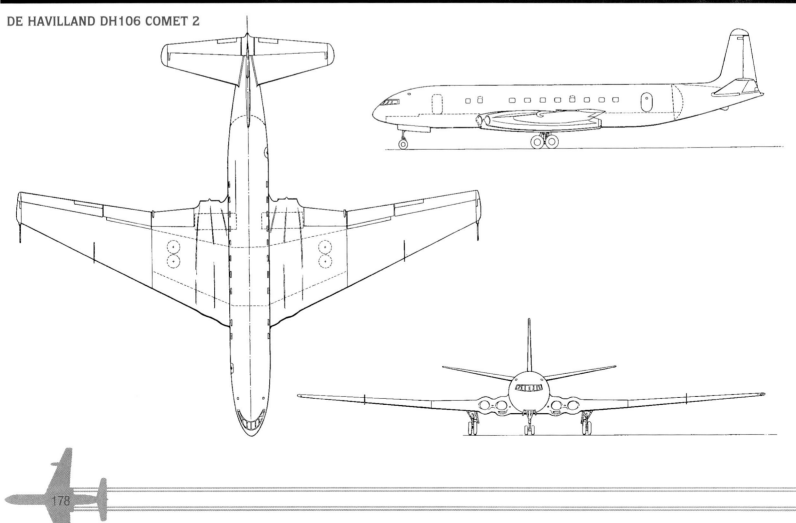

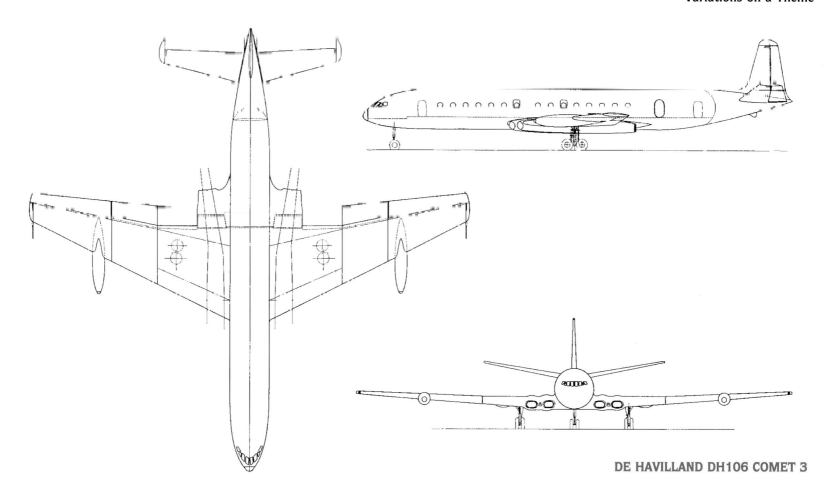

DE HAVILLAND DH106 COMET 3

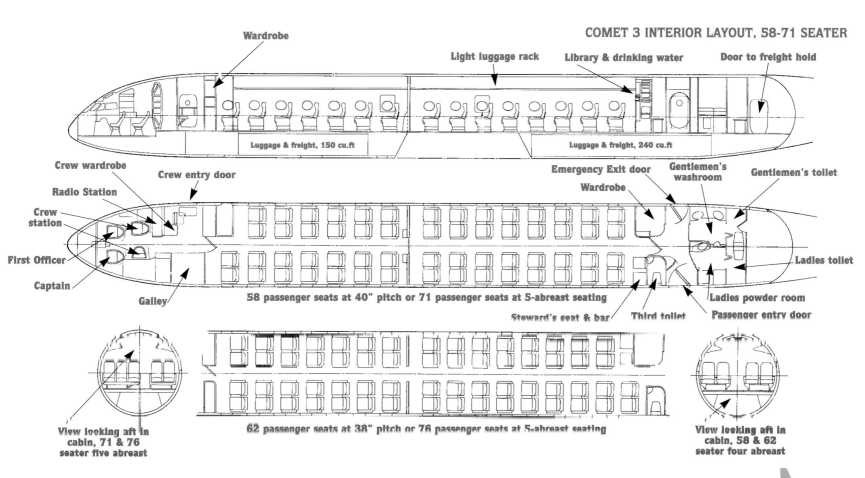

COMET 3 INTERIOR LAYOUT, 58-71 SEATER

Wardrobe

Light luggage rack

Library & drinking water

Door to freight hold

Luggage & freight, 150 cu.ft

Luggage & freight, 240 cu.ft

Crew wardrobe

Crew entry door

Emergency Exit door

Gentlemen's washroom

Gentlemen's toilet

Radio Station

Wardrobe

Crew station

First Officer

Captain

Galley

58 passenger seats at 40" pitch or 71 passenger seats at 5-abreast seating

Ladies toilet

Ladies powder room

Steward's seat & bar

Third toilet

Passenger entry door

View looking aft in cabin, 71 & 76 seater five abreast

62 passenger seats at 38" pitch or 76 passenger seats at 5-abreast seating

View looking aft in cabin, 58 & 62 seater four abreast

DE HAVILLAND DH106 COMET 4

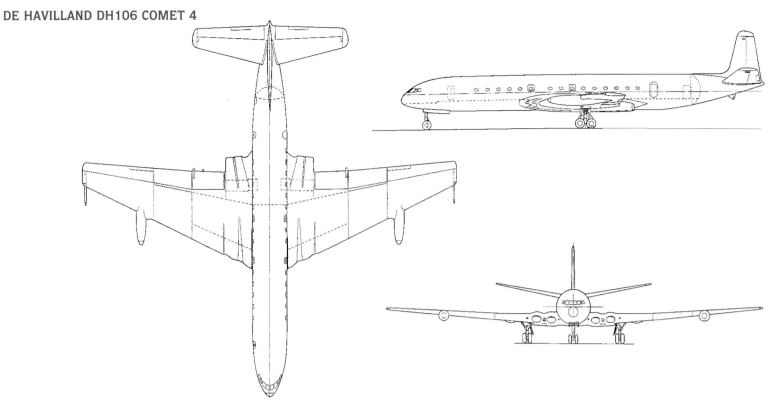

COMET 4 INTERIOR LAYOUT, 58-71 SEATER

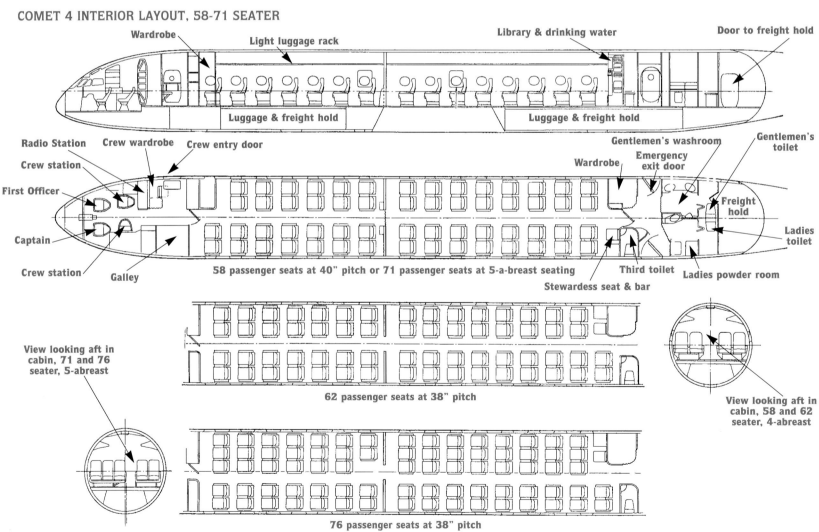

Wardrobe
Light luggage rack
Library & drinking water
Door to freight hold

Luggage & freight hold
Luggage & freight hold

Radio Station
Crew wardrobe
Crew entry door
Gentlemen's washroom
Gentlemen's toilet

Crew station
Wardrobe
Emergency exit door

First Officer
Freight hold

Captain
Ladies toilet

Crew station
Galley
58 passenger seats at 40" pitch or 71 passenger seats at 5-a-breast seating
Third toilet
Ladies powder room

Stewardess seat & bar

View looking aft in cabin, 71 and 76 seater, 5-abreast

62 passenger seats at 38" pitch

View looking aft in cabin, 58 and 62 seater, 4-abreast

76 passenger seats at 38" pitch

THE DE HAVILLAND COMET SERIES 4

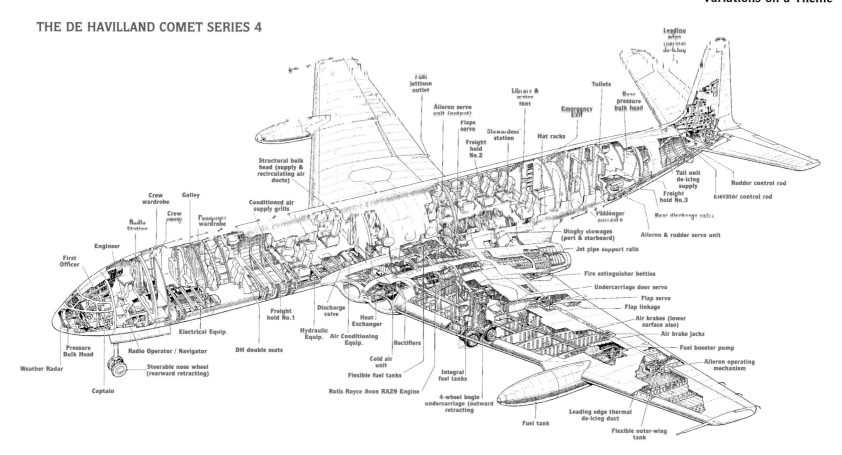

Fuel jettison outlet
Aileron servo unit (output)
Flaps servo
Freight hold No.2
Stewardess' station
Library & water font
Hat racks
Emergency Exit
Toilets
Rear pressure bulk head
Leading edge thermal de-icing
Tail unit de-icing supply
Rudder control rod
Elevator control rod
Structural bulk head (supply & recirculating air ducts)
Rear discharge valve
Passenger entrance
Aileron & rudder servo unit
Crew wardrobe
Galley
Crew entry
Conditioned air supply grills
Dinghy stowages (port & starboard)
Jet pipe support rails
Radio Station
Passenger wardrobe
Engineer
Fire extinguisher bottles
Undercarriage door servo
Flap servo
Flap linkage
Air brakes (lower surface also)
Air brake jacks
Fuel booster pump
First Officer
Freight hold No.1
Discharge valve
Heat Exchanger
Rectifiers
Pressure Bulk Head
Radio Operator / Navigator
Electrical Equip.
Hydraulic Equip.
Air Conditioning Equip.
DH double seats
Cold air unit
Aileron operating mechanism
Weather Radar
Steerable nose wheel (rearward retracting)
Flexible fuel tanks
Integral fuel tanks
Captain
Rolls Royce Avon RA29 Engine
4-wheel bogie undercarriage (outward retracting)
Fuel tank
Leading edge thermal de-icing duct
Flexible outer-wing tank

THE DE HAVILLAND COMET SERIES 4A

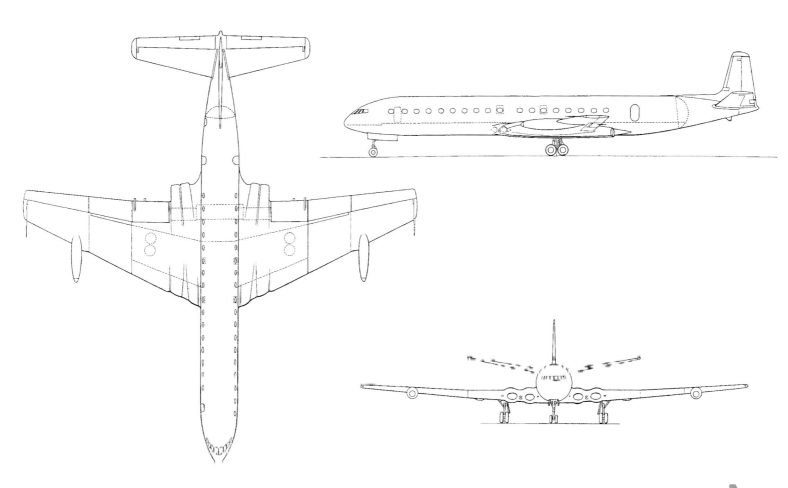

THE DE HAVILLAND COMET SERIES 4B

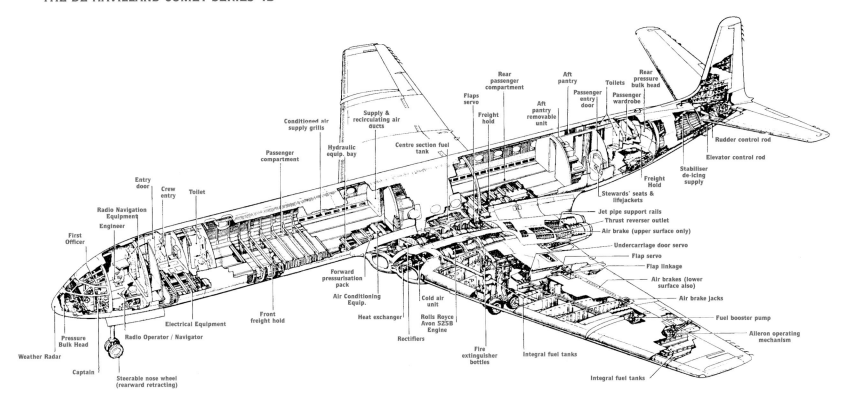

Rear passenger compartment
Aft pantry
Toilets
Rear pressure bulk head
Flaps servo
Freight hold
Passenger entry door
Passenger wardrobe
Aft pantry removable unit
Rudder control rod
Supply & recirculating air ducts
Elevator control rod
Conditioned air supply grills
Centre section fuel tank
Stabiliser de-icing supply
Hydraulic equip. bay
Freight Hold
Passenger compartment
Stewards' seats & lifejackets
Entry door
Crew entry
Toilet
Jet pipe support rails
Thrust reverser outlet
Radio Navigation Equipment
Air brake (upper surface only)
Engineer
Undercarriage door servo
First Officer
Flap servo
Flap linkage
Air brakes (lower surface also)
Forward pressurisation pack
Air brake jacks
Air Conditioning Equip.
Cold air unit
Fuel booster pump
Weather Radar
Pressure Bulk Head
Radio Operator / Navigator
Electrical Equipment
Front freight hold
Heat exchanger
Rolls Royce Avon 525B Engine
Aileron operating mechanism
Captain
Front freight hold
Rectifiers
Fire extinguisher bottles
Integral fuel tanks
Steerable nose wheel (rearward retracting)
Integral fuel tanks

COMET 4B GENERAL LAYOUT

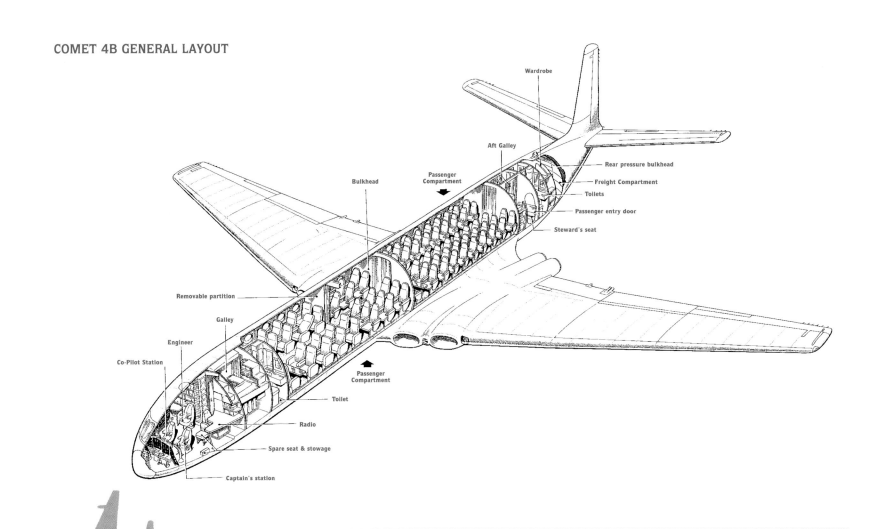

Wardrobe
Aft Galley
Rear pressure bulkhead
Passenger Compartment
Freight Compartment
Bulkhead
Toilets
Passenger entry door
Steward's seat
Removable partition
Galley
Engineer
Co-Pilot Station
Toilet
Radio
Passenger Compartment
Spare seat & stowage
Captain's station

PRINCIPAL EXTERNAL FEATURES

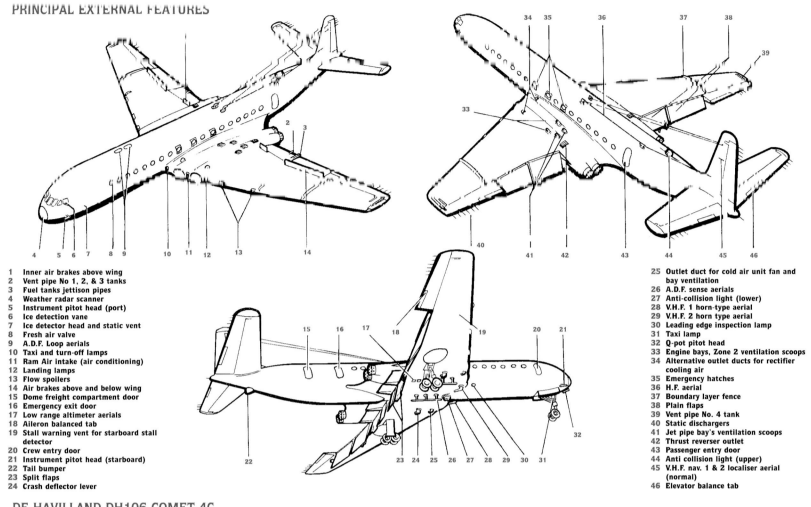

1 Inner air brakes above wing
2 Vent pipe No 1, 2, & 3 tanks
3 Fuel tanks jettison pipes
4 Weather radar scanner
5 Instrument pitot head (port)
6 Ice detection vane
7 Ice detector head and static vent
8 Fresh air valve
9 A.D.F. Loop aerials
10 Taxi and turn-off lamps
11 Ram Air intake (air conditioning)
12 Landing lamps
13 Flow spoilers
14 Air brakes above and below wing
15 Dome freight compartment door
16 Emergency exit door
17 Low range altimeter aerials
18 Aileron balanced tab
19 Stall warning vent for starboard stall detector
20 Crew entry door
21 Instrument pitot head (starboard)
22 Tail bumper
23 Split flaps
24 Crash deflector lever

25 Outlet duct for cold air unit fan and bay ventilation
26 A.D.F. sense aerials
27 Anti-collision light (lower)
28 V.H.F. 1 horn-type aerial
29 V.H.F. 2 horn type aerial
30 Leading edge inspection lamp
31 Taxi lamp
32 Q-pot pitot head
33 Engine bays, Zone 2 ventilation scoops
34 Alternative outlet ducts for rectifier cooling air
35 Emergency hatches
36 H.F. aerial
37 Boundary layer fence
38 Plain flaps
39 Vent pipe No. 4 tank
40 Static dischargers
41 Jet pipe bay's ventilation scoops
42 Thrust reverser outlet
43 Passenger entry door
44 Anti collision light (upper)
45 V.H.F. nav. 1 & 2 localiser aerial (normal)
46 Elevator balance tab

DE HAVILLAND DH106 COMET 4C

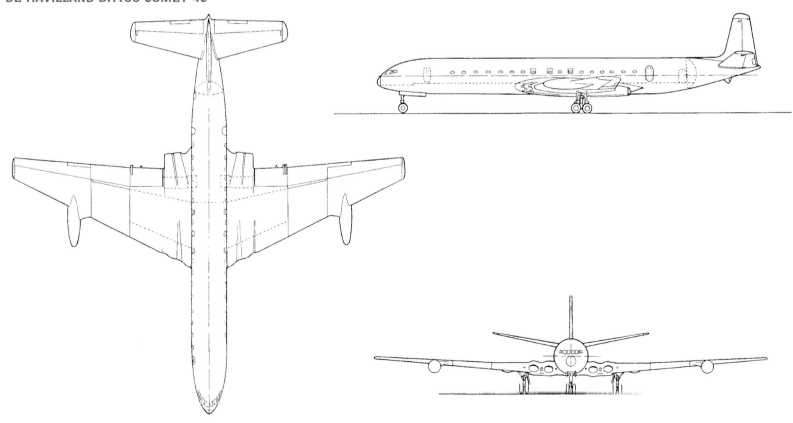

COMET 4C INTERIOR LAYOUT, 79-81 SEATER

PASSENGER ROLE (79 SEATS)

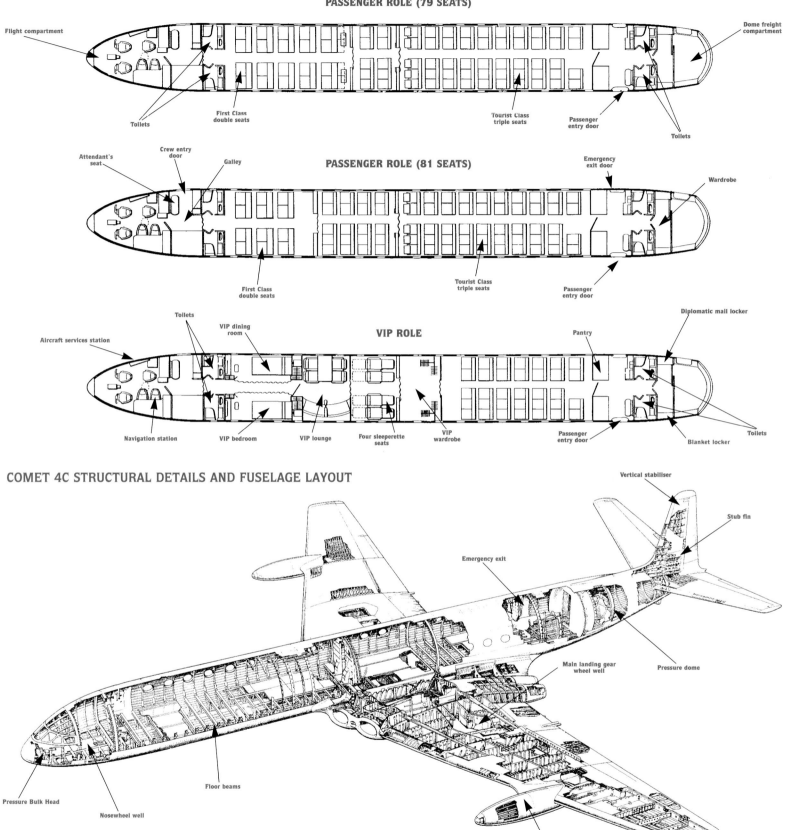

Flight compartment

Dome freight compartment

Toilets

First Class double seats

Tourist Class triple seats

Passenger entry door

Toilets

PASSENGER ROLE (81 SEATS)

Attendant's seat

Crew entry door

Galley

Emergency exit door

Wardrobe

First Class double seats

Tourist Class triple seats

Passenger entry door

VIP ROLE

Toilets

VIP dining room

Diplomatic mail locker

Pantry

Aircraft services station

Navigation station

VIP bedroom

VIP lounge

Four sleeperette seats

VIP wardrobe

Passenger entry door

Blanket locker

Toilets

COMET 4C STRUCTURAL DETAILS AND FUSELAGE LAYOUT

Vertical stabiliser

Stub fin

Emergency exit

Main landing gear wheel well

Pressure dome

Floor beams

Pressure Bulk Head

Nosewheel well

Pod tank

PRODUCTION LIST

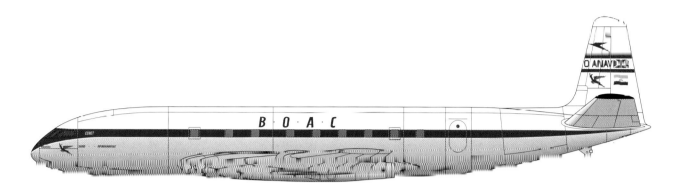

DH 106 COMET PRODUCTION

c/n	Srs	Regn	f/f
06001	1	G-ALVG	27.7.49

MoS prototype ex G-5-1, Sprite take-off trials 7.5.51, to RAE 1953 for structural testing.

06002 1 G-ALZK 27.7.50
2nd MoS prototype handed over 2.4.51 ex G-5-2, route-proving and test programmes, dismantled at Hatfield March 1957.

06003 1 G-ALYP 9.1.51
d/d 8.4.52 to BOAC, 1st production aircraft, 1st commercial jet flight 2.5.52, crashed off Elba 10.1.54.

06004 1 G-ALYR 28.7.51
d/d 17.5.52 to BOAC, badly damaged at Calcutta 25.7.53 and pieces returned to LAP. Used for water tank tests by RAE Farnborough, June 1955.

06005 1 G-ALYS 8.9.51
d/d 4.2.52 to BOAC, to RAE for systems and buffet tests after accidents, scrapped 1955.

06006 2X G-ALYT 16.2.52
MoS owned prototype Series 2 with Avon engines, also anti-icing tests on Avon RA29 for Comet 4. To Halton 15.6.59 as 7610M for instruction, engines removed autumn 1966 and airframe scrapped September 1967.

06007 1 G-ALYU 13.12.51
d/d 6.3.52 to BOAC. First Far East service 12.8.52. Structural test in water tank at RAE August/September 1954, to Pengam Moors, Cardiff, for passenger escape trials and fuselage to Stansted Fire School in 1962.

06008 1 G-ALYV 9.4.52
d/d 23.4.52 to BOAC. Broke up in violent storm after take-off from Calcutta 2.5.53.

06009 1 G-ALYW 25.2.52
d/d 14.6.52 to BOAC. To RAE for structural tests, scrapped in June 1955. Fuselage section stored Abingdon as XV238.

06010 1 G-ALYX 9.7.52
d/d 25.7.52 to BOAC. To Hatfield for prolonged engine running tests then RAE where dismantled in June 1955. Parts to Lasham 3.93

06011 1 G-ALYY 10.9.52
d/d 23.9.52 to BOAC. Lost off Stromboli near Naples 8.4.54 while on charter to South African Airways.

06012 1 G-ALYZ 23.9.52
d/d 30.9.52 to BOAC. Last production Series 1. Damaged beyond repair in take-off from Rome 26.10.52.

06013 1A CF-CUM 10.8.52
1st series 1A to CPA, Empress of Vancouver, but delivered to BOAC as G-ANAV, LAP to Farnborough 24.5.54 and flown with extensive strain gauging August/September 1954, dismantled 1955 and nose section to Science Museum, London.

06014 1A CF-CUN 24.12.52
d/d 2.3.53 to CPA, Empress of Hawaii, but crashed 3.3.53 at Karachi on delivery flight to Sydney.

06015 1A F-BGSA 13.11.52
d/d 11.12.52 to UAT. First proving flight Paris to Dakar 27.12.52, withdrawn 12.4.54. Broken up 1961.

06016 1A F-BGSB 21.1.53
d/d 19.2.53 to UAT, withdrawn from use 12.4.54. b/u Paris 1961.

06017 1A 5301 21.2.53
d/d 19.5.53 to RCAF, converted to 1XB September 1957, retired 3.10.64. Sold to Bob Quigley aircraft sales in 1965. Sold to Dallas Airmotive Inc. in 1967. Parts used to restore 5301, forward fuselage section preserved at Rockliffe Air Museum.

06018 1A 5302 25.3.53
d/d 4.6.53 to RCAF, modified to 1XB post Comet 1 crashes, retired 3.10.64 became CF-SVR, to Miami as N3735 January 1968, stored and broken up in 1975.

06019 1A F-BGSC 15.4.53
d/d 30.4.53 to UAT, damaged beyond repair at Dakar 25.6.53 after skidding off runway.

06020 1A F-BGNX 6.5.53
d/d 12.6.53 to Air France, returned to UK 27.6.56 as G-AOJT and dismantled at RAE, Farnborough. Fuselage to Mosquito Aircraft Museum 20.3.85, now in poor condition.

185

c/n	Srs	Regn	f/f

06021   1A   F-BGNY   22.5.53
d/d 7.7.53 to Air France, operated first service 26.8.53 Paris-Rome-Beirut. Returned to UK as G-AOJU, converted to 1XB February 1957, became XM829 at A&AEE for Decca/Dectra trials, retired to Stansted Fire School 20.2.64, burnt autumn 1970.

06022   1A   F-BGNZ   16.3.53
d/d 22.7.53 to Air France, returned to UK as G-APAS, converted to 1XB March 1957, then G-5-23 and XM823 with de Havilland Propellers and then later Hawker Siddeley Dynamics. Retired to Shawbury 8.4.68 then to Cosford as 8351M for preservation at Aerospace Museum.

06023   2   G-AMXA   29.8.53
d/d 17.2.58 to RAF as XK655. First production Mk 2 converted to 2R for 51 Sqn. Ferried to Strathallan 22.11.74. b/u Strathallan 90, nose to Gatwick Spectators Terrace 1996.

06024   2   G-AMXB   3.11.53
d/d 8.6.56 to 216 Sqn as XK669 f/f 9.12.55. Converted to T2 for 216 Sqn. Later named Taurus, con. to C2 1957. Retired to Brize Norton in 1967 for AQM training, fire dump 1968 and burnt 1969.

06025   2   G-AMXC   25.11.53
d/d 12.7.57 to RAF as XK659. Converted to 2R for 51 Sqn. Ferried to Duxford 10.1.75 to join the Imperial War Museum collection. b/u in 1992.

06026   2   G-AMXD   20.8.54
d/d 3.9.56 to BOAC as 2E for RA29 engine trials, MoS owned. Became XN453 and d/d RAE Farnborough for long range radio air development. b/u 2.73.

06027   2   G-AMXE   18.7.55
d/d 19.4.57 to 51 Sqn, became XK663. w/o 13.9.57.

06028   2   G-AMXF   12.3.56
d/d 7.6.56 to 216 Sqn as T2, became XK670, later became C2 Corvus and retired at Lyneham 29.11.66 as 7926M for fire rescue training. Burnt 1968.

06029   2   G-AMXG   16.7.56
d/d 22.8.56 to 216 Sqn as C2, XK671, Aquila. Last flight Gibraltar to Lyneham 28.1.67, retired to Topcliffe as 7927M. b/u.

06030   2   G-AMXH   21.8.56
d/d 14.9.56 to 216 Sqn as C2, XK695, Perseus, and converted to 2R November 1961 and d/d 51 Sqn 8.3.63. as XK659. Allocated to 192 Squadron 12.7.57, d/d Watton 14.3.58. Wfu 8.4.74, ferried to Ringway 13.5.74, transported to the Pamona Dock, Manchester as an annexe to a Bar. Nose to Mosquito Aircraft Museum 96.

06031   2   G-AMXI   29.9.56
d/d 14.11.56 to 216 Sqn as C2, Orion, became XK696. Lyneham to Watton 27.10.66 and grounded for training, dismantled 1967 and scrapped November 1969.

06032   2   G-AMXJ   17.11.56
d/d 12.12.56 to 216 Sqn as C2R Cygnus, became XK697. To 51 Sqn 1.3.67 and coded 'D' in 1971. Wfu 20.12.72. Remained at Wyton as a static a/c for Air Scouts. Broken up in Dec. 1987.

06033   2   G-AMXK   10.7.57
d/d 26.8.57 to BOAC as 2E for RA29 engine trials, BOAC owned, to MoS and used for Smiths' autopilot development at Hatfield. Became XV144 3.66, f/f as such 6.10.66 and d/d to BLEU Bedford 18.11.66. Retired to Farnborough for spares 18.5.71.

c/n	Srs	Regn	f/f

06034   2   G-AMXL   13.12.56
d/d 9.1.57 to 216 Sqn as XK698 C2 Pegasus. Last 216 Sqn operation 1.4.67. Retired to 27 MU at Shawbury 8.6.67 and moved to St Athan 25.4.69 as 8031M and scrapped.

06035   C2   XK699   2.2.57
d/d 20.2.57 to 216 Sqn as C2 Sagittarius. Retired to Henlow 19.6.67 as 7971M. To Lyneham for gate 6.87.

06036   2
MoS owned static test airframe. Water tank tests.

06037   C2   XK715   26.4.57
d/d 22.5.57 to 216 Sqn as C2 Columbia. Retired early 1967 to Cosford as 7905M. b/u 5.73.

06038
Hatfield. Spare fuselage to Chester.

06039
Hatfield. Half built for LAV. b/u

06040
Hatfield. Half built for LAV. b/u

06041
Hatfield. Part assembled for Panair do Brasil. b/u

06042
Hatfield. Part assembled for JAL. b/u

06043
Hatfield. Part assembled for JAL. b/u

06044
Hatfield. Part assembled for JAL. b/u

06045   C2   XK716   6.5.57
d/d 7.5.57 to 216 Sqn as C2 Cepheus. 1st Chester Comet. Retired to Halton June 1967 as 7958M. b/u

06046
Chester. Part assembled. Stored for spares.

06047
Chester. Part assembled. Stored for spares.

06048
Chester. Scrapped 1959.

06049
Chester. Scrapped 1959.

06061
Belfast. Allocated to UAT.

06062
Belfast. Allocated to UAT.

06063
Belfast. Allocated to Air France.

06064
Belfast. Allocated to Air France.

c/n	Srs	Regn	f/f

06065
Belfast. Allocated to Air France.

06066
Belfast. Allocated to Air France.

06067
Belfast. Allocated to Air France.

06068
Belfast. Allocated to Air France.

06100   3   G-ANLO 10.7.54
Prototype Series 3. Series 4 development flying, modified to 3B to test Mk 4B wings. t/f 21.8.58. Became XP915 and delivered to BLEU Bedford 21.6.61. Damaged 19.4.71 when hit by Trident 3 on approach, but repaired. Retired 1972.

06101
Fuselage used for structural test, Comet 4 customer mockup and stored outside at Hatfield 1962. Used as Nimrod canopy mockup and finally broken up at Hatfield 23.8.66.

06401   4   G-APDA. 27.4.58.
Constructed Hatfield. d/d 24.2.59. to BOAC as G-APDA.Sold to MA 9.12.65 9M-AOA. Registered 9V-BAS with MSA. Sold to Dan Air 11.69.

06402   4
Air frame for water tank tests.

06403   4   G-APDB 27.7.58.   Constructed Hatfield. d/d 30.9.58 to BOAC as G-APDB.
Sold to MA 11.9.65
registered 9M-AOB. Sold to
Dan Air 10.69. Preserved
Duxford Aviation Society 2.97.

06404   4   G-APDC. 23.9.58.
Constructed Hatfield. d/d 30.9.58 to BOAC as G-APDC. Sold to MA 10.65 registered 9M-AOC. Registered 9V-BAT with MSA. Sold to Dan Air 8.69. b/u 4 75.

06405   4   G-APDD 5.11.58
Constructed Hatfield. d/d 18.11.58 to BOAC as G-APDD. Sold to MA 8.11.65, registered 9M-AOD. Sold to Dan-Air 10.69. Leased to EAA as 5Y-AMT for 9 mths and returned to Dan-Air.

06406   4   G-APDE. 20.9.58.
Constructed Chester. d/d 2.10.58 to BOAC as G-APDE. Sold to MA 5.10.65, registered 9M-AOE, then 9V-BAU. Sold to Dan-Air 11.69. Leased to EAA as 5Y-ALF for 9 mths and returned to Dan-Air.

06407   4   G-APDF 11.12.58
Constructed Hatfield. Allocated to BOAC but d/d to MoD as XV814. To A&AEE 1.3.67 for spares use. b/u Boscombe Down 3.97.

06408   4   LV-PLM 27.1.59
Constructed Chester. d/d 2.3.59. to AA, registered LV-AHN, named Las Tres Marias. Sold to Dan-Air 12.71 and b/u 3.73.

06409   4   G-APDH 31.11.58.
Constructed Chester. d/d 6.12.58 to BOAC as G-APDH. Leased to MSA, w/o at Singapore 21.3.64 when undercarriage failed.

06410   4   LV-PLO 25.2.59
Constructed Hatfield. d/d 18.3.59 to AA, named Lucero de la Tarde, reregistered LV-AHO, w/o 30.3.60 at Ezeiza airport during crew training.

c/n	Srs	Regn	f/f

06411   4   LV-PLP 04.0.00
Constructed Hatfield. d/d to AA 2.5.59, named El Lucero del Alba, reregistered LV-AHP. Disappeared off Asuncion.

06412   4   G-APDK 2.1.59
Constructed Chester. d/d to BOAC 12.2.59. Sold to Dan Air 19.5.66. Leased to EAA as 5Y-ALD from 9.1.70 to 21.3.70. Last flight 7.5.73 to Lasham Air Scouts. b/u 9.80.

06413   4   G-APDL 27.4.59
Constructed Hatfield. d/d 6.5.59 to BOAC. Sold to Dan-Air 14.1.69. Leased to EAA as 5Y-ADD from 8.10.65 to 3.67. w/o at Newcastle 7.10.70 in wheels up landing during training.

06414   4   G-APDM 21.3.59.
Constructed Chester. d/d 16.4.59 to BOAC as G-APDM. Operated BOAC's last Comet service 24.11.65. Leased to MEA 3.67 as OD-AEV, then leased to MSA 1.68 as 9V-BBJ.
Acquired by Dan-Air 1969.

06415   4   G-APDN 29.5.59
Constructed Hatfield. d/d to BOAC 10.6.59. Sold to Dan-Air 10.67. Crashed near Barcelona 3.7.70.

06416   4   G-APDO 29.4.59
Constructed Chester. d/d to BOAC 14.5.59. Sold to Dan-Air 26.5.66. Last flight 2.7.73. b/u Lasham 6.74.

06417   4   G-APDP 29.5.59.
Constructed Chester. d/d 11.6.59 to BOAC as G-APDP. Leased to MSA 30.11.67 as 9V-BBH. Sold to Dan-Air 13.2.69. To RAE as XX944 22.3.73, wfu 4.75.

06418   4   G-APDR 9.7.59
Constructed Chester. d/d to BOAC 20.7.59. Sold to Mexicana 3.12.64, registered XA-NAZ, reregistered XA-NAP. Sold to Channel Airways for spares 25.6.71. To Stansted Fire School 6.72.

06419   4   G-APDS 6.8.59
Constructed Chester. d/d to BOAC 14.8.59. To MoD 30.1.69 as XW626. Stored Thurleigh 12.93, b/u 4.94.

06420   4   G-APDT 2.10.59
Constructed Chester. d/d to BOAC 19.10.59. To Mexicana 25.11.65 as XA-POW. Reregistered as XA-NAB. To Heathrow for BOAC cabin crew trainer, 19.12.69. To BAA for fire rescue training 4.80. b/u 8.90.

06421   4B   G-APMA 27.6.59
Constructed Hatfield. d/d to BEA 20.12.59. as 'Sir Edmund Halley'. Last BEA Comet flight 31.10.71. wfu 1.72. b/u Heathrow 7.72.

06422   4B   G-APMB 17.8.59
Constructed Hatfield. d/d to BEA 9.11.59. as 'Walter Gale'. Sold to Channel Airways 15.6.70. Gatwick Handling instructional a/c Gatwick 9.97.

06423   4B   G-APMC 1.10.59
Constructed Hatfield. d/d to BEA 10.11.59. as 'Andrew Crommelin' Operated by Olympic from 5.60 to 9.69. To BEA Airtours 12.3.73. To Dan-Air, Lasham, 2.11.73 for spares.

06424   4C   XA-NAR 31.10.59
Constructed Hatfield. Started as 4B G-APMD, ntu. Registered G-AOVU for ARB and FAA flights. d/d to Mexicana 8.6.60 named Golden Aztec. Wfu Mexico City 12.70, to Westernair as N999WA 17.7.73. To Everett College WA 1.00 and preserved at Museum of Flight, Seattle, 9.97.

c/n   Srs   Regn   f/f
06425   4C   XA-NAS   3.12.59
Constructed Hatfield. Started as 4B G-APME, ntu. Reregistered G-AOVV for ARB and FAA flights. d/d to Mexicana 14.1.60. wfu Mexico City 12.70, to Westernair as N999WA 8.73. wfu Chicago O'Hare 5.79. b/u 93. Some parts remain 1995.

06426   4B   G-APMF   5.1.60
Constructed Hatfield. d/d to BEA 27.1.60. as 'William Finlay'. To BEA Airtours 1.4.70. To Dan-Air 3.1.70. wfu for spares 11.74. b/u 2.76.

06427   4   G-APDG   12.11.59
Constructed Chester. d/d to BOAC 28.11.59. To Kuwait Airways 19.12.66 as 9K-AC1.To Dan-Air 9.70. Last flight 2.5.73, wfu and b/u at Lasham, 6.74.

06428   4   G-APD1   7.12.59
Constructed Chester. d/d to BOAC 19.12.59. Sold to Aerovias Ecuatorianas 13.3.66. Registered HC-ALT. wfu and stored Miami 3.68, b/u 2.78.

06429   4   G-APDJ   23.12.59
Constructed Chester. d/d to BOAC 11.1.60. To Dan-Air 14.4.67, wfu Lasham 28.11.72, b/u for spares 6.74.

06430   4   LV-POY   15.2.60
Constructed Hatfield. d/d to AA 8.3.60. Reregistered LV-AHR and named Alborada, Arco Iris. Crashed Sao Paulo, Brasil on 23.11.61.

06431   4   VP-KPJ   14.7.60
Constructed Chester. d/d to EAA 25.7.60. Reregistered 5X-AAO. Sold to Dan-Air 16.11.70 for spares. b/u 2.73.

06432   4   LV-POZ   18.2.60
Constructed Chester. d/d to AA 19.3.60. Reregistered LV-AHS and named Las Tres Marias, Alborada. Sold to Dan-Air as G-AZLW, 23.11.71. wfu 2.3.73, b/u Lasham for spares.

06433   4   VP-KPK   28.7.60
Constructed Chester. d/d to EAA 6.9.60. Reregistered 5H-AAF. Sold to Dan-Air for spares 1.71. b/u 2.73.

06434   4   LV-PPA   20.7.60
Constructed Chester. d/d to AA 26.7.60. Reregistered LV-AHU and named Centaurus. Sold to Dan-Air as G-AZIY b/u 1978.

06435   4B   G-APMD   17.3.60
Constructed Hatfield. d/d to BEA 29.3.60. as 'William Denning'. To BEA Airtours 31.3.70. To Dan-Air 12.9.72. wfu for spares 10.75. b/u 78.

06436   4B   G-APME   26.4.60
Constructed Hatfield. d/d to BEA 10.5.60. as 'John Tebbutt'. To BEA Airtours 7.8.70. To Dan-Air 24.2.72. wfu 2.5.78. b/u 5. 6.79.

06437   4B   G-APYC   7.4.60
Constructed Hatfield. d/d to Olympic Airways 26.4.60. Re-registered SX-DAK, named Queen Frederica. To BEA 14.8.69. To Channel Airways 26.1.70. Airline went bankrupt, to Dan-Air 6.4.72. Retired to Kemble 4.12.78 for SAS training. b/u 82.

06438   4B   G-APYD   3.5.60
Constructed Hatfield. d/d to Olympic Airways 14.5.60. Re-registered·SX-DAL, named Queen Olga. To BEA 1.9.69. To Channel Airways 26.1.70. Airline bankrupt, to Dan-Air 14.4.72. Last service 23.10.79. Retired to Science Museum store at Wroughton 1.11.79 for preservation, 9.96.

06439   4C   SU-ALC   21.5.60
Constructed Chester. d/d to Misrair 10.6.60. Crashed 2.1.71 on approach to Tripoli.

06440   4B   G-APZM   30.6.60
Constructed Hatfield. d/d to Olympic Airways 14.7.60. Reregistered SX-DAN, named Queen Sophia. To BEA 3.70. To Channel Airways 14.5.70. Airline bankrupt, to Dan-Air 17.4.72. wfu 11.78. b/u for spares at Lasham 9.80.

06441   4C   SU-ALD   15.6.60
Constructed Chester. d/d to Misrair 29.6.60. Crashed in sea 28.7.63 on approach to Bombay.

06442   4B   G-APMG   25.7.60
Constructed Hatfield. d/d to BEA 31.7.60. as 'John Grigg'. To BEA Airtours 16.3.70. To Dan-Air 19.1.73. wfu 11.77. b/u at Lasham for spares 4.78.

06443   4C   XA-NAT   7.10.60
Constructed Hatfield. d/d to Mexicana 29.11.60. as 'Golden Knight'. Crash landed Mexico City 1.12.70. Sold to Westernair as N777WA 5.73. Preserved at Mexico Airport. Derelict.

06444   4C   SU-ALE   22.11.60
Constructed Chester. d/d to UAA 23.12.60. Crashed 9.2.70 on take-off from Munich.

06445   4C   OD-ADK   3.12.60
Constructed Hatfield. d/d to MEA 19.12.60. Reregistered OD-ADR. Destroyed Beirut Airport 28.12.68.

06446   4C   OD-ADQ   4.2.61
Constructed Chester. Registered G-ARJH. d/d to MEA 15.2.61. Reregistered OD-ADQ. Destroyed Beirut Airport 28.12.68.

06447   4B   G-ARD1   18.3.61
Constructed Hatfield. d/d to Olympic 25.3.61. Reregistered SX-DAO, 16.4.68. To BEA 5.11.69. To Channel Airways 16.4.70. To Southend for spares 21.9.71. b/u 4.72.

06448   4C   OD-ADS   5.3.61
Constructed Chester. d/d to MEA 14.3.61. Destroyed Beirut Airport 28.12.68.

06449   4B   G-ARCO   5.4.61
Constructed Hatfield. d/d to BEA 13.4.61. as 'John Hind'. Crashed in sea off Turkey 12.10.67.

06450   4C   OD-ADT   9.3.61
Constructed Chester. d/d to MEA 18.3.61. To Dan-Air at Lasham for spares 4.10.73. b/u 6.74.

06451   4B   G-ARCP   11.4.61
Constructed Hatfield. d/d to BEA 19.4.61. To BEA Airtours 22.5.70. To Dan-Air as G-BBUV, 19.12.73. wfu 12.78. at Lasham and b/u for spares 10.79.

06452   4B   G-ARJK   4.5.61
Constructed Chester. d/d to BEA 15.5.61. To BEA Airtours 5.3.70. To Dan-Air 5.10.73. Last flight 1.11.76 to Lasham. b/u for spares 10.77.

06453   4B   G-ARGM   27.4.61
Constructed Hatfield. d/d to BEA 6.5.61. To BEA Airtours 31.3.70. To Dan-Air for spares 1.11.73. b/u 6.75.

c/n	Srs	Regn	f/f

06454 4C SU-ALL 30.5.61
Constructed Chester. d/d to UAA 13.6.60, wfu at Cairo D.0.77. Sold to Dan-Air for spares.

06455 4B G-ARJL 11.4.61
Constructed Hatfield. d/d to BEA 31.5.61. To Olympic Airways 2.64. To BEA Airtours 31.3.70. To Dan-Air for spares 9.11.73 and wfu.

06456 4B G-ARJM 8.6.61
Constructed Chester. d/d to BEA 26.6.61. Crashed after take-off from Ankara 21.12.61.

06457 4 ST-AAW 5.11.62
Constructed Hatfield. d/d to Sudan Airways 14.11.62. wfu at Khartoum 10.73. To Dan-Air as G-ASDZ 2.6.75.
b/u for spares 10.75.

06458 4C SU-ALM 30.6.61
Constructed Chester. d/d to UAA 15.7.61. wfu 6.4.76. To Dan-Air as G-BEEX 14.10.76 for spares. b/u at Lasham 8.77.

06459 4B G-ARJN 21.7.61
Constructed Hatfield. d/d to BEA 4.8.61. To BEA Airtours 25.3.70. To Dan-Air 15.2.73. b/u 11.78.

06460 4C G-AROV 21.8.61
Constructed Chester for BOAC. d/d to AA 27.4.62. Registered LV-PTS, reregistered LV-A1B and named President Kennedy. Sold to Dan-Air 20.10.71. wfu 3.78 and b/u at Lasham 10.78.

06461 4C SA-R-7 29.3.62
Constructed Hatfield for King Saud. d/d 15.6.62. Crashed in the Italian Alps 20.3.63 en route from Geneva to Nice.

06462 4C SU-AMV 25.3.62
Constructed Chester. d/d to UAA 6.4.62. wfu 31.5.76. To Dan-Air as G-BEEY 9.76 for spares. b/u at Lasham 9.77.

06463 4C ST-AAX 8.12.62
Last Comet Constructed Hatfield. d/d to Sudan Airways 21.12.62. To Dan-Air as G-BDIF 21.12.62. wfu 11.79 and b/u for spares 10.80.

06464 4C SU-AMW 3.4.62
Constructed Chester. d/d to Misrair 16.4.62. Crashed in Thailand 19.7.62.

06465 4C 9K-ACA 14.12.62
Constructed Chester. d/d to Kuwait Airways 18.1.63. Leased to MEA 1.69. To Dan-Air as G-AYWX 4.71. wfu 3.78 b/u at Lasham 10.78.

06466 4C SU-ANC 8.12.62
Constructed Chester. d/d to Misrair 22.12.62. wfu 16.12.75. To Dan-Air as G-BEEZ 9.76 for spares. b/u at Lasham 11.77.

06467 C4 XR395 15.11.61
Constructed Chester. d/d to 216 Sqn 1.6.62. Retired 2.7.75 to 60 MU Leaconfield. To Dan-Air as G-BDIT 4.9.75. wfu 11.80. Ferried to Blackbushe 6.81. b/u 7.84.

06468 C4 XR396 28.12.61
Constructed Chester. d/d to 216 Sqn 12.3.62. Retired 3.7.75 to 60 MU Leaconfield. To Dan-Air as G-BDIU 3.9.75. wfu 10.80. b/u Bitteswell 7.81. Nose section to Kinloss for 8882M.

06469 C4 XR397 17.1.62
Constructed Chester. d/d to 216 Sqn 15.2.62. Retired 30.6.75 to 60 MU Leaconfield. To Dan-Air as G-BDIV 3.9.75. wfu 11.79 and b/u at Lasham.

06470 C4 XR398 13.2.62
Constructed Chester. d/d to 216 Sqn 16.3.62. Retired 1.7.75 to 60 MU Leaconfield. To Dan-Air as G-BDIW 3.9.75. Last Comet commercial flight 9.11.80. Ferried to Dusseldorf 7.2.81 for preservation at Hermeskeil Museum, Germany.

06471 C4 XR399 20.3.62
Constructed Chester. d/d to 216 Sqn 26.4.62. Retired 4.7.75 to 60 MU Leaconfield. To Dan-Air as G-BDIX 3.9.75. wfu 10.80 and ferried to Scottish Museum of Flight, East Fortune, 30.9.81, for preservation.

06472 4 VP-KRL 12.3.62
Constructed Chester. d/d to EAA 10.4.62. Reregistered 5Y-AAA. To Dan-Air 2.71 for spares. b/u 2.73.

06473 4C XS235 26.9.63
d/d to BLEU Bedford later A&AEE Boscombe Down 2.12.63. Named Canopus. Flying laboratory for navigational equipment. Last operational flight 14.3.97. Retired to Bruntingthorpe 30.10.97. Awaiting permission to fly from CAA.

06474 4C 9K-ACE 17.12.63
Constructed Chester. d/d to Kuwait Airways 2.2.64. Leased to MEA 1.69 to 7.69. To Dan-Air as G-AYVS 8.4.71. wfu at Lasham 1.77 and b/u 4.78.

06475 4C SU-ANI 4.2.64
Constructed Chester. Last Comet completed. d/d to UAA 26.2.64. Crashed Addis Ababa 14.1.70.

06476 4C XV147 25.10.65
Constructed Chester. Nimrod prototype for MoD. Registered G-5-1 for ferry flight to Woodford. Powered by Rolls-Royce Avon engines.

06477 4C XV148 23.5.67
Constructed Chester. Nimrod prototype for MoD. Powered by Rolls-Royce Spey engines.

SPECIFICATIONS OF COMETS 1 & 2

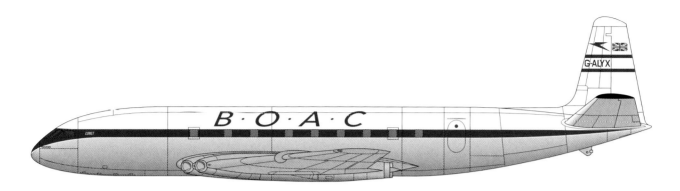

DE HAVILLAND DH108 COMET 1   DE HAVILLAND DH108 COMET 2

Length: .... 93' 0" (28.35m)	Length: .... 96' 7" (29.44m)
Wing Span: .... 115' 0"(35.05m)	Wing Span: .... 115' 0" (35.05m)
Height: .... 28' 5" (8.66m)	Height: .... 28' 5" (8.66m)
Wing area: .... 2,015 square feet (187.2 square metres)	Wing area: .... 2,015 square feet (187.2 square metres)
Tailplane span: ...... 42' 8" (13.0m)	Tailplane span: ...... 42' 8" (13.0m)
Wheel track: .... 28' 5" (8.66m)	Wheel track: .... 28' 5" (8.66m)
Wheelbase: .... 31' 11" (9.73m)	Wheelbase: .... 34' 11" (10.64m)
MTOW: 105,000lb (47,628kg)	MTOW: 120,000lb (54,432kg)
Fuel capacity: .... 6,000 Imperial gallons	Fuel capacity: .... 6,900 Imperial gallons
Engines: .... 4 DH Ghost DGT3 Engines	Engines: .... 4 Rolls-Royce Avon Mk 118 Engines
Static thrust: 5,000lbs	Static thrust: 7,000lbs
Cruising speed: 490mph (790km/h)	Cruising speed: 490mph (790km/h)
Cruising height: ..... 35,000 to 40,000 feet	Cruising height: ..... 35,000 to 40,000 feet
Range with Max Payload: .... 2,140 miles (3,450 km)	Range with Max Payload: .... 2,500 miles (4,000 km)
Passenger accommodation: .... 36 - 48 seats	Passenger accommodation: .... 44 - 48 seats

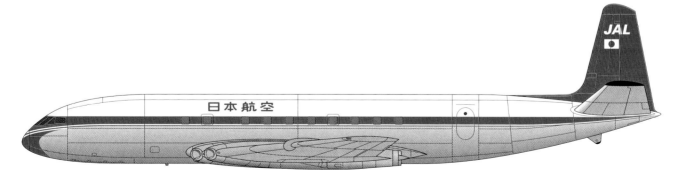

SPECIFICATIONS OF COMETS 3 & 4

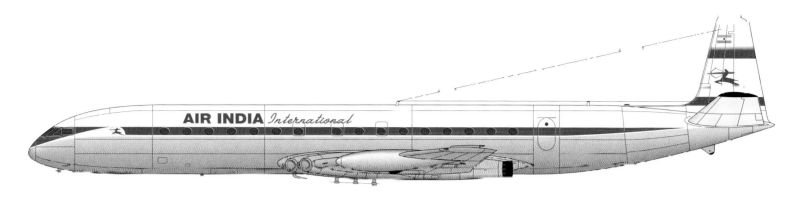

DE HAVILLAND DH108 COMET 3

DE HAVILLAND DH108 COMET 4

Length: .... 111' 6" (33.98m)		Length: .... 111' 6" (33.98m)
Wing Span: .... 115' 0"(35.05m)		Wing Span: .... 115' 0"(35.05m)
Height: .... 28' 5" (9.0m)		Height: .... 28' 5" (9.0m)
Wing area: .... 2,121 square feet (197 square metres)		Wing area: .... 2,121 square feet (197 square metres)
Tailplane span: .... 47' 5" (14.45m)		Tailplane span: .... 47' 5" (14.45m)
Wheel track: .... 28' 2" (8.58m)		Wheel track: .... 28' 2" (8.58m)
Wheelbase: .... 46' 8" (14.22m)		Wheelbase: .... 46' 8" (14.22m)
MTOW: 120,000lb (54,432kg)		MTOW: 162,000lb (73,483kg)
Fuel capacity: .... 19,365 Imperial gallons		Fuel capacity: .... 19,365 Imperial gallons
Engines: .... 4 Rolls-Royce Avon Mk502 Engines		Engines: .... 4 Rolls-Royce Avon Mk524 Engines
Static thrust: 10,000lb		Static thrust: 10,500lb
Cruising speed: 500mph (800kp/h)		Cruising speed: 503mph (805kp/h)
Cruising height: .... 30,000 to 42,000 feet		Cruising height: .... 30,000 to 42,000 feet
Range with Max Payload: .... 2,600 miles (4,160 km)		Range with Max Payload: .... 3,225 miles (5,190 km)
Passenger accommodation: .... 58 - 76 seats		Passenger accommodation: .... 58 - 81 seats

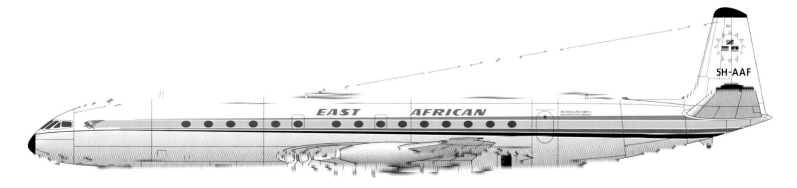

SPECIFICATIONS OF COMET 4A & 4B

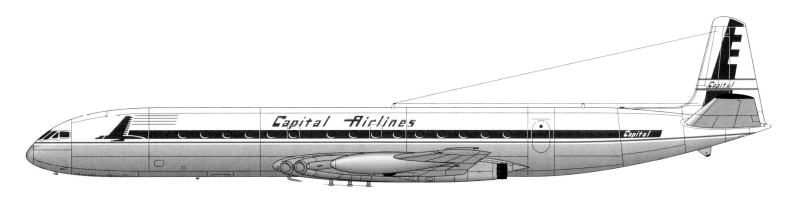

DE HAVILLAND DH108 COMET 4A

DE HAVILLAND DH108 COMET 4B

	Comet 4A	Comet 4B
Length:	114' 10" (34.78m)	118' 0" (35.90m)
Wing Span:	107' 10" (32.86m)	107' 10" (32.86m)
Height:	28' 5" (8.66m)	29' 6" (8.99m)
Wing area:	2,059 square feet (191.28 square metres)	2,059 square feet (191.28 square metres)
Tailplane span:	47' 7" (14.51m)	47' 7" (14.51m)
Wheel track:	28' 2" (8.56m)	28' 2" (8.56m)
Wheelbase:	50' 0" (15.24m)	53' 2" (16.19m)
MTOW:	152,500lb (69,174kg)	157,960lb (71,650kg)
Fuel capacity:	7,800 Imperial gallons	7,812 Imperial gallons
Engines:	4 Rolls-Royce Avon Mk524 Engines	4 Rolls-Royce Avon Mk525B Engines
Static thrust:	10,500lb	10,500lb
Cruising speed:	522mph (840km/h)	532mph (851km/h)
Cruising height:	23,500 feet (7,160m)	23,500 feet (7,160m)
Range with Max Payload:	2,730 miles (4,395km)	2,600 miles (4,000km)
Passenger accommodation:	70 - 92 seats	84 - 99 seats

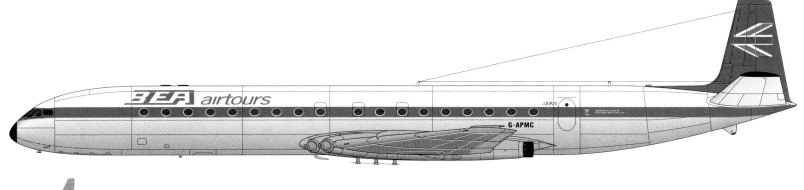

SPECIFICATIONS OF COMET 4C

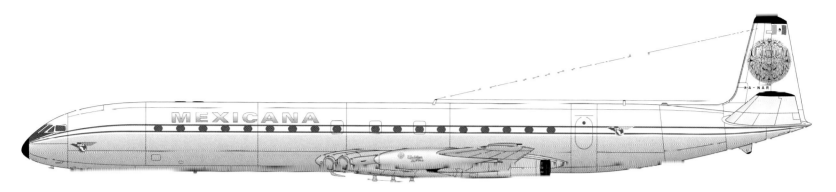

DE HAVILLAND DH108 COMET 4C

Length:	118' 0" (35.97m)
Wing Span:	115' (35.05m)
Height:	29' 6" (8.99m)
Wing area:	2,121 square feet (197 square metres)
Tailplane span:	47' 7" (14.53m)
Wheel track:	28' 2" (8.59m)
Wheelbase:	46' 8" (14.22m)
MTOW:	162,000lb (73,483kg)
Fuel capacity:	8,900 Imperial gallons
Engines:	4 Rolls-Royce Avon Mk525B Engines
Static thrust:	10,500lb
Cruising speed:	500mph (800km/h)
Cruising height:	30,000 to 40,000 feet.
Range with Max Payload:	2,820 miles (4,538km)
Passenger accommodation:	72 - 102 seats

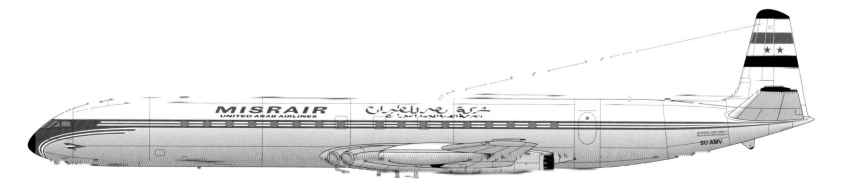

SPECIFICATIONS OF COMET BOMBER AND COMET 5

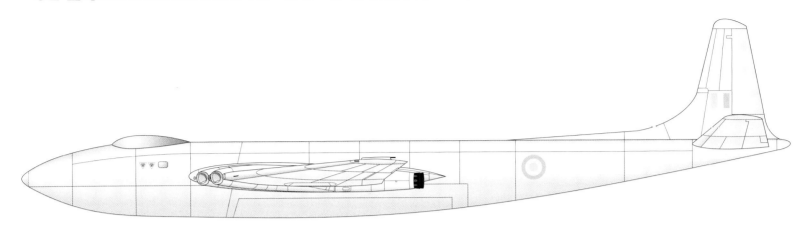

DE HAVILLAND DH111 COMET BOMBER

DE HAVILLAND DH118 COMET 5

Length: .... 95' (28.95m)	Length: .... 121' 4" (37.03m)
Wing Span: .... 115' (35.05m)	Wing Span: .... 124' 9" (38.10m)
Max weight 104,500lb (47,401kg)	Height: .... 29' 5" (9.0m)
Fuel capacity .... 4,350 gallons (11,265Ltrs)	Take Off Weight 193,00lbs (87,544kgs)
Engines: .... 4 D H Goblin or Ghost	Fuel capacity .... 11,000 gallons
Static thrust........................... 5,700lb	Engines: .... 4 Rolls Royce Conways
Bomb load: 6,000lb (2,722kg)	Cruising speed: 560mph (901km/h)
Cruising speed: 500mph (800km/h)	Cruising height: .... 30,000 to 40,000feet.
Cruising height: .... 35,000 to 45,000 feet.	Range with Max Payload: .... 5,900 miles (9,495km)
Range with Max Payload: .... 3,350 miles (5,391km)	Passenger accommodation: .... 120 - 174 seats

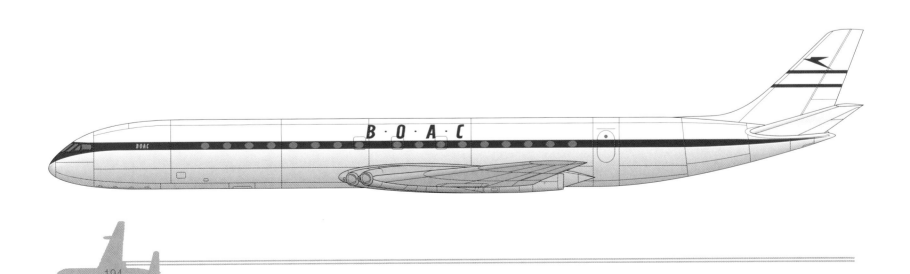

REFERENCES

[1] On 15th May 1941 the compact little Gloster E 28/39 flew for the first time at Cranwell. Frank Whittle had invented the turbojet engine in 1929 and had started testing an engine in 1937. A second Gloster prototype took to the air on 21st April 1942.

[2]: By the time the Comet 1 had made its maiden flight, the basic price of a fully equipped and furnished Comet 1 was quoted as £450,000 without the radio equipment. Wings of Change by J M Ramsden, Aeroplane Monthly, September 1989.

[3]: The aircraft designers were R. E. Bishop and R. M. Clarkson and the engineers were F. B. Halford and J. S. Moult.

[4]: According to some sources, 06002 was never actually registered as G-5-2.

[5]: It was during these trials that the aircraft reached the world altitude record of 59,446ft on 23rd March 1948.

[6]: J M Ramsden op.cit.

[7]: See Viscount, Comet & Concorde by Stewart Wilson, page 101.

[8]: Stewart Wilson, op.cit., page 131.

[9]: A J Fairbrother, March 1999.

[10]: A J Fairbrother, March 1999.

[11]: Naturally aged aluminium copper alloys were best in terms of their toughness and fatigue properties but they were the lowest in terms of their ultimate strength. Artificially aged aluminium copper alloys were stronger but their toughness and fatigue properties were reduced, and artificially aged aluminium zinc alloys were the strongest and yet offered the least in terms of toughness and fatigue resistance.

[12]: From the memoirs of M V Parker, 1999.

[13]: Letter from Julia Wood — formerly an employee at BOAC's Airways House HQ — 20th March 1999.

[14]: Letter from Diana Gatchfield, née Furness, 21st March 1999.

[15]: Diana Gatchfield op.cit.

[16]: Diana Gatchfield op.cit.

[17]: Comet Highway by Henry Hensser MBE.

[18]: Diana Gatchfield, op.cit.

[19]: J M Ramsden op.cit.

[20]: Conversation with Captain J A Perry, 24th March 1999

[21]: Letter from Captain Jeffrey Grey (Retired) 18th November 1998. Report released by the Brazilian Air Ministry.

[22]: Captain A J Angus, 5th March 1999.

[23]: The information contained in this report remains the property of the Turkish Ministry of Communications.

[24]: Francis Mseka, March 1999.

[25]: Eric McCarthy, 31st March 1999.

[26]: Eric McCarthy, 31st March 1999.

[27]: From the memoirs of M V Parker, 1999.

[28]: From the memoirs of M V Parker, 1999.

[29]: M V Parker op.cit.

[30]: M V Parker op.cit.

[31]: M V Parker op.cit.

[32]: M V Parker op.cit.

[33]: The information contained in this report remains the property of the Spanish Air Ministry.

[34]: Communication from Captain Bryn Wayt, 19th March 1999.

[35]: Conversation with Francis Mseka, 17th March 1999.

[36]: Information concerning the plans to restore XS235 to flying condition has been taken from the National Air Pageant Comet Campaign Update of January 1999.

CLOSE-UP DETAIL SECTION

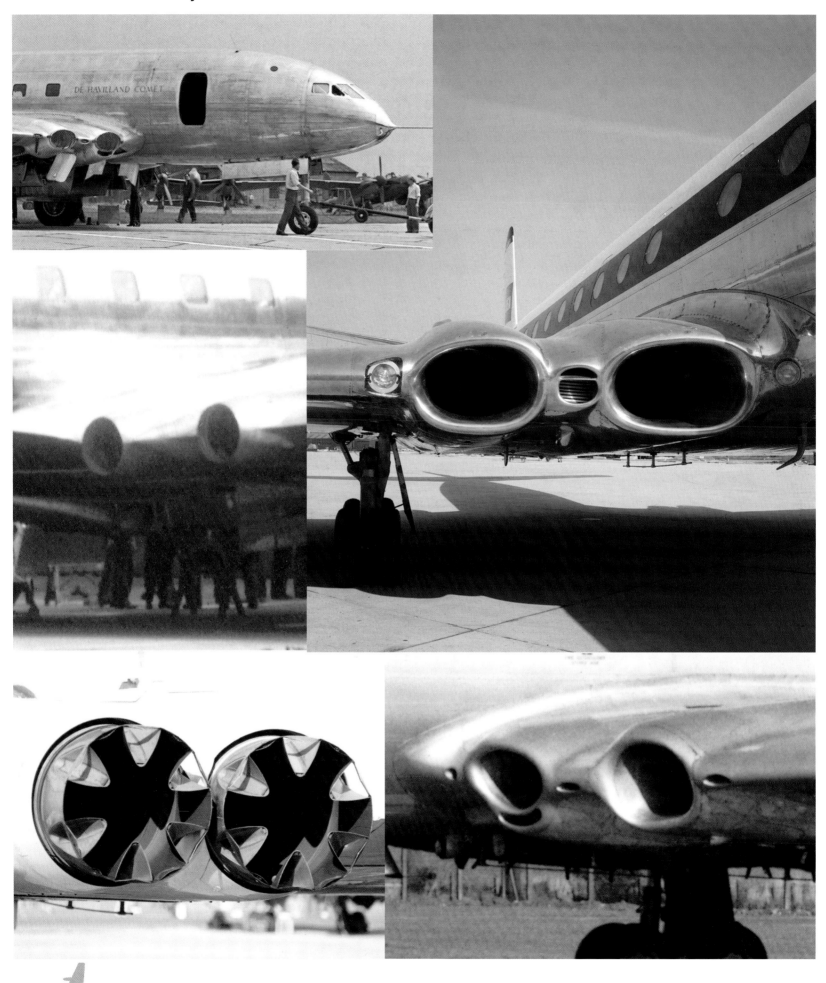

BIBLIOGRAPHY

LIST OF ILLUSTRATIONS

PERIODICALS & JOURNALS

The de Havilland Gazette Nos 50~124

BOOKS

Gunston, Bill (Ed) Chronicle of Aviation (Chronicle Communications Ltd, London, 1992)

Simons, Graham The Spirit of Dan–Air Services (G M F Enterprises, 1993)

Spring, Ivan Winged Springboks 1934 to 1996 (Spring Air CC, South Africa, 1996)

Streetly, Martin World Electronic Warfare Aircraft (Jane's Publishing Company Ltd, 1983)

Wilson, Stewart Viscount, Comet & Concorde (Aerospace Publications Pty Ltd, 1996)

MAGAZINES

Flight (23.3.50; 17.10.52; 22.10.54)

The Aeroplane (5.52; 2.5.52; 24.10.58; 24.10.58)

Bentley, John Flight International 'Navigating in the Cold' (29 June, 1967)

Birtles, Philip J Aircraft Illustrated 'The Hawker Siddeley Comet 4C' (August, 1970)

Birtles, Philip J Aircraft Illustrated 'De Havilland Comet' (May, 1972)

Birtles, Philip J Aircraft Illustrated 'The de Havilland Comet 4B' (March, 1975)

Bowyer, Michael J F Air Pictorial 'Comet Bomber Project – The de Havilland D.H.III, a contender in the early V-bomber stakes' (September 1987) pp 354~357

Bowyer, Michael J Aviation News 'A Comets Tale' (22 May ~ 5 June 1992) pp 26~29.

Burney, Allan Aircraft Illustrated 'Tail–end of the Comet' (February, 1981)

Dyer, Sqn Ld Gordon, MBE Flight International 'Southern Sortie – Boscombe Down's Comet Navigates in the Antarctic' (20 August, 1970)

Dorman, Geoffrey British Test Pilots No 4 'Group Captain John Cunningham, D.S.O., D.L.C'

Kunert, Roger Air Pictorial 'Summer In Mexico' (January, 1979)

March, Peter R Aircraft Illustrated 'Singapore Airlines' (January, 1978)

Prins, François Air Enthusiast 'World Beater – Homage to the DH 106 Comet' (November~December, 1998)

Ramsden, J M Aeroplane Monthly 'Wings Of Change' (September, 1989)

Reavell, K C, Air Pictorial 'The Comet 4 Series' (September, 1964)

Rawlings, J D R Air Pictorial 'By Dan–Air Comet to Teneriffe' (August, 1970)

Stroud, John The Journal of Commerce and Shipping Telegraph 'London to Bombay Via Beruit' (3rd November 1961)

Ward, M A Air Pictorial (11.71; 8.12.71; 1.79; 1.79; 2.79)

NEWSPAPERS

The Times [about the Elba Crash] (22.1.54; 6.2.54; 10.2.54; 17.2.54; 22.2.54; 18.3.54; 28.5.54; 30.7.56)

GLOSSARY & ABBREVIATIONS

A&AEE:	Aeroplane and Armament Experimental Establishment at Boscombe Down
ADF:	Automatic Direction Finder
AFB:	Air Force Base
APU:	Auxiliary Power Unit
ARB:	Air Registration Board. Now replaced by CAA.
Astro-fix:	Use of the stars to calculate position using sextants or astro-compass
AUW:	All up weight
AWACS:	Airborne Warning and Control System
BAA:	British Airport Authority
BEA:	British European Airways
BLEU:	Blind Landing Experimental Unit
B.O.A.C:	British Overseas Airways Corporation.
B.C.P.A:	British Commonwealth Pacific Airlines: Airline founded 24th June 1946 by Australian, New Zealand and UK governments to operate services from Australia and New Zealand to the US and Canada
B.S.A.A	British South American Airways: A British nationalised airline created in 1946 and later merged with BOAC
BST:	British Summer Time
b/u:	Broken up
BUA:	British United Airlines
Busbar:	Main electrical power distribution lines
Canard:	An aircraft with tailplane mounted in front of wing Chargeurs Reunis S.A.: French Shipping company
Check 1,2,3,4:	Aircraft maintenance checks
c.g.:	Centre of gravity
C.L.Max:	Coefficient of lift
CPA:	Canadian Pacific Airlines
d/d:	Delivery date
Decca:	Hyperbolic navigation
Diametral:	Located on or forming a diametric
Dielectric:	Insulator
DME:	UHF distance measuring equipment which gives slant distance to a beacon
Doppler:	Navigation radar — measures aircraft groundspeed and drift angle
DRA:	Defence Research Agency, Farnborough
Efflux:	Exhaust trails
Elapsed time:	Flying time plus stopovers, between the point of departure and the final destination
Elint:	Electrical Intelligence
Engine Numbers:	The port outboard engine was Number 1, the port inboard was Number 2, the starboard inboard Number 3 and the starboard outboard Number 4
FAA:	Federal Aviation Authority US equivalent of the British Civil Aviation Authority
Flutter	Dangerous oscillation of an aircraft, or part of, caused by the interaction of aerodynamic forces
GPO:	General Post Office
IAS:	Indicated Air Speed
IATA:	The International Air Transport Association

ICAO.	International Civil Aviation Organisation
ICAN:	International Commission on Air Navigation
ILS:	Instrument landing system
Impeller:	Vaned rotating disc of a centrifugal pump or compressor
Intertropical Convergence Zone:	Verging trade winds along the equator causing rising air currents and low atmospheric pressure
ISA:	International Standard Atmosphere
IT:	Inclusive tour
KLM:	Royal Dutch Airline (Koninklijke Luchtvaat Maatschappij voor Nederland an Kolonien)
LAP:	London Airport (Heathrow)
Leis:	A garland of Flowers.
Loran:	Long-range Navigation system
MAP:	Ministry of Aircraft Production, which later became the Ministry of Supply
MATS:	Military Air Transport Service
MoD:	Ministry of Defence
MoS:	Ministry of Supply, formerly the Ministry of Aircraft Production
MP:	Member of Parliament in the UK
MTOW:	Maximum take-off weight
Paraffin:	Also known as kerosene
QDM:	Magnetic Heading
RAAF:	Royal Australian Air Force
RAE:	Royal Aircraft Establishment
RAF:	Royal Air Force
Ram pressure:	Increased pressure in forward-facing aircraft inlet/duct as a result of forward aircraft speed
RAPCON:	Radar Approach Control
RAS:	Rectified Air Speed
RMI:	Radio Magnetic Indicators
Sigint:	Signals Intelligence
SKAT:	Seychelles-Kilimanjaro Air Transport
Slip crew:	A crew pre-positioned en route
Slipstream:	The stream of air forced backwards by an aircraft's propeller
s.t.:	static thrust
SWG:	Standard Wire Gauge. A notification for the diameters of metal rods or thickness of metal sheet ranging from 16 mm to 0.02 mm
Tacan:	Tactical air navigation
UHF:	Ultra high frequency
USAF:	United States Air Force
V Bombers:	The three British Jet Bombers developed in the 1950s for RAF service under Ministry of Supply specification B9/48.
V2:	Take-off safety speed
VOR:	VHF omnidirectional range - navigation system
wfu.	Withdrawn from use
w/o:	Written off

Index

SCOVAL
PUBLISHING LTD